"It's delightful to have this volume of essays address a vital theme while honoring a wise mentor and beloved friend. Insights from these excellent contributors can promote the practice of evangelical hospitality that many of us have experienced from Dennis Okholm."

—DANIEL TREIER, Wheaton College

"*To Be Welcomed as Christ* is a fitting tribute to Dennis Okholm, whose wide-ranging interests are well represented in this volume. But what ties them all together is Okholm's commitment to the Christian monastic heritage, whose influence is likewise diffused throughout the church and across the Christian tradition. Just as monasticism is a gift to the church, so is Okholm, and his influence in institutions and individuals will continue to flourish and bear much fruit."

—GREG PETERS, American Benedictine Academy

"*To Be Welcomed as Christ* is truly a welcoming and spiritually rich book. It is also a well-deserved tribute to theologian, friend, and conscience of evangelicalism Dennis Okholm. The diverse set of significant contributors introduce and elaborate on major themes of theological and relational hospitality true to Okholm's life and ministry. It is a delightful and edifying book."

—ROBERT A. FRYLING, author of *The Leadership Ellipse: Shaping How We Lead by Who We Are*

This delightful collection of essays addresses hospitality, friendship, and community in the life of the church. Each chapter is beautifully written, honest, thoughtful, uplifting, hopeful—a true testimony to Okholm's passion for theological reflection and community flourishing.

—LYNN H. COHICK, Northern Seminary

"This rich collection of essays presents dimensions of a Christian faith that can be hospitable, humble, and capacious. The distinctive voices here manifest the Christ-bearing aroma of Dennis Okholm, in whose honor these reflections have been so deservedly gathered. Nicholas Scott-Blakely does a fine job as editor presenting essays that intensify our hunger for that hospitable wisdom of God, whose friendship is meant to mark all our communion."

—MARK LABBERTON, Fuller Theological Seminary

"This beautiful collection models profoundly hospitable collaboration, illuminating Dennis Okholm's theology as good news: welcome in contrast to the exclusion, distortion and condescension of much of the Western intellectual tradition. In the spirit of Barth, McClendon, and—supremely—Jesus Christ, these essays place theology in that long narrative of the God whose Spirit opens all difference and conflict into an awareness of the beautiful friendship the Father extends to us all in his Son."

—ANDREW TEAL, University of Oxford

To Be Welcomed as Christ

To Be Welcomed as Christ

PURSUING A HOSPITABLE EVANGELICALISM

ESSAYS

IN HONOR OF

DENNIS OKHOLM

Edited by

Nicholas Scott-Blakely

PICKWICK *Publications* · Eugene, Oregon

TO BE WELCOMED AS CHRIST
Pursuing a Hospitable Evangelicalism

Pickwick Publications
An Imprint of Wipf and Stock Publishers
199 W. 8th Ave., Suite 3
Eugene, OR 97401

www.wipfandstock.com

PAPERBACK ISBN: 978-1-5326-7446-4
HARDCOVER ISBN: 978-1-5326-7447-1
EBOOK ISBN: 978-1-5326-7448-8

Cataloguing-in-Publication data:

Names: Scott-Blakely, Nicholas, editor.

Title: To be welcomed as Christ : pursuing a hospitable evangelicalism / edited by Nicholas Scott-Blakely.

Description: Eugene, OR : Pickwick Publications, 2022 | Includes bibliographical references.

Identifiers: ISBN 978-1-5326-7446-4 (paperback) | ISBN 978-1-5326-7447-1 (hardcover) | ISBN 978-1-5326-7448-8 (ebook)

Subjects: LCSH: Ockholm, Dennis L. | Evangelicalism.

Classification: BR118 .T63 2021 (print) | BR118 .T63 (ebook)

To Dennis,
our friend, teacher,
and brother in Christ

All guests who present themselves
are to be welcomed as Christ,
for he himself will say:
"I was a stranger and you welcomed me" (Matt 25:35).
– *The Rule of St. Benedict* –

Table of Contents

Contributors

Justin Ashworth is Assistant Professor of Theology at Azusa Pacific University. He has published articles in *Political Theology, Modern Theology,* and *Scottish Journal of Theology* and is the author of the forthcoming *Belonging without Borders: The Ethics of Borders and the Mission of God.*

Vincent Bacote is Associate Professor of Theology and Director of the Center for Applied Christian Ethics at Wheaton College (IL). His publications include *The Political Disciple* and *The Spirit in Public Theology: Appropriating the Legacy of Abraham Kuyper.*

Jennifer M. Buck is Assistant Professor of Practical Theology at Azusa Pacific University. Her publications include *Reframing the House, Distinct: Quaker Holiness in Everyday Life,* and *Bad and Boujee: Toward a Trap Feminist Theology.*

Ellen T. Charry is Professor Emerita of Theology at Princeton Theological Seminary. Her publications include *By the Renewing of Your Minds, God and the Art of Happiness,* and *Psalms 1–50: Sighs and Songs of Israel.* She is currently working on *Who is the Israel of God?: Healing the Christian-Jewish Debate.*

Rodney Clapp is an editor at Cascade Books. His most recently authored book is *New Creation: A Primer on Living in the Time between the Times.*

David Fugoyo-Baime is Vice Chancellor of Africa Renewal University in Buloba, Uganda. He received his PhD in Biblical Studies from Africa International University in Nairobi, Kenya and has published on the book of Judges, Christian leadership in South Sudan, and was a contributor to the *Africa Study Bible.*

Todd Hunter is founding bishop of the Anglican diocese of Churches for the Sake of Others. He is the author of *Christianity Beyond Belief, Giving Church Another Chance, The Outsider Interviews, The Accidental Anglican, Our Favorite Sins,* and *Our Character at Work.*

Craig Keen is Professor Emeritus of Systematic Theology at Azusa Pacific University. His publications include *The Transgression of the Integrity of God: Essays & Addresses* and *After Crucifixion: The Promise of Theology.* The book, *Sanctity: Standing Up to the Coming of God,* is forthcoming.

Scot McKnight is Professor of New Testament at Northern Seminary and serves as Canon Theologian for the Diocese of Churches for the Sake of Others, Anglican Church in North America. His publications include *The King Jesus Gospel, Reading Romans Backwards,* and *Pastor Paul.*

Michael McNichols is Affiliate Assistant Professor of Intercultural Studies at Fuller Theological Seminary where he served as Director of Fuller Orange County for thirteen years. His publications include *Shadow Meal: Reflections on Eucharist* and *Atonement at Ground Zero: Revisiting the Epicenter of Salvation.*

Robert L. Millet is Professor Emeritus of Religious Education at Brigham Young University. Among his publications are *A Different Jesus?: The Christ of the Latter-day Saints* and *Talking Doctrine: Mormons and Evangelicals in Conversation,* co-edited with Richard J. Mouw.

Richard J. Mouw is Senior Research Fellow at the Henry Institute for the Study of Religion and Politics at Calvin College and Senior Professor of Faith and Public Life at Fuller Theological Seminary, where he served as president for twenty years. He has written numerous books including *All That God Cares About, Restless Faith, Adventures in Evangelical Civility, Uncommon Decency, Calvinism in the Las Vegas Airport,* and *The Smell of Sawdust.*

Robert C. Roberts is Distinguished Professor Emeritus of Ethics at Baylor University. His most recent book is *Emotions in the Moral Life,* and he is currently at work on *Kierkegaard's Psychology of Character.*

Nicholas Scott-Blakely is a PhD Candidate in Christian Ethics at Fuller Theological Seminary where he works for the Institute of Faith and Public Life.

Benet Tvedten, OSB, was the oblate director at Blue Cloud Abbey in Marvin, South Dakota from 1977 until its closure in 2012. He is now a member of Assumption Abbey in Richardton, North Dakota. His books include *How To Be a Monastic and Not Leave Your Job* and *The View from a Monastery*.

Introduction

Nicholas Scott-Blakely

IN JANUARY 2013 I began the first week of my senior seminar in theology at Azusa Pacific University. That day, I scribbled on my notepad two key questions raised by the professor that helped frame our semester together: "What kind of person do you want to become? What will help form you into that person?" These questions were meant to point us to the topic of the seminar: friendship and community. Dennis Okholm, our beloved professor, taught us that friendships and the communities that constitute a person's life are of paramount importance for self-understanding and human flourishing. Indeed, our friendships are central to the task of Christian theology. Friendships and communities are gifts from God that help humans understand themselves as deeply loved and befriended by God.

Okholm was trying to instill in us that beyond the practical formation one encounters among one's friends, the task of Christian theology is meaningless apart from the concreteness and particularity of one's own community and friends. It is through these relationships that we learn to see the world in ways that would otherwise be skewed or hidden. The way people live out their lives ideally corresponds to this vision—a vision we cannot develop without our friends.

The theological emphasis Okholm places on friendship and community is focused on the particular community of the church. In most contexts throughout Christian history, churches are the primary hub for the moral and theological formation of Christians. Okholm's focus on the community of the church is stressed in his *Learning Theology through the Church's Worship*. He coins the memorable phrase, "liturgical ophthalmology," in order to identify the ways in which humans view the world through different lenses shaped by their contexts and relationships. Gathering together in the church for worship, humans are formed over time to view the world through a Christian lens.[1] Just as an ophthalmologist helps diagnose, treat, repair, and heal one's vision, God forms, corrects, influences, and instructs the church through its liturgy, Scripture, and God's presence in the life of the community. Without these influences, people are unable to fully see the world as God intends it to be seen. As Okholm writes, "We do not *see* reality the way God created it and is in the process of redeeming it merely by *looking* at our lives and the world. Seeing requires correction—in this case, correction made possible by God's revelation in the incarnation, in Scripture, and in Christ's church."[2] This correction is possible because individuals gather together in friendship and the community of the church.

The formation that occurs through the work of liturgical ophthalmology matters to Okholm because Christian identity is meant to impact how one lives in the world as an individual and in community with others. Christian identity is not based solely on affirming propositions about God or undergoing experiences in relation to God; rather, baptism into the Christian life involves being inducted into a story that entails corresponding practices and language conducive to that story. The Christian lens acquired through life in the community of the church impacts beliefs and also forms how community members are meant to act in the world; one's theology *and* ethics should be impacted by the ways in which church communities recount and relive the story into which the community and its members have been baptized.[3] Life together in these communities becomes the way in which Christians test their theology, witnessing to the world what they believe by how their beliefs are translated into acts of loving service in the world.

However, participation in the Christian story is not automatic; it is a choice. Humans can live by different stories and be shaped to see the world through different lenses—from the vantage of capitalists, Republicans, Democrats, Buddhists, nationalists, vegans, communists, and many others. More often than not, conflicting stories compete for

1. This is not to suggest that there is a univocal Christian lens; rather, united by minimal commitments such as the Nicene Creed, Christians in all their diversity can be shaped by their particular communal gatherings to see the world in ways inspired by the trinitarian God attested to in Scripture and the ongoing life of the church.

2. Okholm, *Learning Theology*, 2.

3. Okholm, *Learning Theology*, 6.

ultimate loyalty, and it is a challenge to be cognizant of which stories one prioritizes at any given moment. It is even more difficult to do this alone, without the influence and support provided by one's community and friends.

The importance of friendship and community in Christian theology is ultimately significant because of what the Christian life entails and the direction Christians believe history is going. The Christian story invites humans from a multitude of contexts to live with hope and expectation, actualizing the coming kingdom of God in the present. Okholm captured the church's task well during a lecture given at Fuller Theological Seminary:

> It's like this, when my kids were really young and we would get to Thanksgiving, their language and behavior began to change. It's because something was coming—Christmas! That's the way the church should be living—in such a way that people look at the church and say, "You all are living in such a way as if something else is coming that isn't here yet."

One of the points Okholm was trying to make is that the church's communal life is influenced by the eschatology it holds. The church's task, he believes, is to live in ways that bring God's future into the present— a future in which God's justice and love restores and heals the world, ushering in a new creation. What Okholm offers to Christians in his own context is an approach to theology based on his own friendship with God and a life immersed in the community of the church.

To Be Welcomed as Christ

Okholm's theological journey is difficult to summarize because of the numerous communities with which he has invested his life. His own context in the Christian story has involved leadership as an academic theologian in largely white evangelical Christian spaces, and as an ordained minister. He was raised Baptist, received his PhD from Princeton Theological Seminary, ordained into the Presbyterian Church (USA) for twenty-seven years, became an Oblate with the Order of Saint Benedict in 1989, and is now a Canon Theologian for the Diocese of Churches for the Sake of Others in the Anglican Church of North America. In addition to his former role as professor of theology at Wheaton College for fourteen years and his current role as professor of theology at Azusa Pacific

University since 2003, he also taught periodically at Fuller Theological Seminary and Young Life Training Institute and preached and lectured around the United States and in Canada, Sudan, Kenya, and Romania.

In all of these rolls, Okholm has committed himself to, as he has said in numerous personal conversations, "filling the pews of the church with theologically and biblically literate members." The intention of this book is to give a glimpse into the decades Okholm has invested in others to bring that goal into fruition. It is by no means comprehensive, but it attempts to commend some of the multi-faceted ways he has tried to help his Christian communities flourish.

One of the primary ways he has done this is by building bridges between his own communities and that of others who have come to know Jesus in their own ways. Okholm does this not only out of a sense of curiosity in the ways God is at work in the lives of others, but also out of a genuine desire to be a hospitable person. His hospitality extends outwards as he befriends others, serving and educating communities into which he is invited, and it also flows inwards as he makes room in his own life to receive those same gifts from others.

This theme of hospitality in relation to Okholm's own life and stream within Christianity motivates the title of this book: *To Be Welcomed as Christ*. It specifically comes from chapter fifty-three of St. Benedict's *Rule*, "The Reception of Guests," where Benedict establishes how Benedictine communities should treat guests of the community: "All guests who present themselves are to be welcomed as Christ, for he himself will say: 'I was a stranger and you welcomed me' (Matt 25:35)."[4] Okholm is no stranger to treating guests in this way; he has graciously welcomed strangers into his own community of faith and has also received this gift of hospitality as he has been brought into diverse communities of which many evangelicals are otherwise ignorant or apathetic. His willingness to welcome strangers into his own evangelical communities and his excitement to learn from different branches of the Christian church by participating in communities other than his own is a model in dire need of imitation.

Hospitality extended to others is mutually beneficial. As much as it is a gift to receive one's hospitality, the person extending it is also transformed. Spending his life with others outside of his own flock has encouraged Okholm to try to see others as God sees them. He writes in *Monk Habits for Everyday People*: "If we could genuinely practice

---

4. Benedict, *The Rule*, 73. Thanks to Rick Cummings for suggesting that the title of this book should be rooted in this chapter from St. Benedict's *Rule*.

Benedict's brand of hospitality, welcoming each guest to our churches as the visitation of Christ, it might transform our guests as well as us. Instead of making the other into my image, I am invited to see the other as one who is made in God's image and for whom Jesus Christ died."[5]

Okholm's theological emphasis on friendship is important to this posture of hospitality because of the love that is at the core of his extension of friendship to others. This love is motivated by the hospitable love extended by God to the world through Jesus Christ. Extended to others in friendship, Liz Carmichael writes that this love has "its focus on the person and what they may become. . . . The love of friendship is creative of personhood, rejoicing in each person's potential and suffering when that potential is missed or marred. Love is God's way of creating and revealing goodness."[6] Through individual and communal friendships, hospitable love is extended and a bridge is built that enables one another to receive and witness the ways that God is at work in the lives of others.

As often as Okholm encouraged hospitality in his own communities, he was also enhancing the lives of people in communities other than his own. Sister Michaeleen Jantzer, one of the Benedictines responsible for introducing Okholm to the Benedictine way, wrote a letter to me in April 2020 reflecting on her friendship with Okholm. She wrote that the Christian denominational differences between her and Okholm "have enhanced our friendship." These differences and the way in which Okholm has chosen to live out his own faith, she writes, "has enriched my ability to live my own Catholic faith."

Okholm has sought a life for evangelicals that is enriched by the presence of other Christians. In his own life, this has taken time, patience, and stability, but the effort has helped him come to know and enjoy God more fully in the company of others. In another passage from *Monk Habits*, he uses the phrase "Crockpot Christianity" to describe the stability he learned from the Benedictines: "I stew slowly in one place until I become what God intended."[7]

---

5. Okholm, *Monk Habits*, 82.

6. Carmichael, *Friendship*, 197–98.

7. Okholm, *Monk Habits*, 96.

Pursuing a Hospitable Evangelicalism

This book is motivated by Okholm's hospitality and his goal of filling the church with biblically and theologically literate Christians. It contains a small sampling of Okholm's care for the life of the church, his desire for evangelicalism to be a more hospitable home for all within its fold and in relation to other communities, and his desire for friendship to have a more prominent role in theological and biblical reflection. Each of these authors is tapping into a strand of Okholm's passions and commitments that make his life compelling and hospitable to a wide array of people in the church and the academy. Each contributor has the pleasure of knowing Okholm professionally and personally and chose to contribute in order to continue carrying on elements of his work in their own contexts.

While Okholm has expressed his personal dismay to me and others over the current state of American evangelicalism, his lifelong commitment to evangelicalism has been characterized by a deep love and passion for the church as well as his inclusion of people often neglected by white mainstream evangelicalism. Okholm's awareness of and passion for the diversity of the kingdom of God has led him to pursue dialogue with Mormons; make room for women and people of color in traditionally white male spaces; form friendships and learn from Benedictines through meals, pints, and worship; and offer the liturgical imagination of Anglicanism and his own love for the church to the many students he teaches in predominantly evangelical spaces.

Although Ellen Charry is not an evangelical, her opening chapter captures the task of theology and the responsibility such work entails that has often characterized Okholm's life. Her distress over the rupture between the ancient spiritual and modern academic approaches to the purpose of theology is aimed at the promotion of a flourishing life. Theology's fundamental task that is deeply in need of retrieval is to "help the community help people know, love, and enjoy God better so that the communities to which they contribute may flourish." Flourishing corresponds not to a set of propositional claims but to a beautiful life that is lived in the context of one's own community.

Todd Hunter focuses on the centrality of the church as the particular community out of which Christians extend hospitality to all people—the same hospitality that they have been extended by the head of the body, Jesus Christ. Hunter suggests a trinitarian framework that grounds the church's nature and purpose from which Christians can participate in God's ongoing purposes to redeem and restore the world.

Justin Ashworth attempts to salvage what he sees as problematic enactments of God's mission in the world due to the ways evangelical understandings have been fused with right-wing politics. Taking cues from trinitarian doctrine and Latin American liberationist hermeneutics, Ashworth offers a different evangelical approach to God's mission to redeem the world in ways that are liberating, justice-oriented, and communal.

Vincent Bacote, Jennifer Buck, and Richard Mouw focus on the potential within evangelicalism to be a more hospitable home than it has been historically. Evangelical communities have not reached their full potential because of those within who have excluded, marginalized, or ignored those who are deemed to be different. However, each author plumbs resources within and beyond evangelicalism not to condemn it but to help it flourish. The diversity of expression and relatively traditionless nature of evangelicalism allows for constant renewal and rejuvenation if leaders and communities are willing to listen and recognize the ongoing need to make evangelicalism a home for all who desire.

Bacote challenges the white supremacy permeating evangelical spaces, arguing that it jeopardizes the core theological commitment of evangelicalism. Bacote envisions an evangelicalism that can truly be a home for all—and that the centrality of the Bible provides an anchor upon which evangelical practice and belief can be held accountable. Following this call for evangelicalism to become its best self, Buck offers an overview of women in Scripture and a selection throughout the history of the church that have been neglected by mainstream evangelical theologians. Her overview of these women is a step toward rediscovering women who have been pushed to the margins despite the compelling ways they have chosen to follow God for the sake of others.

Writing with decades of evangelical interfaith dialogue experience, Mouw identifies the lack of a robust theology of interfaith dialogue as a major stumbling block for evangelicals, hindering them from approaching people of different religious traditions with a genuine curiosity and willingness to learn. Rather than treating interfaith dialogue as a covert operation in evangelism, Mouw proposes a humble and theologically motivated approach to interfaith dialogue that relies on friendship with those who would otherwise be strangers, as well as a sustained trust in the work of the Holy Spirit in lives beyond those within the bounds of the Christian Church.

Robert Millet, Professor and Dean of Religious Education at Brigham Young University and deeply involved in Mormon–evangelical dialogue with Mouw and Okholm, gives his own account of the decades of dialogue he co-led with Mouw. Millet's assessment embodies the characteristics of interfaith dialogue that Mouw espouses. He suggests that even in the midst of profound differences between his own community and the evangelical community with which he was in dialogue, the similarities between the two communities were both a cause for celebration and opportunities for further introspection. Both communities came to a deeper understanding of their own convictions in light of their friendship with the other and grew in their awareness of God's presence in one another's communities.

Okholm has also been at the forefront of introducing evangelicals to Benedictine spirituality. His own pursuit of it beginning in the 1980s led him to become an Oblate in the Order of Saint Benedict and also to emphasize the ways in which friendship, community, and virtues sustain the Christian life. These were not emphases absent from his theological outlook before experiencing them through his friendships with Benedictines, but they did take on a more pronounced form in his theological trajectory.

Motivated by this trend in Okholm's work, Rodney Clapp focuses on the practice of "remonking" the church; a challenge to renew one's own community that he extends to all Christians. Resisting the stereotypical dismissal of monasticism as an elitist or sectarian way of life meant for only a select few Christians, Clapp identifies ancient modes of monasticism as well as newer adaptations among Protestants and evangelicals, believing they have the potential to bring about deep renewal in the life of evangelical communities.

Scot McKnight provides a compelling Pauline theology of friendship, suggesting that at the core of Paul's pastoral ministry was the conversion of friendship into siblingship—a conversion constituted by nurturing friends into co-workers for the sake of the gospel. Nurturing these siblings was Paul's goal in his ministry; one that was deeply practical and aimed at helping his brothers and sisters grow in the virtues emulated by Christ.

David Fugoyo-Baime, originally from South Sudan and now residing in Uganda, highlights the strong resonance African Christians have with the type of friendship extended to all by Jesus because of a shared cultural value on friendship. In Fugoyo-Baime's context the term *Wiri*

Nina is used to identify one's closest friends as sharing the same significant bond one has with one's own sibling. *Wiri Nina* is correlated with
Christian friendship in order to underscore the unity all Christians are
meant to share as siblings in Christ's body.

Craig Keen argues that the language and logic of the market, and of
Christian friendship, are at best contradictory, and at worst mutually exclusive. The love of Christ and his commission for Christians to love their
neighbors and enemies alike is a challenge and rebuke to the nefarious
tendencies of market-driven ideology. Is friendship integral to discipleship, or will Jesus's cross lead his followers away from the happy life of
friendship to one that is always giving oneself to the despised, lonely, and
forgotten of the world?

Following the importance of virtues in Benedictine spirituality,
Robert Roberts's contribution focuses on the virtue of humility, exploring whether or not one is able to be proud of the progress one has made
in living a life of humility. Although this may be paradoxical, he suggests
that distinguishing vicious pride from pride that is virtuous makes it possible for a Christian to feel proud of the progress one has made toward
virtuous humility. Pride in one's humility is appropriate as one aims at the
sort of virtues that are constitutive of a flourishing community; a pride
that builds up the community of which the individual is a part.

Michael McNichols's concluding chapter focuses on Dennis
Okholm, attempting to better capture the ways in which his life has
attempted to model the hospitality that is offered to all by Christ. Mc-
Nichols highlights Okholm's "hospitable reach" that has led him into a
multi-faceted vocation of teaching and ministry, as well as an openness
to different streams of Christianity. As McNichols writes, "Hospitality is
not simply a thing that he does as the occasion arises; hospitality is, for
Dennis, a practice of his life."

Finally, a brief epilogue is written by Brother Benet Tvedten, one of
the key Benedictines responsible for encouraging Okholm to become an
Oblate in the Order of Saint Benedict. Br. Benet's epilogue is his reflection
on the unexpected journey that Okholm and other Protestants have taken
into Benedictine spirituality and community—a journey responsible for
decades of prayerful friendship between he and Okholm.

Each entry in this book (and many more that could have been included) is written by a person who has experienced the ways in which
Okholm goes into communities without presuming he has everything
to offer—a novel trait among academics. His warmth and humility has

often made others feel comfortable to share their gifts with him. Okholm is open to being formed by the gifts of God he finds in other people and communities. This openness has allowed him to fill many pews not only with biblically and theologically literate Christians, but with friends who seek to embody and share his curiosity, kindness, and hospitality with others.

⌖

This project began in 2014 and has progressed in anticipation of Dennis Okholm's retirement. Since 2014 I have had the pleasure of connecting with many of Dennis's closest friends and colleagues from around the world. Each conversation and email about Dennis stretched my understanding of the number of communities he has impacted and how many colleagues and former students he has turned into friends. Immense gratitude is in order for the multitude of people who helped with this project, especially Trevecca Okholm, Justin Ashworth, Rodney Clapp, Michael McNichols, and many of Dennis's former students and colleagues who took the time to identify the key traits that make Dennis's approach to theology and love for the church so compelling. Additionally, each contributor was a pleasure to work with and enthusiastically embraced the opportunity to honor Dennis's work. I appreciate the time they invested in writing their respective chapters and the care and thoughtfulness that went into their work.

A special note of gratitude is due to Rick Cummings, who helped edit the entirety of this book and was a support and sounding board for me throughout the many years it took to bring this project into fruition. I have witnessed from both Dennis and Rick that the task of theology is meaningless apart from one's friends. Thanks also to my wife, Ellen Summerfelt, who was a constant presence and encouragement. This book would not have happened without the gift of time that she gave me to invest in this project from beginning to end.

I do think I would have stayed in the church whether or not I had met Dennis Okholm. However, my love for theology and desire for the church to flourish is indebted to him. Thank you, Dennis, for nurturing me in the faith, instilling within me a hospitable approach to theology and people, and for the ongoing gift of friendship.

Bibliography

Benedict. *The Rule of St. Benedict*. Edited by Timothy Fry. Collegeville: Liturgical, 1981.

Carmichael, Liz. *Friendship: Interpreting Christian Love*. London: T. & T. Clark, 2004.

Okholm, Dennis. *Learning Theology through the Church's Worship*. Grand Rapids: Baker Academic, 2018.

———. *Monk Habits for Everyday People: Benedictine Spirituality for Protestants*. Grand Rapids: Brazos, 2007.

1

Theology as a Healing Art

Ellen T. Charry

Dennis Okholm repairs damaged bridges. Task-oriented, future-directed Americans are particularly prone to neglecting the past, relinquishing custom, and seeking novelty, ignoring the need for healing. Perhaps trained by the advertising industry selling products based on planned obsolescence cultivates craving novelty interested in keeping pocketbooks open and the economy afloat. To this, Okholm says, wait a minute. As one of my own teachers taught me, just because they didn't have computers, doesn't mean that you are smarter than those who've come before. Perhaps the contrary dependent as we are on machines to do our thinking for us. We speak of "the wisdom of the ages" for a reason. Indeed. At bottom, Okholm is inviting us to consider just that wisdom. He is calming underlying Protestant anger at the corruption of the medieval church that took on a life of its own yet is now anachronistic. His reconsideration of monasticism is a humble penitential move for Protestant doctrine and practice. Sometimes looking back enables moving forward. While the Catholic instinct is to repair what has gone awry, the Protestant instinct has been to get rid of it. Enough time has now elapsed since righteous indignation drove the Protestant Reformation that evangelicals may see that in running to fresh ground they discarded valuable treasures. Indignation may by now have run its course unless we indoctrinate students into the sixteenth century's theological problems as their own at the expense of current theological needs. Indeed, penitential humility became the chief virtue of western monasticism. Okholm's work exemplifies it.

Damaged bridges are not only between the Great Church and Protestantism that Okholm's retrieval of Benedictine spirituality and patristic psychology addresses.[1] Other bridges were damaged between church and culture with modernity—perhaps itself born of Protestant rejectionism—that also charted a fresh way forward. So, for example, Okholm is offering a way to get from the modern evangelical notion of faith as assent to intellectual propositions to faith as the cultivation of "the law of the Spirit of life in Christ Jesus" as Paul understood the purpose of following Christ according to Romans 8:2: "For the law of the Spirit of life in Christ Jesus has set you free from the law of sin and of death."[2] In this particular case, Okholm is reclaiming the ancient notion that following the Anointed Savior is not assenting to a set of ideas that enable one to live forever or escape eternal punishment but to a beautiful life. He is healing theology of its rationalist cognitive obsession back into beauty.

The point of this reflection on theology is not to besmirch or regret modernity but to recognize that every strength has its weakness. In creating modern science, medicine, and technology, some valuable things fell by the wayside—beauty, truth, and goodness chief among them. We do not have to, indeed, cannot choose sides between modern science and the value of goodness and beauty as true wisdom of God because embracing science and technology does not preclude admitting that we do not need the wisdom of God. In this we are no different from the pre-moderns. This essay hopes to contribute to the bridge-repairing effort, particularly repairing the break within theology itself between the ancient spiritual and modern academic understandings of what it is and does.

What Is Theology?

Theology is a notoriously slippery word. Assuming that the world is intelligible, it became reasoned thought seeking the truth about god and the things of god. I use the lower case "g" here to indicate that theology is larger than reflection on the God of Israel whom Jews, Christians, and

---

1. See Okholm's *Monk Habits* and *Dangerous Passions*.

2. Unless otherwise noted, all biblical quotations in this volume are from the New Revised Standard Version (NRSV).

Muslims worship. Plato, Aristotle, Zeno, and Epicurus were theologians, although they did not know of the biblical God. As reasoned thought, theology aims at human flourishing through an intentional life based on the orderliness of the world grounded in god. Theology's chief task is to help society flourish by enabling individuals to flourish. Christian theology assumes that that is not going too well and aims to heal the fault.

As conversation, theology is a human word, one hopes a lucid word, a vulnerable word. And as a vulnerable human word about god and the things of god it invites discussion, correction, and repair. Theology is thus a conversation across the ages, gathering up the wisdom of each, known primarily by assessing and (re)interpreting its honored texts, that the wisdom of the ages may refresh and guide each generation.

Working within a classical theistic heritage that keeps God at its center, Christian theology itself became a tradition that abides by certain conventions that both preserve the heritage and give each generation fresh access to it. Christian theological convention adopted Greek philosophical categories that describe the ancient notion of perfection as divine attributes rather than the biblical ones listed at Exodus 34:6 (paraphrased at Jonah 4:2): "The LORD passed before [Moses], and proclaimed, 'The Lord, the Lord, a God merciful and gracious, slow to anger, and abounding in steadfast love and faithfulness.'" Christian insistence on divine perfection removed God from history making it difficult for theology to make sense of God entering history as a Judean carpenter.

Leaving that logical conundrum aside for now, theology has other work to do. Since it is undertaken to help people, heal people so that they understand themselves and the world salutarily, it requires interpretation of the culture in which it resides. So, theology looks in two directions simultaneously, seeking to interpret the culture to the tradition and the tradition to the culture. To do this well, theology esteems the literature, stories, and practices of its particular heritage and puts these in conversation with contemporary needs and society's circumstances.

From this perspective, theology is a helping profession like auto mechanics, pharmacy, social work, dietetics, medicine, and law—before the last two became business ventures. They all seek or sought to keep people safe and functioning well in order to secure societal well-being. Theology seeks to heal society that individuals may flourish and to heal individuals that society may flourish. This is a mutually enhancing cycle. Morally and economically healthy societies foster individual flourishing and flourishing individuals enable morally, spiritually, and socially flourishing societies. To this end, theology is the self-observing physician of religious communities, correcting and repairing them when criticisms from outside the community or current in the general culture are sufficiently persuasive for insiders to recognize that certain beliefs or practices are or have become corporately or individually harmful. The task here is self-reflection unto self-repair, not polemic to bolster itself against an alternative interpretation of the texts that constitute the tradition.

The medicinal function of theology is not to adapt the tradition to current tastes but to examine its doctrines and practices to enable the heritage to be its best self so that it will form people for excellent lives. One current example is the secular ecology movement that enables Christians to understand the biblical doctrine of creation better. Genesis 1:28: "God blessed them, and God said to them, 'Be fruitful and multiply, and fill the earth and subdue it; and have dominion over the fish of the sea and over the birds of the air and over every living thing that moves upon the earth.'" The blessing has an ugly underside for it seems to permit the exploitation of animals and perhaps of the earth itself. Once ecological awareness is raised however, ecologically attuned biblical texts make a stronger impression. Deuteronomy 20:19 on the conduct of war is one: "If you besiege a town for a long time, making war against it in order to take it, you must not destroy its trees by wielding an ax against them. Although you may take food from them, you must not cut them down. Are trees in the field human beings that they should come under siege from you?" Another ecologically attuned text is Deuteronomy 22:6–7: "If you come on a bird's nest, in any tree or on the ground, with fledglings or eggs, with the mother sitting on the fledglings or on the eggs, you shall not take the mother with the young. Let the mother go, taking only the young for yourself, in order that it may go well with you and you may live long."

At the same time, secular culture is capable of deforming or harming people. When this happens, the theologian becomes the attorney for the heritage, interpreting its salient teaching to those outside the community in terms that they can grasp, as well as to insiders who entertain similar questions or experiences. An example is the question of whether Christians may participate in war. The question was first discussed by Augustine of Hippo who coined the term "just war."[3] He judged that Christians may be soldiers under certain conditions. "Christians could

3. Augustine, "Securing the Peace of Babylon," 162–83.

serve in the army as long as it was for just reasons such as obeying the commands of God, the righting of wrongs or in pursuit of a better state of peace. In addition, soldiers were required to obey the legitimate orders of their superiors."[4] Augustine's concern for just conditions for war reverberates unto our own day. Aspects of it remain controversial but that too has been a helpful stimulus for wider consideration of how a general culture receives theological reflection.

Following the master bishop, Aquinas the monk discussed the notion of just war at *Summa Theologiae* 2.2.40.[5] He sustained the master's judgment that Christians may soldier but developed three criteria to judge a war to be just: It must be formally, legally declared. It cannot be a private war. That is homicide. It must be defensive, not offensive, although he permits ambush to catch the enemy off-guard. Expanding on Augustine, it must be undertaken for the sake of establishing peace, not for self-aggrandizement or cruelty. These conditions aim to strictly control the desire for revenge or to cause harm to personal adversaries. Aquinas's opinion was highly respected in the sixteenth into the seventeenth century. Two Christian theologians, Francisco Suarez and Hugo Grotius, both advanced just war theory in the international arena as international law was aborning.

These Christians set in motion wider currents for international reflection on humanitarian considerations of conduct of war. Thus, Christian theology contributed to the Geneva Conventions, legal treaties on internationally agreed upon standards for humanitarian treatment and rights of wartime prisoners, protections for the wounded and sick, and treatment of refugees that were signed in 1949 in response to the Second World War. Developing Christian reflection on war further, the National Conference of Catholic Bishops issued a pastoral letter on war and peace in 1983 in response to the buildup of nuclear weapons stockpiles.[6]

Augustine's criteria for what constitutes a war that Christians may soldier for in good conscience seeded much further reflection. Christianity's just war principles went on to shape modern just war theory far beyond Christianity. Here we have an example of theology being the attorney for the heritage. Here theology is meeting its responsibility by

---

4. Lee, "Selective Memory," 309–22.

5. Question 2.2.40 has four articles. His primary contribution to just war theory is in Article 1. Article 2 provides for military chaplains.

6. National Conference of Catholic Bishops, *The Challenge of Peace*.

making its case for the well-being of society at large by elaborating its humanitarian values for public use.

Here we see two basic roles for theology. As physician, it is self-critical, examining the heritage for weaknesses that have harmed and may yet harm individuals or communities. In this role, theology also examines the intellectual framework in which beliefs and practices were formulated. If they have ceased to edify and become demoralizing because the intellectual climate has rendered them obscure and abstruse, reframing becomes necessary. In dusting off arcane language and actions, theology functions as Christianity's physician by repairing and re-presenting doctrines and practices so that they enhance the flourishing of its members. As attorney, theology both defends the tradition to its critics and goes public carrying its gifts to a wider world speaking an edifying word in language that the latter can understand. Thus, theology faces in two directions simultaneously both for the common good. While it is important to clarify evasive ideas for intellectual acuity theology's primary task is to edify both the community and those beyond. Here the goal is to enable God to be seen as the life-giving power for living that enhances the common good. This is the pastoral, spiritual, and moral function of theology to which we now turn.

Theology's Formation and Deformation

The burden of this argument is that theology—in the narrow sense of exegeting doctrines and practices for the sake of the flourishing of individuals and society—has lost its focus. Normatively speaking it is both an intellectual and a spiritual activity. Modernity, however, threw theology into crisis because it unseated the worldview, the intellectual foundation on which Christianity was built. This was a three-tiered universe divided into heaven, earth, and hell in which the world we know and the lives we live are lived in only one of three tiers and not the most important of them. In modernity heaven and hell evaporated rendering classical Christian eschatology unintelligible. To regain intellectual credibility theologians turned to the coherence of ideas (the picture puzzle image is again apt) to demonstrate the "truth" of Christianity because they could no longer rely on the correspondence notion of truth where theological claims made in the visible world were assumed to correspond to items in an invisible world beyond time-space.

Modernity destroyed the view that biblical narratives and claims have actual referents in an invisible realm of reality, rendering them untrue. In response to this crisis, modern theology moved to claiming that truth depends not on referring to reality in another realm of existence but on the coherence of ideas presented. This gave birth to systematic theology that rests its truth claims on the integrity of all Christian claims around a single idea. Modern systematic theology assumed that demonstrating intellectual coherence was the only thing necessary to save Christianity's credibility. This eclipsed the pastoral, spiritual and edifying tasks of theology especially in its Protestant forms. Rebuilding that bridge is Dennis Okholm's project.

The spiritual or pastoral task of theology requires the psychological perspicuity to invite people into an intentionally godly life. One must consider the possible effects doctrines and practices might have on those who take them seriously. The larger task of theology then is to help the community help people know, love, and enjoy God better so that the communities to which they contribute may flourish. As noted, theology is a public-spirited endeavor. It calls for recalibrating doctrines and practices not only when they lose intellectual cogency but also when they become psychologically or emotionally harmful to persons and communities.

Augustine's *De Trinitate* distinguished theology's "scientific" task from its sapiential or spiritual task. Its first half articulates the Christian doctrine of God from scripture and logic while its second half is Augustine's moral psychology, its *sapientia*, its spirituality. Theology's *scientia* is the biblical, historical, factual, or rational content of the tradition. It distills and clarifies knowledge (*scientia*) about the triune God for its usefulness to Christians. Augustine's challenge in part two of *De Trinitate* is to render the cognitively mind-numbing doctrine of the trinity spiritually useful. The baptismal creed's three articles themselves intend to display the divine triplicity but it can easily be read as presenting three gods. The burden of his argument is not only to explain that the three are one God, the God of Israel, but also to explain that by seeing the one God we can discover ourselves as the image of God that is our proper identity and dignity—the true beauty of who we are in God. That is using *scientia* to *sapientia*. Augustine carries the intellectual deposit of the faith into the inner life—knowing, loving, and enjoying our identity as the image of God enables a stellar life.

Exegeting this doctrine for its perspicuity alone, as if clarity and coherence without existential and emotional appeal suffice for a godly life misses theology's goal of fully engaging people about the quality of their moral and spiritual life. Identifying a set of propositions to be assented to in order to win salvation through intellectual compliance may be intellectually elegant but it is not necessarily emotionally alluring. Doctrine must involve more than cognition to shape a whole self for a beautiful life. It must press beyond *scientia's* confines. God must be able to (re)form the self with social and emotional strengths and virtues. Theology must produce *sapientia*. For one who images God, biological attributes and socio-economic distinctions become instrumental to a higher purpose. One's higher self enables one to use these material strengths in service to a God-guided life that benefits the common weal. To this end, doctrinal exegesis must enable one to experience oneself as participating in and becoming an agent of the redemption of the cosmos through life in, with, and through God. This cannot be done without cognition but neither is cognition sufficient to the task.

The union of *scientia* and *sapientia* began to weaken when theology moved from monastic cathedral schools into the medieval university of Paris in the twelfth century and was academized. The following century Thomas Aquinas produced his powerfully influential *Summa Theologiae*, dividing his complete interpretation of Christian theology into three parts.[7] At the very beginning (1.1.1) he defines theology's goal as human well-being (*salutem*) for which we need to be instructed by divine revelation that gives knowledge from God because philosophy is limited to human reason. The well-being he has in mind is beyond what reason can achieve. "Above all because God destines us for an end beyond the grasp of reason" interpretation of divine revelation is requisite. Part I presents the *scientia* of the first article of the Creed.

Part II of the *Summa Theologiae* is Aquinas's massive character ethics running to thirty-three volumes. It is analogous but not comparable to Augustine's turn to the inner life with his moral psychology that promotes a salutary life. Perhaps because Aquinas was a university professor and not a functioning bishop as Augustine was, ethics itself is offered in argumentative form as the whole *Summa Theologiae* is. At its outset he

7. The *Summa Theologiae* has a highly dialectical structure of treatises, topically ordered around a major theme. Each topical treatise is written as a series of questions to the topic, and each question is comprised of sub-questions or articles. Each article states the question, gives objections to the implied answer to the question, then brings an authority who weighs in on the other side of the objections. Thomas then offers his answer to the two sides of the argument. Each article closes with his reply to each of the opening objections.

elaborates what he said at 1.1.1. Here the moral well-being of human life is happiness (*felicitas*). That can be achieved imperfectly in this life, but perfect bliss is only achievable after this life. One should keep in mind that Aquinas also wrote of assent to doctrines contributing to Christian identity.

While Aquinas detailed many virtues in Part II, the presentation was philosophically precise rather than emotionally inviting, as was scholasticism more broadly. At the same time, we should remember that as a monk Aquinas lived the life of prayer, although he was assigned the intellectual work of Inquisition to defend orthodoxy against the Albigensians. Doctrinal theology that encourages moral and spiritual well-being began to be eclipsed by rationalism. While this shift was motivated by the appropriate desire to keep beliefs and practice from veering off into psychologically harmful extremes, it effectively though perhaps inadvertently marginalized theology's sapiential task.

Modern science emerged in the seventeenth century and quite transformed both truth and knowledge. Classically, knowledge was to beauty, truth, and goodness all of which were morally and spiritually freighted. Whatever is beautiful or true or good can give the soul greater capacity to understand God, self, others, and the world more deeply. They enable ascent to God so that one becomes morally beautiful, true to the best she can be, and stretching into the goodness of God. Beginning with Locke and Descartes, modernity stripped beauty and goodness from truth and transformed it into correct information about things that are verifiable and quantifiable. Knowledge was no longer expected to yield wisdom but only information.[8] *Scientia* no longer aimed to help people experience the wisdom of God but to improve the quality of life. Knowledge was transformed from morally and emotionally uplifting, to being the result of analyzing facts. Scientists are not concerned with beauty and goodness but humanists aim to expand the soul. And that is not quantifiable. Scientists and humanists have difficulty understanding one another. Theology, having lost its sapiential interest and being unable to compete with modern knowledge lost its way.

With the crisis of modernity, Christianity became unintelligible. In response it sought to modernize by trying to scientize. Having already been academized by medieval and later Protestant scholasticism, when the modern research university was formed in Berlin, theology presented

8. Taylor, *Sources of the Self.*

itself as a science in order to demonstrate its appropriateness there. Friedrich Schleiermacher literally wrote the book on this (1810, second edition 1830) when he assumed the professorship in theology at the new University of Berlin.[9] He defined theology as a "positive science" whose various disciplines join together to govern the church's faith in cultivating consciousness of God. For this he designated two types of theologian—the academic whose task is the philosophical, historical, and doctrinal elucidation of Christian beliefs and practices (theology in the narrow sense); the other the minister whose task is proper administration of the local church. "Science" here refers to the rational, orderly methods that rely on the actual historical experience of Christianity to talk about a way of being conscious of God that aims to provide skilled Church leadership.

To these ends Schleiermacher created the modern "theological encyclopedia," the organization of many theological disciplines into three divisions or departments: philosophical theology, historical theology, and practical theology. Most divinity schools and seminaries that train professional ministers retain some aspects of this three-fold division. As a result of the proliferation of theological subdisciplines and their literature, it becomes impossible or at least intimidating to think and write outside one's area of specialization, creating a silo effect among faculty members of any school. Theological education of clergy becomes disunified, with students needing to figure out what the study of John has to do with preaching on John or whether the Incarnation has anything to say to struggling single mothers.

Today when religious studies eschews any edificatory function and the study of religion has become a social science and no longer a humanistic discipline, one of the *Geisteswissenschaften*, theology considered as a positive science cannot sustain—perhaps not even recognize—edificatory, character building responsibility to help people know, love, and enjoy God. Research universities (as well as undergraduate institutions) may have religious studies departments but these are to impart information not lift the soul to God. Theology, because it is value laden, a normative rather than a descriptive enterprise, may be disrespected or disallowed and be considered inappropriate for a university whose purpose may be to advance knowledge for its own sake, rather than for the sake of the flourishing of its students and teachers who themselves are uplifted by their studies or the communities to which they will contribute. Theology

9. Schleiermacher, *Brief Outline on the Study of Theology.*

is considered inappropriate in such institutions because of the fear that it would seek to influence students about how they are to live, for theology is interested in those for whom it is written, seeking to help them live a wise and beautiful life that enables God's other creatures to flourish. The fear is that the university would usurp the role of parents, assuming that parents do not benefit to additional help and that college freshman no longer need parental or comparable guidance. If school is not to guide but only to inform, religion courses at best function as institutional maintenance for the traditions studied, if that. This concern may be at work in the home-schooling movement, but that is not possible at the college/university level.

On the other hand, fear of authoritarian indoctrination into a particular way of belief and practice is real and it is dangerous in doctrinaire institutions where elasticity in religious commitment and identity is lacking. Yet, how are the young to even consider a godly life without exposure to any alternative to the marketplace? The question of elasticity within religious communities and their practices of formation is difficult to discuss. That will have to await a different opportunity. Suffice it to say here that no musical instrument plays but one note.

So, classical normative theology as practiced by Augustine held that knowledge is to produce wisdom—the ability to use oneself and the world adeptly, constructively, respectfully to enhance creation's flourishing. Wise living is intentional rather than haphazard living, that one may use oneself beautifully for God's pleasure, one's own pleasure, and that of others and all of creation. That construal of theology's responsibility was lost in modernity when the spiritual and moral meaning of truth lost its footing and verifiable and quantifiable information replaced it. Beauty and goodness lost their footing even in the fine arts and were largely replaced by the author's self-expression.

In the mid-nineteenth century, poet and literary critic, Matthew Arnold, seeing that historicism had emptied religion of its formative, uplifting, and consoling power, proposed that religion would and should be replaced with poetry. "More and more mankind will discover that we have to turn to poetry to interpret life for us, to console us, to sustain us."[10] Arnold's work was directed to British "men of letters" like himself; that is a small world indeed. Despite Arnold's attempt to hold onto meaning and moral formation through English poetry, literary criticism has

10. Arnold, "The Study of Poetry," 2.

turned on poetry itself, deconstructing it analogous with historicism's deconstruction of Christianity. Art as formation to moral beauty as the goal of education is unintelligible in today's universities. Education is largely vocational instruction and is uninterested in those being instructed. Formation of a wise and beautiful self gave way to filling the mind with competing ideas and quantifiable facts.

At this point, it must be clearly said that one essential role of the arts, as is the case with theology also, is to offer discerning criticism of society that it avoid harming its members. Yet the line between constructive criticism and harmful criticism is a fine one, especially when criticism is driven by anger, frustration, and deep dissatisfaction with current arrangements. Revolutions all face this question. It is one reason why revolutionaries may not be the best administrators of an institution once the offending structure is overthrown.

The preceding contextualizes theology's role among the humanities, including the arts that, like theology, have societal flourishing at heart. For the most part, theology fell in with the modern view that stripped knowledge of spiritual aspirations. This was recognized as a problem by the President of Princeton Theological Seminary, Benjamin Breckinridge Warfield in 1911 when he delivered "The Religious Life of Theological Students." Warfield worried that the historical consciousness of theological studies was undermining student piety as they came to realize that Christianity was forged over time. Not wanting to impugn his faculty, Warfield implored students to attend area churches on Sunday where he hoped preaching might repair any damage done by growing historical consciousness. Yet he ignored the fact that the preachers to whom he commended the students were in fact the products of precisely the modern academic studies that his faculty were teaching current students. Biblical, historical, and theological disciplines were already severed from spiritual edification. The biblical historians, church historians, and historically attentive theologians and ethicists were not interested in the edificatory potential of the doctrinal ideas being forwarded. Separation of theological studies into disciplines and subdisciplines destroyed the possibility that the Bible should edify its readers.

Theology in the narrow traditional sense of interpreting doctrines (dogmatic and systematic theology) became informational study and lost its calling to help people as medicine, clinical psychology, and social work do. Further, it lost its humanistic orientation where, like the study of literature and poetry, the ancient understanding of philosophy, and study of languages and the fine arts, it aims at the expansion of the soul and the cultivation of wisdom.[11] While theology works through a substantial body of literature with technical vocabulary, tradition, and recommended methods, it is not like cooking or sewing where one follows a recipe but more like an art. When I say art, however, I do not mean in the modern sense where the artist is primarily expressing her own ideas, personality, creativity, or virtuosity. I use art in the classical sense that the clinical practice of medicine is an art that is in service to a higher goal than self-expression. A fine health care professional is using the art of medicine not to express herself, but to serve the patient with the best means at her disposal. Medicine requires the art of giving. I understand theology similarly to employ the truth of God made known to the Jewish people, the Christian Church, and the Islamic Umma to carry God's creatures into an excellent life for their sake and for the sake of the communities to which they contribute. On these terms, modern Christian systematic and dogmatic theology are in an abnormal state, perhaps even in a state of apostasy, having truncated their interest in—and thereby abandoned—their sapiential responsibility.

Repairing the Broken Bridge

I have argued that Augustine of Hippo established the normative dynamic of theology: knowledge is to wisdom. The reason to examine Christianity in detail is to enable Jesus-believers to become wise by understanding Christianity adeptly in order to walk a beautiful Christian life. With monasticism, the dominant strategy for this in the west became inducing fear and cultivating humility, even cringing humility to promote morally healthy societies.

Perhaps in the high Middle Ages with the embrace of Aristotle, but certainly later with the emergence of modern science, theology backed off from the Augustinian conviction that the intellectual guardians of the faith promote the spiritual and moral wisdom of those under their care. This is vividly illustrated by Protestant theology that eschewed the spiritual writers, spiritual direction, and the edificatory function of theological exegesis—to the point that Christian psychology became an obtuse

11. Philosophy, like theology, experienced dramatic transformation in modernity. Ancient philosophy is moral philosophy laying out various visions of what the good life is and how to live it. See Annas, *The Morality of Happiness*; Hadot, *Philosophy as a Way of Life*.

undertaking. Protestant pietism voiced objection to this direction creating the modern holiness traditions, particularly Wesleyan Methodism. Protestant scholasticism in both Lutheran and Calvinist forms ignored the soul, speaking only to the mind as if people could be persuaded of Christianity by cognition alone. If this amounts to apostasy—and I believe abandonment of the soul does—what are we to do now? How are we to repair the breach?

The initial step of repair is the most difficult. It is to admit that the theological disciplines that impart information about God but not guidance for an excellent life with God are truncated. The next step will have to be customized to each discipline's particular needs, for each will need to examine and ascertain the effects its truncated teaching has on those who receive it. Then it will have to ascertain how prepared its practitioners are to address the lacunae in the standard presentation of the material being presented. Where existential, psychological, interpersonal, and spiritual acumen are lacking, even naming them will be difficult for those whose piety is purely cognitive and not experiential.

Theology aims to help as medicine does and has analogues to four features of clinical medicine that make for successful treatment: (1) It has a body of knowledge that must be mastered, interpreted, and adeptly applied. (2) It must look to the accumulated experience of the community to inform us of the practical impact of its doctrines and practices over time and to correct and reshape them when they prove harmful, ineffective, or simply wrong. (3) The theologian must employ discerning judgment about how to interpret beliefs and practices received by the culture in which they are interpreted. (4) It requires the moral integrity and interpretive skill of its practitioners to assure that the beliefs and practices of the tradition really induce a flourishing life that is God's hope for us.

The task of theology is to improve the community's beliefs and practices. It works indirectly rather than directly as medication or surgery do. Theology is an interpretive discipline in the humanities, not the sciences. By reflecting on and critically examining the heritage and the culture of its day, it both speaks to and listens to the general culture in order to contribute its insights and to be strengthened by the general community that God may be glorified.

Theology is as much a spiritual exercise as it is an intellectual undertaking. Spiritual virtues are necessary for all learning, including theological learning. Discerning theology requires specific virtues: It requires acceptance of being accompanied by minds other than one's own; it requires making friends with strangers, even assumed enemies. It requires humility, courage, respect, charity, silence, forgiveness, discipline, and surrender, patience, hope, and prayer. All of these virtues are also necessary for a well lived life. Consider now the virtues required for defending and correcting one's theological community:

> *Humility*: Learning requires the learner to assume that the people whose ideas she encounters have something to teach; that is, that you lack something that they have. To learn from someone—even things they did not mean to teach—you must assume that the author was at least as intelligent, thoughtful, and sensitive as you are. Indeed, in all probability the writer has spent more time in reflection on these matters than you have.

> *Courage*: Study and learning might change you, challenge your most cherished beliefs, even the cause you seek to advance. Courage in this sense is the courage to become vulnerable, to open yourself to ideas you do not want to face, to thinkers you have been led to believe led your community astray, to those who oppress you. Learning requires the courage to be humbled by strangers and enemies as well as to express theological truths even if they are discounted by the larger community.

> *Respect*: To learn, one must genuinely respect otherness. Otherness of intellectual climate, historical circumstance, agenda. One must respect that with which one disagrees; respect the texts and problems with which people previously struggled, even if they stumbled. They probably have more relevance to our day than at first meets the eye.

> *Graciousness*: Being gracious and charitable is the opposite of being vindictive, spiteful, and holding grudges. Scoffing, spite and revenge are defense mechanisms hoping to ward off criticism and new ways of thinking. Without graciousness, however, it is impossible to learn because one is so prideful that there seems nothing to learn or even if there is one fears that one might be brought down a peg by listening to it (Prov 1:22b).

> *Silence*: To learn you must be able to listen, reflect, and ponder what you read without responding to it. Ideas must penetrate you, even those that are alien or at first repugnant. The assiduous mind will probe what this strange idea meant/means to

those who hold it. Consider what this offensive idea teaches you about yourself, how it might humble you.

Forgiveness: To forgive truly means to be arrested by the other perspective, not simply to motion toward acceptance superficially without consequence. Who would be satisfied with that? Forgiveness means taking the other's position seriously, perhaps for the first time. One must begin all over again, having absorbed a different perhaps even odious take on the matter. Without the ability to forgive, the person's gifts will certainly pass you by and you will be left alone, unable to grow, locked in the prejudices you brought with you. Forgiving requires deep spiritual strength.

Discipline: Learning requires disciplined concentration, perseverance until an opaque paragraph breaks open its fruits; it requires being alone and quiet for sustained periods of time, just saying no to being sociable; it requires being well-organized mentally, physically, and economically. There must be adequate time for study and reflection on the material. It requires mental preparedness. Your whole life must be in good running order. You cannot study if your life or your mind is in confusion.

Surrender: Learning requires recognizing and surrendering prejudices and ignorance; learning pierces defensiveness, the need to be right. It may mean surrendering heroes who do not stand up under scrutiny as well. It may require the vulnerability to be converted to whatever you want most to avoid: the patriarchal Christian tradition, liberalism, modernism, conservatism, feminism. Find a mentor.

Patience: Learning requires patience with oneself. The material will be alien and impenetrably difficult. Learning requires endurance and grace in the face of difficulty and failure. It requires patience through the confusion, inner conflict, and uncertainty learning can produce. Learning also requires patience and respect for others, as noted above: respect for one's teachers and colleagues who see things radically differently; patience in dealing with the conflicts that may develop among colleagues, and within yourself. Pray when you are in conflict or angry.

Hope and prayer: To be truly vulnerable to learning you will need hope that on the other side of conflict and uncertainty all will be well. Hope that even if you come out of your study at a different place than you began, that God will lead you where you are to go, and faith that where you are being led is right and proper.

In conclusion, theology is divine service pursuing a God-guided life. At its best, Christianity has a holistic not a dualistic view of human personhood. God created us with bodies and minds. The mind encompasses ideas and emotions. Both thinking and feeling are to know, love, and enjoy God by enhancing the flourishing of the creatures of God. A working definition of theology as the physician and attorney of the heritage is that it is sustained self-critical reflection on a religious or spiritual heritage (in this instance Christianity) that reviews its revered texts and practices to center the community on God and on the things of God that it may foster beautiful lives for its members and the flourishing of the communities to which they contribute.

Bibliography

Annas, Julia. *The Morality of Happiness*. Oxford: Oxford University Press, 1993.

Arnold, Matthew. "The Study of Poetry." In *Essays in Criticism: Second Series*. New York: Macmillan, 1888.

Augustine. "Securing the Peace of Babylon." In *The Political Writings of St. Augustine*, edited by Henry Paolucci, 118–83. Chicago: Regnery, 1996.

National Conference of Catholic Bishops. *The Challenge of Peace: God's Promise and Our Response: A Pastoral Letter on War and Peace*. Washington, DC: United States Catholic Conference, 1983.

Hadot, Pierre. *Philosophy as a Way of Life*. Translated by Michael Case. Oxford: Blackwell, 1995.

Okholm, Dennis. *Dangerous Passions, Deadly Sins: Learning from the Psychology of Ancient Monks*. Grand Rapids: Baker Academic, 2014.

————. *Monk Habits for Everyday People: Benedictine Spirituality for Protestants*. Grand Rapids: Brazos, 2007.

Lee, Peter. "Selective Memory: Augustine and Contemporary Just War Discourse." *Scottish Journal of Theology* 65.3 (2012) 309–22.

Schleiermacher, Friedrich. *Brief Outline on the Study of Theology*. Translated by Terrence N. Tice. Atlanta: John Knox, 1977.

Taylor, Charles. *Sources of the Self: The Making of the Modern Identity*. Cambridge: Harvard University Press, 1989.

Warfield, Benjamin Breckinridge. "The Religious Life of Theological Students." In *Selected Shorter Writings of Benjamin B. Warfield, vol. 1*, edited by John E. Meeter, 411–25. Nutley: Presbyterian and Reformed, 1970.

2

To Be Welcomed as Christ—Into the Church

Todd Hunter

[I]t is impossible to become and to be a Christian apart from the church. To be a Christian is to be a part of Christ's body. The church is the community in which faith is born, nourished, lived out, and proclaimed.[1]

FOR THE MANY YEARS I have known Dennis Okholm, one thing has been clear: Dennis, as the quote above reveals, loves the church. The whole church. The best churches and churches who do not show up on anyone's *best* list. Dennis does not just love the *idea* of the church. His commitment is not to ecclesial or theological abstractions. His practice of church is grounded in the real lives of named people in concrete congregations. At the church where Dennis and I have served, Holy Trinity Anglican Church, Dennis and his wife, Trevecca, are legendary for their hospitality—hospitality that they extend to students who adore them, church members, and first-time visitors alike.

It is this combination of love for the church and welcoming generosity that form the basis for this chapter: *to be welcomed as Christ—into the church*. In this day of great cynicism regarding the church, Dennis' love of it in mission, corporate worship, and personal hospitality is both right and a deliverance from the suffocating contempt that strangles so many imaginations about the God-purposed goodness of the church. The church is something that welcomes people from all walks of life. Such

1. Okholm, *Learning Theology*, 180.

30

acts of relational and spiritual hospitality are core to the will of God for the church.

What Is the Church?

There are four common ways of describing the church. The first is through what is commonly known as the four marks or attributes of the church: *one, holy, catholic,* and *apostolic.* These traditional bits of Christian eccle-siology come from the Nicene-Constantinopolitan Creed completed at the First Council of Constantinople in AD 381. *One* speaks to the es-sential unity of the church. *Holy* denotes the church as called, elected, and separated out for God's purposes. *Catholic* describes the church's univer-sal nature. *Apostolic* is both a *grounding* word—church is centered in the teaching and practices of the apostles—and a *sending* word: the church, like the apostles, is the sent, missionary people of God.[2]

A second common definition says that there is a church where *the word is rightly preached and the sacraments are rightly administered.* A third way of demarcating the church adds to word and sacraments the notion of *church discipline*—an intense focus on right doctrine and obe-dience as a way to ensure the unity of the church. A fourth elaboration of church adds to word, sacrament, and discipline *the central role of the episcopacy*—of bishops in apostolic succession playing a unique role in constituting the church. The main strands of the church—Eastern Or-thodox, Roman Catholic, Lutheran, Reformed, Free Churches, evangeli-cal, and Pentecostal/Charismatic—all have their own adjustments to the above descriptors and add to them their own distinctive elements.[3]

Such definitions are fine as far as they go—but static labels are not sufficient for something meant to be as dynamic as the body of Christ in action on earth. Without minimizing accurate theological definitions, and without denying the importance of the visible, institutional, and sac-ramental elements of church, the definitions above can stick in people's thoughts as merely academic, creating a non-vibrant imagination of the church. At worst, approaching the church as something to be analyti-cally categorized can provide the means for people to conceptualize the centrality of the church while simultaneously failing to participate in the activities of Christ who is at work in the world primarily through the

2. See Van Engen, *God's Missionary People.*
3. See Kärkkäinen, *An Introduction to Ecclesiology.*

church. Charles Van Engen has helpfully suggested that the descriptors one, holy, catholic, and apostolic can be imaginatively construed as both *gifts* and *tasks*; they can be made *adverbs* instead of *adjectives*.[4]

Inert characterizations of the church are in jeopardy of leaving out Jesus's kingdom agenda. Jesus announced, proclaimed, and taught about the kingdom; he demonstrated its effect and its reality in his deeds of power, healing, deliverance, raising the dead, authority over nature's storms, etc. In his way of being in the world, he embodied the obedience and ethics implicit in the rule and reign of God. Whatever else the church might be, it needs to find its meaning and purpose within the person, work, and teaching of Jesus.

The church's foundation is the Triune God who tasks the church with being God's cooperative friends in the world. Notions of the Trinity are crucial for an intuitive sense of what it means to be the church. The Trinity implies relationship. It also implies a movement outward to the other members of the Trinity and to the world. The church is caught up into both those realities: love for the trinitarian God and an outward love for both the members of the church and for the world. Each person in the Godhead informs what the church is in both aspects of *being* and *doing*.

The Father

It is the eternal purpose of the Father to have a people for himself—a purpose that God ordained before the creation of the cosmos. This is seen in creation, in the partnership God envisioned with Adam and Eve, in the calling of Abraham and Israel, in God's deliverance of Israel from Egypt, in the sending of the Son and the Spirit, in the creation of the reconstituted Jew-plus-Gentile people of God (the church), and in the promise that the people of God will rule and reign with him forever in the new heavens and the new earth. This divine intentionality and self-sending points and pulls the church toward God's *telos*—the completion or fulfillment of his eternal purposes. The alignment of the church with the Father entails the transformation of ontological realities, an overall life-ethic, and practices of obedience to his purposes.

4. Van Engen, *God's Missionary People*, 64–65.

The Son

Jesus is God's *word* to us; he is both the explanation and model of God's purposes. He is humanity as God intended. The writer of Hebrews tells us this in narrative form:

> Long ago, at many times and in many ways, God spoke to our fathers by the prophets, but in these last days he has spoken to us by his Son, whom he appointed the heir of all things, through whom also he created the world. He is the radiance of the glory of God and the exact imprint of his nature, and he upholds the universe by the word of his power. (Heb 1:1–3a ESV)

Karl Barth wrote, "the body of Christ derives from Jesus Christ—because of him it exists as his body; apart from Jesus Christ there is no other principle or *telos* to constitute and organize and guarantee the body of Christ."[5] Furthermore, as Okholm sums it up: "The character of the church's mission emerges out of its place in God's history-of-salvation. It emerges from that history's center—Jesus Christ—in which the church has been chosen before the foundation of the world, and then moves out to the world to participate in God's redemption of the cosmos."[6]

The person and work of Jesus are fundamental to who the church is and what the church does. *Being* is expressed as we seek spiritual formation into Christlikeness. The mission of the church finds its expression only as it follows Jesus. Eugene Schlesinger has written that a missional ecclesiology is one that recognizes that mission is not one among the church's various activities or programs, not an optional feature that the church may or may not elect to engage; rather, mission constitutes the essence of the church: "One adheres to Jesus precisely by engaging in his mission."[7] Christopher Wright rounds out my imagination for Jesus-centered mission (and discipleship) saying:

> Mission, as articulated in the Great Commission, is the reflex of the new covenant. Mission is an unavoidable imperative founded on the covenantal Lordship of Christ our King. Its task is to produce self-replicating communities of covenantal obedience to Christ among the nations. And it is sustained by the

5. Barth, *Church Dogmatics* 4/1:663.
6. Okholm, "Reformed Ecclesiology," 5.
7. Schlesinger, *Missa Est!*, 11.

enduring covenantal promise of the presence of Christ among
his followers.[8]

Thus, I want to commend an ecclesiology in which *church, mission,*
and *kingdom* find their coherence in the person of Jesus. The centrality of
Jesus means that the church must commit itself to *Christoformity.*

A compelling vision for the church can be seen in the way Peter
joins being and doing:

> But you are a chosen race, a royal priesthood, a holy nation, a
> people for his own possession, that you may proclaim the excel-
> lencies of him who called you out of darkness into his marvel-
> ous light. Once you were not a people, but now you are God's
> people. (1 Pet 2:9–10a ESV)

"A chosen race, a royal priesthood, a holy nation, a people for his own
possession" implies *being.* What we *are* proceeds but is tightly connected
to what we *do:* "that you may proclaim the excellencies of him who called
you out of darkness." Wright says, "the Bible as a whole presents the
universal God with a universal mission announced to Abraham . . . accomplished in anticipation by Christ . . . to be completed in the new creation. Whatever mission God calls us to must be a participation in this."[9]
Wright says further that the call to be the people of God "is universal, but
it remains uncompromising in its particularity regarding Jesus."[10] We see
this played out when Peter, facing intense persecution, said: "Salvation
is found in no one else, for there is no other name under heaven given
to mankind by which we must be saved" (Acts 4:12 NIV). Consider also
the power of the revelation to John regarding the absolute uniqueness of
Jesus: when all of cosmic history was at stake, John, in his vision, looked
around and saw that

> no one in heaven or on earth or under the earth could open the
> scroll or even look inside it. I wept and wept because no one was
> found who was worthy to open the scroll or look inside. Then
> one of the elders said to me, "Do not weep! See, the Lion of the
> tribe of Judah, the Root of David, has triumphed. He is able to
> open the scroll and its seven seals." (Rev 5:3–5 NIV)

8. Wright, *The Mission of God,* 355.

9. Wright, *The Mission of God,* 252.

10. Wright, *The Mission of God,* 246.

So far I have said that the definition of church consists of ontological participation in the life of Christ and thus acting as his cooperative friends, his kingdom-agents. The word *ontological* is a philosophical term that refers to how one defines existence, the nature of being, or how things are related to one another. For our purposes here, I mean to call attention to the notion that Christ is the head of the church (see Ephesians and Colossians) and that we find our existence and the nature of our being—individually and corporately as the church—as Christ's body. Just as my limbs obey the thoughts of my mind to walk or to pick up a pen, the body of Christ is meant to learn and discern the will of our head. We are meant to move, speak, think, and shape our attitudes based on impulses from the head, carried to us by the Spirit, and enabled by grace. Pulling this together in terms of the particularity of Christ called for by Wright, and in the kingdom terms that Jesus taught, we could say the church is:

- The people of the reign of King Jesus
- The anticipatory sign of the coming final rule of the King
- The servant of the kingdom, spreading the knowledge of the rule of King Jesus, who is now present and available to anyone who will apprentice themselves to him

People who prioritize the ontology of the church may wish that these descriptions place a stronger emphasis on the ontological realities between Christ the head and his body, the church. Let it be said that the *is, essence,* and *nature* of the church are essential preconditions to the *work* of the church. Serving as a sign, foretaste, and instrument, the church is more than its functional purpose—but the church is not less!

The Holy Spirit

The Holy Spirit is the person and power that animates every aspect of participation in the life and work of Jesus. Each activity named above is made possible because of the authority, power, gifts, and fruit given by the Holy Spirit. If it is true that the church is constituted by the sending of the Son and the Spirit, then any ecclesiology must take the words of Jesus seriously—words that Jesus spoke to his disciples as a way for them to understand the goodness and rightness of his soon departure. For our purposes here, I want to note how the ascension of the Son and the sending of the Spirit are two crucial strands of the divine narrative:

"Nevertheless, I tell you the truth: it is to your advantage that I go away, for if I do not go away, the Helper will not come to you. But if I go, I will send him to you" (John 16:7 ESV). Other translations put it this way:

- It is *expedient* for you that I go away (KJV)

- It is *profitable* (good, expedient, advantageous) for you that I go away (AMPC)

- It is to your *advantage* that I go away (NRSV)

- I am going to do what is *best* for you. That is why I am going away (CEV)

- It is for your *good* that I am going away (NIV)

That all sounds counterintuitive! I imagine Jesus's first followers heard his words with more than a little confusion. How could his departure be *good*, an *advantage*? That question raises key expository questions: To what do we suppose Jesus was conscious when he spoke those words? What effect did he intend them to have? Jesus's words were the key to stitching together the sending of the Son and of the Spirit. Despite the paramount importance of Jesus, the Son of God, by his own words, which he roots in the will of the Father (John 14:25, 15:26; Luke 24:49; 11:13; etc.), the story of God and the church is not complete in Jesus. The church finds its sense of self, meaning, purposes, and practices within the framework of the whole Trinity.

Let's try to give an answer to the two questions above: *To what do we suppose Jesus was conscious when he spoke those words?* First, he was being *obedient*. Jesus was thoroughly and determinedly embedded in his Father's story. This relational reliance on the unfolding of his Father's will is what gives rise to the many times Jesus says statements like: "For I have come down from heaven, not to do my own will but the will of him who sent me" (John 6:38 ESV). Second, he was *teaching*. Jesus was a patient and effective rabbi who explained things to his disciples in ways that he deemed best. Jesus wanted his friends to understand what was happening to him, but as a good leader Jesus also knew his ascension would prompt the question from his friends: "What will this mean for me?" Anticipating this question with empathy is what prompts in Jesus the adjectives about his departure: *good*, an *advantage*, and *profitable*. Third, Jesus was *comforting* his friends. Jesus's divine conformity is not robotic; he is not an automaton. Jesus is deeply personal—to the twelve then and to the church now. To lose the relationality of Jesus is to lose Jesus entirely. He is not a doctrine. He is not a Platonic ideal. Jesus is not confined to black ink on the pages of systematic theology. As a *person*, he is *social*. He feels the hearts of his friends. He knows his obedience is their pain, grief, and loss.

What effect did he intend his words to have? His obedience was a model for the twelve, intended to spark in them similar obedience. His teaching was meant to both inform them and to form in them the same kind of relational reliance on the Spirit that he enjoyed with his Father. His effort to comfort the twelve was meant to stabilize, ground, and center them in the reality that God has the whole unfolding story in his strong and loving hands—even the shocking twists in the story: death, resurrection, and ascension.

Before we leave these words of Jesus and their intended effect, a related teaching of Jesus, while imaginative and evocative, has always remained out of my complete grasp: "Very truly, I tell you, the one who believes in me will also do the works that I do and, in fact, will do greater works than these, because I am going to the Father" (John 14:12 NRSV). Those words seem like they should be paradigmatic for the church but they often seem absent from informing the church's mission. These words seem "too good to be true," "beyond our imagination," or "not something for which we can devise a program." I want to emphasize that the church must find its meaning in the ascension of Jesus and the sending of the Spirit. Jesus was conscious of something concrete when he said "very truly." The concreteness must find a home in the church's "belief" so that the church can do the "greater works" of which he spoke.

There are many other texts that depict an interactive relationship with the Holy Spirit, thus shaping the underlying imagination and daily practices of the church. To cite just a few, 2 Corinthians 1:22 says the presence of the Spirit in the life of the church is an important *seal* and *guarantee* of the work of the Father in the church. In a similar vein, in Ephesians 1:14, Paul says the Spirit is the guarantee of the church's full spiritual inheritance to come in Christ. Romans 5:5 says it is the Spirit who lets our hearts know just how very much God loves us. Jesus said the sending and receiving of the Spirit was a missional imperative (Luke 24:49); John 20 records the moment Jesus breathed on his friends, filled them with the Spirit, and sent them into the world "in the same manner" the Father had sent him. (There is that narrative "stitch" of the Spirit again, joining the church to Jesus.) The passages in Romans 12, 1 Corinthians

12—14, and Ephesians 4 reveal the ways in which the Spirit was working in the church—just as Jesus had promised. Galatians 5 gives us the rich imagery of the Spirit producing in the church the character and ethic of the kingdom.

I understand and have empathy for the many Christians who don't quite know what to do with the person and work of the Spirit. The wind and fire of Acts 2 seem very distant from a world marked by Bluetooth and artificial intelligence; claims to Spirit-giftedness can seem forced, weird, or self-serving. However, it was *Jesus* who said it was better for him to go away so the Spirit would come to the church—to lead us, guide us, give us authority, empower us, engift us, and en-fruit us. For the church there is everything to gain from a robust conversational relationship with the Holy Spirit—and there is nothing to fear. For instance, when you are trying to discern a way forward in life it might be a great time to receive a gift of discernment from the Spirit. When counseling someone it would be a great moment to receive a gift of wisdom or discernment. We are simply trying to cultivate a readiness for whatever Jesus meant when he said the Holy Spirit would bring us truth (John 14:17) and "will teach you everything, and remind you of all that I have said to you" (John 14:26). Such a life is not "Pentecostal" or "Charismatic"; it is, according to Jesus, basic, normative Christianity. As Jesus said: "If you then, who are evil, know how to give good gifts to your children, how much more will the heavenly Father give the Holy Spirit to those who ask him!" (Luke 11:13).

God's purposes, especially as embodied, taught, and modeled by the kingdom words and works of Jesus and the sending of the Spirit, are the major source of imagination for discipleship and church life. We simply cannot imagine the Father's intentions for the people of God unless we see these people in relation to the kingdom of God at work in the world and as an overflow of God's eternal trinitarian life—his absolute love and free self-giving for the other. Eugene Schlesinger describes well the relational and worshipful dynamic that undergirds the church's activity in the world:

> Just as Jesus was attuned both to the Father and the broken world, the church maintains this dynamic tension—in worship and mission. . . . These are not to be pitted against each other, but are to be harmonized in one consistent life/church. Mission is not a second stage that unfolds alongside or after the liturgy,

but is itself part of the liturgy's internal logic. Worship and mission are *distinguishable*, but not *separable*.[11]

This trinitarian framework is the source of the church. From this trinitarian perspective the church learns its practices, ethic, and *telos*. A trinitarian reality forms that into which we are welcomed and welcome others. This participation with the Father, Son, and Holy Spirit is both communal and personal, and, as such, it shapes an imagination for discipleship to Jesus.

Church as Discipleship

Participation in the enduring life of the Trinity is not a heavy burden to put on the church. Notions of active being or the academic definitions I cited need not produce the kind of anxious, fear-of-culture activities that have caused so many people to leave the modern church. In the scheme I have in mind here—the church as an outcome of the ruling and reign of God—both *origin* and *agency* belong to God. That knowledge should fill the church with peace. It is now becoming widely paradigmatic that whatever we may mean to say about mission or being *missional*, we are describing something that is of grace. Whatever the church may do, it is connected to the mission of God in human history.[12] Wright joins thinking and action well by grounding the church's *deeds* in God's *being*:

> Fundamentally, [the church's] mission (if it is biblically informed and validated) means our committed participation as God's people, at God's invitation and command, in God's own mission within the history of God's world for the redemption of God's creation.[13]

Dallas Willard is similarly helpful in rooting *action* in *being*. In a number of different contexts, I would often hear Willard speak about the *divine conspiracy*: God's plan to intervene in human history and overcome evil with good, in order to create an all-inclusive community of loving persons with Godself as the prime sustainer and most glorious inhabitant of the community.[14]

11. Schlesinger, *Missa Est!*, 1.

12. See Wright, *The Mission of God*.

13. Wright, *The Mission of God*, 22–23.

14. The best place to explore Willard's thoughts on the matter is Willard, *The Divine Conspiracy*.

These notions of church as participating in the continuing life of God on earth form the basis and fundamental practices of discipleship. As Willard wrote: "a disciple or apprentice is simply someone who has decided to be with another person, under appropriate conditions, in order to become capable of doing what that person does or to become what that person is."[15] Giving us a further imagination for the church as personal participation in the ongoing life of Jesus, Willard says disciple-ship means that "I am with Jesus by choice and grace, learning from him how to live in the kingdom of God."[16] Further, Willard gives an evocative vision for where participation with Jesus in the church leads: "Those who have apprenticed themselves to Jesus learn an undying life with a future as good and as large as God himself."[17]

While God is always the initiator and we are always joining some-thing already in motion, the church does have vital instrumental agency. But that agency is derived from *election* (the one/few chosen to be a bless-ing to the many), *followership of Jesus*, and *reception of the Spirit*—all of which God is the initiator. The church is governed by the rule and reign of God's kingdom as taught and modeled by Jesus, and it is enabled by the power of the Spirit to participate in the life of the Trinity. The church is meant to join Jesus in his work of proclamation, carrying on his kingdom ministry for the good of others.

The Church in Action

In the sections above I asserted that the church is more than just defini-tions, no matter how coherent or compelling they may be. I argued that fundamental to the *being* of the church is *cooperation* with *God's being*. If that is the case, we need to explore a bit deeper what the church is meant to *do*. First, it bears repeating that it is not my intent to paint the church with a utilitarian brush or to turn her into a mere tool in God's cosmic shed. However, there is an unavoidable and inevitable "do-ness" and "sent-ness" and "go-ness" inherent in the people of God. Paul puts this in a lovely, non-institutional way that is inspirational and relational: "we are God's handiwork, created in Christ Jesus to do good works, which God prepared in advance for us to do" (Ephesians 2:10 NIV). Okholm has put

15. Willard, *The Divine Conspiracy*, 282.

16. Willard, *The Divine Conspiracy*, 283.

17. Willard, *The Divine Conspiracy*, 375.

it this way: "The church exists only as a witness to the One on whom it is dependent—who is its source—who called it into being. Insofar as it ceases to be that witness, it ceases to be the church."[18]

The notion of working alongside and witnessing to God under his grace-based direction and inspiration is a constant theme throughout the Bible: Adam and Eve were tasked with working together with God in his new creation, Noah was chosen to do the work of saving a remnant of humanity, and Abraham was elected as the progenitor of the people of God who are meant to serve his purposes in the world. The other patriarchs, judges, kings, and prophets were likewise called to work with God to stimulate the whole people of God to obedience to their calling. This story line continues throughout Israel's history to John the Baptist, the calling of the twelve, the sending of the Spirit, and the creation of the church.

From this biblical theme, the church's approach to discipleship is informed: the church is meant to exist in continuity with the faith, obedience, love, commitment, trust, and covenant loyalty found in God's people throughout the Bible—Old and New Testament alike. But in my experience, most churches either over-emphasize doing in a way that creates a driven church culture with highly anxious church members, or, often in reaction to such churches, over-accentuate fellowship or personal discipleship. But these are not the only choices for the church; there is a third way.

Elizabeth O'Connor lived and taught a beautiful rhythm for missional living rooted in spiritual transformation into Christlikeness. O'Connor was a close colleague of Gordon Cosby who founded the Church of the Saviour in Washington, DC. Together, they led an exemplary church—a community of people who they guided on a *journey inward* and a *journey outward*.[19] Church of the Savior created, facilitated, and sustained a rhythm of church life that seamlessly blended together teaching on the kingdom, life in the Spirit, the intelligent and targeted use of private and corporate spiritual disciplines, and mission. This mix of mission and formation transformed large elements of their neighborhood and hundreds of people in the church. To my mind, Church of the Saviour is still a "gold

18. Okholm, "Reformed Ecclesiology," 2.

19. See O'Connor, *Journey Inward.*

standard" for what it means to "do" church—through an appropriate, Spirit-guided mix of contemplation and action.[20]

The church's interior work of transformation and external mission for the sake of others is never out of the blue. God's work in the church and in the world is always situated in a given context. The relationship between God's work and the context of any given church has been a difficult riddle for two millennia, and it is to that challenge we now turn.

The Church in Context

Every local church is situated in time and space. There is no such thing as a non-contextualized community of God's people. This means that every generation has the task of unbundling transcendent *essence* from established *forms*. This has to happen in part so that institutional sluggishness does not overwhelm the joyful and playful movement of the Spirit. When I highlight unbundling essence from forms I am sometimes misunderstood as being anti-institutional, a bit too risk-taking, or too permission-giving. I am not anti-institutional; institutions are a given. Instead, I am is *pro-Spirit* and *pro-kingdom*. Institutions have to exist, but they must bend to the movement of the Spirit and to the rhythms of the kingdom, not the other way around.

Are there limits to this creative diversity of the forms of the church? I am not sure. I am neither motivated by pushing boundaries nor by mindless conformity; I am motivated by seeing people come to faith, become followers of Jesus, receive healing and deliverance, and become ambassadors of the kingdom. The creative diversity of the church might only be circumscribed by trinitarian purposes. The bar before which creativity stands might simply be this: does this approach, form, ritual, or method align well with the eternal purposes of God? Does it facilitate the will of God among a given people in a particular time? Where church life is facilitating these things, I am a happy bishop whose mind is bent towards *fruit*, not *limits*.

Pope Francis has given the church some guidance for putting this trinitarian-minded practice on the ground. He has called for

> a missionary impulse for the church capable of transforming everything, so that the church's customs, ways of doing things, times and schedules, languages and structure can be suitably

20. See O'Connor, *Call to Commitment*; Underhill, *Practical Mysticism*.

channeled for the evangelization of today's world rather than for her self-preservation . . . so that in her ongoing discernment, the church can also come to see that certain customs not directly connected to the heart of the Gospel, even some which have deep historical roots, are no longer properly understood and appreciated. Some of these customs may be beautiful, but they no longer serve as means of communicating the Gospel. We should not be afraid to re-examine them . . . if they no longer have usefulness for directing and shaping people's lives.[21]

The challenge of welcoming goes beyond forms of the church which may be more barrier-like than bridge-like. Contextually-derived moralisms are also in play. Every time and place has its own moral angst which makes welcoming *certain* people into the church problematic. Over the course of my life I can think of drugs, long hair, the sexual revolution in its many iterations, birth control, divorce, and, most recently, LGBTQIA+ conversations. Over the last 140 years, evangelicals and fundamentalists have fought over Broadway Sunday/Sabbath curtains (plays), dancing, prizefighting, cards, horse racing, gambling, movies, immigration of non-white ethnicities, and other religions. They have fought against the changing roles of women in society, railed against short skirts, hair styles, makeup, cigarettes, capital punishment, birth control, prohibition, labor movements, social security, sex education, etc. Having a siege mentality, it seems as if some evangelicals and fundamentalists have had a knack for picking losing battles! As part of the evangelical tribe, I have thought about this over the years and I have begun to wonder: Are *fighting* and *winning* kingdom ideals?

Debates over who belongs in the people of God and who does not is not new. This debate often got Jesus in trouble. This scriptural narrative gives us a window into Jesus's experience:

> Now all the tax collectors and sinners were coming near to listen to him. And the Pharisees and the scribes were grumbling and saying, "This fellow welcomes sinners and eats with them." (Luke 15:1–2 NRSV)

Jesus then goes on to tell the parables of the lost sheep, the lost coin, and the lost son. Going back again to our trinitarian grounding, we can note the role of the Father, Son, and Spirit in drawing people in, taking relational risks, giving people a chance, and building bridges—not barriers.

---

21. Schlesinger, *Missa Est!*, xix–xx.

Among the many images that could be cited from scripture, imagine the loving, searching, longing portrait painted below:

- The Father: the waiting, longing, prodigious love of the Father in the parable of the Prodigal Son.

- The Son: Jesus, the Son of Man, who has come to seek and to save that which was lost.

- The Spirit: the Holy Spirit, who is given by God to fill our hearts with his love (Romans 5:5). And when the Spirit comes, "he will convict the world concerning sin and righteousness and judgment" (John 16:8 ESV).

My experience is that the church wants to hold the Trinity in their mind as holy—unspeakably holy, completely set apart, and other. This is correct, but what if a major aspect of divine holiness is the capacity to stay connected to the broken, sinful creation? The attribute of God that allows him to be simultaneously wholly other and still closely associated with fallen creation is both a motive to admiringly love and serve him, joining God to serve and heal the broken creation with which we interact every day.

My vision for the church learning to love their neighbor and enemy is rooted in the behavior of Jesus, which is of course further rooted in Jesus revealing God to us. It is deeply stirring to me that Jesus was not afraid of catching *worldly germs*—either from social and religious outcasts or from lepers or dead bodies. Jesus knew that when he interacted with brokenness of various kinds, he would not become sickened by that brokenness; rather, virtue, power, healing, and deliverance would flow from him to lepers, sinners, and the dead. Were the church to find even a fraction of Jesus's confidence it would transform our relationship to the world. I am moved by the evocative way Brian Zhand put it: "We thought God was a deity in a temple, turns out God is a father at a table . . . pull up a chair and sit with us . . . we will make room for you."[22]

The Trinity, the Church, and Mission

Summing up our work in this chapter, we can say that the church finds grounding, nature, and purpose via a constant reference to the Trinity. Its

---

22. Zhand, *Water to Wine*, 141.

orientation is toward the Gospel of the kingdom as taught, modeled, and demonstrated by Jesus. Its hope, joy, authority, power, gifts, and transformation are aspects of the gift of the Spirit. Mission is of its essence, not an afterthought for the outgoing among church communities. In the first book I wrote, I longed to articulate a brief, compelling way for ordinary Christians to imagine themselves living such a life. I suggested an imagination shaped by:

- Living as cooperative friends of Jesus
- Seeking to live lives of constant creative goodness
- Relying on the power of the Holy Spirit
- Existing for the sake of others[23]

My desire is that lives animated in this manner will lead to many people being *welcomed as Christ—into the Church.*

Bibliography

Barth, Karl. *Church Dogmatics 4/1: The Doctrine of Reconciliation.* Translated by Geoffrey Bromiley et al. Edinburgh: T. & T. Clark, 1956.

Hunter, Todd. *Christianity Beyond Belief: Following Jesus for the Sake of Others.* Downers Grove: InterVarsity, 2009.

Kärkkäinen, Veli-Matti. *An Introduction to Ecclesiology: Ecumenical, Historical, and Global Perspectives.* Downers Grove: InterVarsity, 2002.

O'Connor, Elizabeth. *Call to Commitment: The Story of the Church of the Saviour.* New York: Harper and Row, 1963.

———. *Journey Inward, Journey Outward.* Washington DC: Potter's House Bookservice, 1975.

Okholm, Dennis. *Learning Theology through the Church's Worship.* Grand Rapids: Baker Academic, 2019.

———. "Reformed Ecclesiology: 'The Community of Christ.'" *Theology Matters* 15.1 (2009) 1–6.

Schlesinger, Eugene. *Missa Est!* Minneapolis: Fortress, 2017.

Underhill, Evelyn. *Practical Mysticism.* Los Angeles: Hardpress, 2010.

Van Engen, Charles. *God's Missionary People: Rethinking the Purpose of the Local Church.* Grand Rapids: Baker, 1991.

Willard, Dallas. *The Divine Conspiracy: Rediscovering Our Hidden Life in God.* New York: HarperCollins, 1998.

Wright, Christopher. *The Mission of God: Unlocking the Bible's Grand Narrative.* Downers Grove: InterVarsity, 2006.

Zahnd, Brian. *Water to Wine: Some of My Story.* Spello, 2016.

23. See Hunter, *Christianity Beyond Belief.*

3

Participating in God's Mission

A Proposal at the Boundaries of Evangelicalism

JUSTIN ASHWORTH

"I'M NOT SURE I can call myself evangelical anymore," mused Dennis Okholm, my former teacher, longtime friend, and current colleague at Azusa Pacific University (APU). "I think I will just go with 'disciple of Jesus.'" These words came after Okholm taped a political cartoon to the door of my APU office. The cartoon featured President Donald Trump standing at the foot of the cross with evangelical Christian onlookers fawning over him. The President sees in the t-shaped cross a salute to his own majesty, while the evangelicals see in the President gazing at the cross the pious man God has appointed for a time such as this. When I noticed the cartoon on my office door, I walked over to Okholm's office, laughing—because if you don't laugh, you'll cry—at the insight of the artist and the embarrassment of being identified as evangelical. I remember chuckling and nodding after Okholm probed the possibility of no longer calling himself an evangelical, yet I left the exchange wondering whether I too could make that move.

Dennis Okholm may or may not still feel this way. However, what is important about the exchange is that he pointed to a crucial problem facing US evangelicals: our fusion with right-wing politics.[1] In some cases, that fusion is mere perception; in others, it is very real. Although Okholm

---

1. A fine attempt to survey the US evangelical landscape is the Center for Religion and Civic Culture, "Varieties."

is one of the best representatives of evangelical Christianity that I know, he is embarrassed by some of our fellow evangelicals, and so has difficulty retaining the identifier. This situation is truly dire for those of us who think we need to retain the word *evangelical*.

Around the same time as this conversation with Okholm, I required my upper-level undergraduate students to write an essay on the nature of Christian mission in light of readings from Darrell L. Guder, José Míguez Bonino, and Dana Robert. I thought these texts pointed to both the problems of Christian mission and the possibilities for the term *mission* in our day. I had thought that including a seminal text from one of the most influential of first-generation liberation theologians, José Míguez Bonino, as well as a reading on evangelism's problematic embeddedness in colonialism and imperialism, would help my students see that there are better and worse ways of understanding Christian mission. Most students did see this, but one student wrote a paper stating that we must give up on mission altogether because of its colonialist and imperialist baggage. The word is too compromised, the student said, just like *evangelical*, so any type of Christian faith worth confessing today must abandon the notion of mission and think in terms of serving the world.

Sentiments like Okholm's lament and my student's refusal abound, for they point to the problems of Christian, particularly evangelical, political engagement. At the root of this political engagement is a misunderstanding of Christian mission—not on Okholm's part, though perhaps on my student's part and certainly on the part of many people in the US. To many people, mission smacks of paternalism at best and crusades—evangelistic, military, economic, cultural, or sometimes all of them together—at worst.[2] History is replete with such performances of Christian mission, but we need not accept these as normative. In this essay, I propose a different view of mission and our participation in it, a view that is at once liberationist and evangelical. It is liberationist in its emphasis on the privileged position of the marginalized in the divine economy, as well as on the materiality and communal nature of salvation. Given how Karl Barth and liberation theologians have influenced these reflections, however, my vision may not sit well with many evangelicals: hence the subtitle of this essay. On the other hand, many evangelicals have employed Barth as if he were something like a modern day "church

---

2. See among others Rivera, *Violent Evangelism*; Jennings, *Christian Imagination*.

father,"[3] and Míguez Bonino, one of my chief liberationist interlocutors here, identified as *evangélico*.[4] Thus, while I too disavow right-wing evangelicalism, I also think we can restate this most evangelical of Christian teachings in a way that condemns repulsive, but all-too-common, missionary theologies and practices as unevangelical.

Reducing and Compromising God's Mission

To offer such an account, we must first pinpoint the problems of Christian mission. Darrell Guder highlights the reductionisms and compromises that lead many people to reject the noun *mission* and the adjective *evangelical*. The first reductionism Guder notes is the construal of the gospel as merely the information that individual souls can be spared hell, as if salvation were entirely interior, individual, and future. Second, many churches have confined God's work in the world to the church and its missionaries, thereby leaving little space for the mission of God *outside* the church. If God is to reach the world, in this view, God must work through the church, parachurch ministries, and their missionary representatives. Third, many churches and pastors believe they exist to serve church members and, in Guder's memorable phrase, to tend to the "savedness of the saved." This frequently occurs in evangelical churches that "advertise themselves as 'full-service' congregations and function as purveyors of the religious programs and products their member-consumers want."[5] Finally, many Christian leaders have followed the Christendom tradition of aligning themselves with coercive imperial and state forces in the pursuit of, for example, the free exercise of religion (for some), to work to abolish abortion, and to wage military and culture wars against religious and secular infidels at home and abroad. In this Christendom formation, the church is the chaplain of the state.

Many of us find this constellation of theological imagination and ecclesial practice so antithetical to what we know of Jesus Christ that we too will be tempted to disavow words like *evangelical* and *mission*—if we haven't done so already. But as missional theologians since the middle of

3. Collins Winn notes this curious use and disavowal of Karl Barth among US evangelicals in Collins Winn, "Kingdom," 87n2.

4. Míguez Bonino, *Faces*, vii–viii.

5. Guder, *Called to Witness*, 69. The Center for Religion and Civic Culture designates this brand of evangelicalism "iVangelicalism" ("Varieties").

the twentieth century have insisted, God's mission should not be reduced to individual salvation doled out only through the church, nor should the church's life be reduced to constituency-maintenance or compromised by alignment with imperial power. The next section will reiterate some of the crucial themes emerging from this literature, and the subsequent section will state my view of how human beings *participate* in God's mission.

Restating God's Mission

Statements about God's mission (*missio Dei*) abound among evangelicals, but it is not always clear what this mission is. Is God's mission primarily soteriological—and if so, is salvation the entry of souls into heaven, the redemption of society, or the transformation of the *cosmos*? Or is the *missio Dei* primarily about God's identity, God's sending (from the Latin *missio*) the Son and the Spirit into the world? Still another emphasis is ecclesiological, as in Emil Brunner's claim that "the church exists by mission, just as fire exists by burning." Among evangelicals, these are common expressions and sentiments, yet it is unclear exactly what they mean.

While there are many ways of describing God's mission, my discussion is framed by the work of John G. Flett. As the concept of *missio Dei* developed, says Flett, it clustered around three theological themes: the Trinity, the kingdom of God, and the missionary nature of the church.[6] These themes correspond to the theological, soteriological, and ecclesiological loci for God's mission mentioned above. Flett notes that the initial function of these themes was to criticize reductionisms and compromises like those discussed by Guder.[7] To imagine God's mission as first of all *God's* mission is to distance the true work of God from the imperialist and colonialist legacies of Christendom (Christendom compromise). To imagine God's mission as concerned with the kingdom of God is to say that God's work in the world is more than the mere saving of souls (soteriological reductionism) and wider than the church (ecclesiocentrism). Finally, to imagine God's mission as inaugurating a missionary church is to distance the true, world-serving church from the self-serving, inward-focused churches with which so many of us are familiar (ecclesiological reductionism). Yet, as much as these themes criticize current church

---

6. Flett, *Witness of God*, 36.

7. Flett, *Witness of God*, 37, 51, 64.

realities, they were underdeveloped in the missional literature of the middle- and late-twentieth century.

In this section, I will offer missional sketches of the Trinity and the kingdom of God. My sketch differs from Flett's primarily in my discussion of the kingdom of God and its liberative dimensions. Flett's account of the kingdom is the least developed theme in his constructive proposal, and it lacks reference to how the kingdom Jesus proclaimed and embodied liberated the oppressed, healed the broken, and included the marginalized—all of which are emphasized by liberation theologians. The final section turns to the meaning of participation in God's mission, not to replace Flett's third theme, the missionary nature of the church, but to answer a major question posed by liberation theologians regarding the politics of God's mission. In particular, "what relation is there between salvation and the historical process of human liberation," and indeed between salvation and human action more broadly?[8] I will argue that while we should not equate participation in God's mission with either struggles for justice or faithful church commitment, participation in God's mission entails both active church commitment *and* struggling to make right what has gone wrong in the world.

Trinitarian Missions

We can find a lucid, traditional account of trinitarian missions in Catholic theologian Gilles Emery's work *The Trinity*. There Emery notes the traditional distinction between God's visible and invisible missions. The former refers to the Father's sending the Son to be made flesh (incarnation) and the Father and Son's sending the Holy Spirit upon Jesus Christ and his disciples (baptism and Pentecost, respectively).[9] The invisible missions of the Son and the Spirit are the Son's cultivation of wisdom and the Spirit's cultivation of charity in individuals' hearts. God's invisible missions result in believers' changed actions as they receive the very life of the Son and the Spirit through the church's sacraments.[10]

Thoughtful evangelicals might be attracted to this traditional Thomist account of trinitarian missions because of its theological depth in contrast with the theological anemia of many evangelicals' talk of God

8. Gutiérrez, *Theology of Liberation*, 29.

9. Emery, *Trinity*, 179–83.

10. Emery, *Trinity*, 185–88.

and the moral life. Yet there are several difficulties with this view from a missional standpoint. The first is that the locus of God's saving work is neither the *cosmos* nor communities but individual hearts. To be sure, Emery believes that God's work in us through the Christian community will lead to wiser, more loving action among believers, but the saving work of God is still a matter of individuals being changed. The second issue is the bifurcation of the being of God and the act of God, with the result that the trinitarian missions are necessary only for God's relationship with creatures, not for God's very identity. Here "God's movement into his economy is a second step alongside who he is from all eternity."[11] To be sure, Emery believes human beings need the Father to send the Son and the Spirit because those missions are "revelatory and salvific."[12] But God, it seems, could be the Triune God within Godself, without sending the Son and the Spirit. It is worth pondering whether the Triune God would be *this* God—not the god who could have been but the God who *is*—if the Father had not sent the Son and the Spirit. It seems that we would be talking about a different god—an unknown, hidden god—if we were to say God could have been God without sending the Son to be made flesh and the Spirit to baptize the Son of God and his disciples.

The third, most important deficiency is the absence of the kingdom of God. This is a surprising oversight given that immediately after Jesus's baptism by the Holy Spirit (Mark 1:10) and his return to Galilee from his Spirit-led journey into the wilderness (1:12–13), Jesus proclaimed the good news that "[t]he time is fulfilled, and the kingdom of God has come near" (1:14–15; see also Matt 3:13–4:17). Luke's Gospel does not use the word *kingdom* when Jesus begins his ministry after his baptism (3:21–22) and temptation by Satan (4:1–13), but what he *does* proclaim—as the Spirit of the Lord is (sent?) upon him—is that he is there "to bring good news to the poor. [The Lord] has sent me to proclaim release to the captives and recovery of sight to the blind, to let the oppressed go free, to proclaim the year of the Lord's favor" (4:18–19). At any rate, later in that chapter, Jesus says he "must proclaim the good news of the kingdom of God to the other cities also; for I was sent [*apestelen*] for this purpose"

---

11. Flett, *Witness of God*, 19. Many people will not consider this a flaw. But the question remains for anyone who denies the necessity of the sending of the Son and the Spirit: is God truly the Triune God if God has not eternally known that God would send the Son to be made flesh? Contemporary interpreters of Karl Barth's doctrine of election have debated this question at great length.

12. Emery, *Trinity*, 179.

(4:43). In short, the Father baptized the Son in the Spirit so that the Son might proclaim the reign of the Triune God. There is no purpose to the sending of the Son and the Spirit other than this. Thus, to leave out the kingdom when describing the trinitarian missions is not to describe the trinitarian missions at all.

While these flaws in Emery's account of the trinitarian missions make his view less useful than one might like, we can still take what is good in his view and modify it to serve the missional purposes of this essay. The trinitarian missions are the sending of the Son to be made flesh and the sending of the Spirit to baptize the Son and his community so that they might proclaim the good news of the presence of God's reign in Jesus Christ. God also sends the Spirit upon all people so that they, as individuals and communities, might respond to this gospel in faithfulness. In fact, part of the good news is that God can change our actions so that we serve God's purposes rather than those of Mammon. New social formations are possible because of God's work among us.[13] Thus, included in the sending of Son and Spirit is the conversion of faithless people and peoples to the Triune God. Part of this conversion is our being sent as witnesses—individually and corporately—to the gospel in places where God is already working. Just as God simply is the one who sends the Son and the Spirit, so everyone made a disciple of Jesus Christ is sent as a witness to his work.

Here we have an account of the *missio Dei* steeped in the rich language of trinitarian orthodoxy and infused with the liberationist sense of the centrality of the kingdom of God for Christian faith and theology. (1) God's mission is first the sending of the Son and the Spirit by the Father. (2) The mission of God's Son is to proclaim and embody the reign of the Triune God, about which we learn in the Scriptures. (3) God's kingdom is wider than the church, involving both God's turning of the hearts of non-believers to receive the gospel in faithfulness and God's promise to heal communities and, as I will suggest, all of creation. (4) God's mission incorporates people outside God's people *into* God's people, whose purpose is the same as Jesus's own, namely, to proclaim and embody the Triune God's reign.

---

13. I have taken this insight from Barber, *Diaspora*, 30–31.

The Kingdom of God

What is this kingdom of God? A brief sketch of the meaning of God's reign will suffice to fill out what God accomplishes in the trinitarian missions. In Christian Scripture, the kingdom of God does not initially refer to the future for which God's people long. While the eschatological referent of the kingdom would come to predominate in the Second Temple period and in later theology, the Hebrew phrase *YHWH malak* ("the Lord reigns") means simply that Israel's God is actively reigning. This language is found in many Psalms, but it is also found at the end of Moses's song of praise immediately after crossing the Red Sea: "The Lord will reign forever and ever" (Exod 15:18). This salvific act of God in delivering God's people from Egypt points to several dimensions of the phrase "the Lord reigns."[14] First, God's reign is cosmic, for God commands waters, animals, insects, human beings, and the sun and the moon. However, the Lord has chosen to be king of a particular people, Abraham's descendants. This is the second aspect of God's reign: election. Third, God enacts God's reign in saving God's people, delivering Israel from bondage. Fourth, the salvation God brings is material, not only spiritual. God cares about human beings' well-being *in this life*, and God's victory over imperial oppression and violence displays this concern. Fifth, in freeing Israel from Egypt—and in God's later promises to deliver them from pagan empires—God confronts the imperial orders that oppress people: "the Egyptians shall know that I am the Lord, when I have gained glory for myself over Pharaoh, his chariots, and his chariot drivers" (14:18). Finally, the Lord's reign both evokes praise (Moses's and Miriam's songs) and calls for the people's obedience (ten commandments).

We find these six aspects of God's reign in the story of Jesus.[15] He governs the chaos of storm (Mark 4:35–41) and sea (6:47–52), yet he has come to proclaim and embody God's reign primarily among God's children, not the gentiles, even though there is an important place for the latter (7:24–30; 15:39). Jesus heals people's bodies (3:1–5), feeds the hungry (6:30–44; 8:1–10), and restores people to community (1:40–44), in these ways saving people "from urgent concrete needs" as a sign of

14. Much of what follows leans on Mays, *The Lord Reigns*.

15. This brief sketch accords with the basic reference work of Green, "Kingdom of God/Heaven"; and with the more systematic theological account of Sobrino, "Central Position."

the fullness of the holistic, communal, and cosmic salvation they await.[16] This deliverance "from urgent concrete needs . . . means liberation," says Jon Sobrino, "since the needs from which one is saved are those produced by elements of oppression."[17] In offering people such foretastes of final salvation, Jesus confronts the powers that oppress, marginalize, and harm people, not only with powerful words (2:23–28; 11:15–18; 14:53–65) but also with God's miraculous power to restore what is broken (1:21–28, where word, deed, and authority are equated). The climax of this confrontation is Jesus's resurrection from the dead: "this man . . . you crucified and killed by the hands of those outside the law. But God raised him up" (Acts 2:23–24). Finally, the reign of God calls forth repentance, faith, and a life in accordance with God's work in the world (Mark 1:14–15; Acts 2:37–39).

This sketch of God's kingdom work avoids several problems in western views of mission. First, it shows the material, communal, and cosmic dimensions of the gospel. God is at work to bring healing in the world of nature and society, not only to grant individuals access to heaven. Second, this account of the kingdom avoids the ecclesiocentrism that imagines the church as the sole instrument God uses to bring about salvation. The church is the community created as a witness to God's reign, but God can work in the world apart from the church. Third, to emphasize that the kingdom is God's project, not human beings' project, is to set it against any systematic alignments with human political projects. However, fourth, since God's reign addresses and benefits the marginalized first, some of our political projects will better align with God's political project than others do.[18] Thus, while "[t]here is no *divine* politics or economics," as Míguez Bonino says, "we must resolutely use the best *human* politics and economics at our disposal."[19] The criterion of good and bad political projects is the extent to which "they belong to this new order" of the kingdom of God proclaimed and embodied by Christ.[20]

16. Sobrino, "Central Position," 364.

17. Sobrino, "Central Position," 364. I would have said, "often," where Sobrino said, "those," to indicate that some of the things Jesus made right were not caused by material oppression.

18. Sobrino, "Central Position," 382.

19. Míguez Bonino, *Revolutionary Theology*, 149. Emphasis in original.

20. Míguez Bonino, *Revolutionary Theology*, 141. This criterion parallels Wright's conviction that we can build *for* the kingdom by "accomplishing something that will become in due course part of God's new world." Wright, *Surprised by Hope*, 208.

Participation: Three Dimensions

To speak of human political projects is to gesture toward our participation in God's mission. In Christian theology, the word *participation* has come to mean many things, but Kathryn Tanner's barebones definition of participation as "sharing in something that one is not" can help us determine the meaning of participating in God's mission.[21] There are three dimensions of human beings' sharing in what we are not, two of which concern the trinitarian missions.[22]

The first dimension of our participation in God is ontic: creation necessarily participates in God because we live "a life derived from a God who does not derive from another as [we] do."[23] Creatures naturally participate in God, though only passively so, because God sovereignly created us and sustains, accompanies, and governs us. To speak of ontic participation is simply to say that we are contingent creatures.

Another form of participation, also passive, is what we might call *mystical*.[24] We mystically participate in God by God's condescension to be with us and God's elevating us to be covenant partners with God in Jesus Christ.[25] This is a result of the trinitarian missions. Here it is important

21. Tanner, *Christ the Key*, 7.

22. This definition of participation implies ontological transcendence ("something that one *is* not"). Thus, although I share Reformed hesitations about the language of participation in God because of its associations with deification among Eastern Orthodox, the *analogia entis* among Catholics, and natural theology among Protestants, the term—or one like it—is unavoidable if one believes that God is infinitely different from us and in intimate relationship with us. Barber has made this point, albeit critically, in *Diaspora*, 49–61. Excellent discussions of Barth's engagement with these themes are: Neder, *Participation in Christ*, 12–14, 86–92 (deification); Johnson, "Barth's Rejection" (*analogia entis*); and Flett, *Witness of God*, 163–95 (natural theology in the context of mission).

23. Tanner, *Christ the Key*, 8.

24. I am not entirely happy with the word *mystical*, as it conjures Platonist images of contemplation of, and absorption into, the One. On Barth's hesitation on this score, see Neder, *Participation in Christ*, 78–79. Still, I hope that my emphasis on divine transcendence and divine-human actualism makes clear that I do not conceive such mystical participation in Platonist terms.

25. Barth, *CD* 4/1:128–32; Tanner, *Christ the Key*, 14. Both Barth's and Tanner's theologically rich accounts of the dogmatic structure of our participation in God lack sufficient reference to the socio-politically liberative aspects of God's work in the world. Thus, although they provide the formal dogmatic structure of my argument, liberationists provide much of the material content, especially regarding the nature of God's reign. A similar point is made, though about patristic rather than modern authors, in Sobrino, *Christ the Liberator*, 236.

to distinguish *de jure* from *de facto* participation in God to avoid both the blurring of the Creator-creature distinction and any sense that we effect our union with God, as well as to insist, nevertheless, that we must actively respond to God's participation in the human situation.[26] Our *de jure* participation in God is God's joining God's Son "with our humanity by way of the hypostatic unity of the incarnation before any change in our own attitudes and dispositions comes to reflect that fact."[27] (To this we must add the outpouring of the Spirit.) Our *de facto* participation in God, this "change in our own attitudes and dispositions," both individually and communally, is our free response to God's participation in our situation. This is made possible by God's mission: "God becomes man," said Barth, "in order that man may—not become God, but come to God."[28] God participates in our history so that we might become covenant partners in God's history, God's mission. Indeed, as Barth would later argue, our active participation in Christ as God's covenant partner is the intention of God's active participation in our life in Jesus Christ.[29] God wills to have faithful covenant partners, and God gains them by sending the Son in human flesh and sending the Spirit upon human flesh.

This mention of covenant partners points to the third dimension of participation, which I call *ethical participation*. Theologians disagree about the nature and content of this ethical participation. Immanentist views identify divine agency with specific human activities, construing the latter as the extension of the former. James Cone represents a liberationist version of the immanentist view: "the black revolution is God's kingdom becoming a reality in America."[30] Here human work for liberation simply is God's work in history. The notion of "building the kingdom" is consonant with this view. An equally immanentist view, consonant with the equation of church and kingdom, construes the church as the literal body of Jesus Christ in the world. Hence Robert Jenson's claim: "The church is the body as which Christ confronts his world."[31]

26. Neder, *Participation in Christ*, 18.

27. Tanner, *Christ the Key*, 72.

28. Barth, *CD* 4/2:106.

29. Barth, *CD* 4/2:508.

30. Cone, *Black Theology*, 124.

31. Jenson, "The Church and the Sacraments," 210.

Both views point to human work—in church and society—and confidently equate that work with the work of God.[32]

The precise relationship between divine and human agency has provoked intense debate. Around the time that Cone wrote his words (1970), liberation theologians in Latin America were wondering about the relationship "between the Kingdom of God and the building up of the world."[33] Some (like Juan Luis Segundo) claimed that human achievements toward liberation cause the kingdom to come, while others (like Gustavo Gutiérrez) claimed more modestly that "the process of liberation will not have conquered the very roots of human oppression and exploitation without the coming of the Kingdom, *which is above all a gift*."[34] Jürgen Moltmann rejected the radically immanentist language of Segundo, insisting on some distinction between God's work and our own, the former calling forth the latter. The struggle for liberation is a crucial response to God's reign, but it cannot have "a 'causal character' for the Kingdom of God—even Pelagius never would have said that."[35] Similarly, several theologians have contested Jenson's maximalist claims for the identification of the risen Christ with his church.[36] There must be some distinction between Jesus Christ and the community he calls his own, lest we conflate divine and human agency.

This third dimension of participation in God deserves further reflection because it highlights the political problems mentioned earlier. To secularize our participation in God's mission, as Cone does, or to *ecclesify* it, as Jenson does, is to subject God's mission to human projections, political or ecclesiastical.[37] Yet neither Cone nor Jenson is wrong to see a connection between salvation and rightly ordered human communities, as gifts from God and goals for which we must strive. After all, the purposes of the trinitarian missions were to proclaim and embody God's healing reign over bodies, communities, and creation and to gain

32. To call the church a human work is not to deny that it is also a divine work but to acknowledge the church's humanity.

33. Gutiérrez, *Theology of Liberation*, 29.

34. Gutiérrez's quote comes from *Theology of Liberation*, 104. Emphasis added. On Segundo, see Míguez Bonino, *Revolutionary Theology*, 139–40.

35. Moltmann, "Liberation Theology," 58.

36. See Webster, "Church"; and Plantinga Pauw, *Church in Ordinary Time*.

37. J. C. Hoekendijk coined the term *ecclesify*, which is often cited in missional literature. Sobrino calls it "the ecclesialization of the kingdom of God" (*Christ the Liberator*, 335).

covenant partners who likewise proclaim and embody that healing. This is again de jure and de facto participation in God's mission: Christian mission is how people "participat[e] . . . in what God himself 'is' and *therefore* in what God 'does.'"[38] The Triune God "enables, demands, and incorporates the 'partner' God has chosen" into God's healing work in the world as a foretaste of that final cosmic healing for which God's people long.[39] In short, we participate actively in God's work as we ourselves work in the world in ways that correspond to (and are enabled by) God's own work, ways that are in fact Christ living his life in and through us.

A lingering question remains for people still uncertain about mission: what is evangelism, which is perhaps the heart of Christian mission?[40] What do we proclaim? This is a good question to ask in light of evangelicalism's sense of the urgency of Christian proclamation. Míguez Bonino offers an account of proclamation that is consistent with this holistic view of participation in God's mission. For Míguez Bonino, evangelism is "a call to repentance, faith, and discipleship," nothing less than "*the invitation to participate in faith in the very life of the triune God and hence in the totality of what God has done, is doing, and will do to fulfill God's purpose of being 'all in all.'*" Since God promises to be all in all—individually, communally, and cosmically, not only spiritually and ecclesially—"all evangelization should be . . . an announcement of God's justice and a call to practice and serve it." Thus, any evangelistic message that does not speak to how God confronts the myriad horrors that oppressed peoples face, as is the case with much evangelical proclamation and practice, "does not deserve to be called evangelical."[41]

What kind of proclamation does deserve to be called evangelical? It must involve at least (1) telling the world that the Father has sent the Son and the Spirit to proclaim and embody God's healing reign; (2) emphasizing God's "'option for the poor' as the criterion of interpretation of the reign of Jesus Christ and of the mission of the kingdom";[42] and (3)

---

38. Míguez Bonino, *Faces*, 139. I emphasize Míguez Bonino's "therefore," which makes our action necessary, not the "and," which could be seen as dividing the being from the action of God.

39. Míguez Bonino, *Faces*, 141.

40. Just as important as the question *what* we proclaim is the question *how* we proclaim it—with (literal or metaphorical) sword in hand or from the foot of the cross? Alas, I don't have the space to develop this theme here.

41. Míguez Bonino, *Faces*, 144. Emphasis in original.

42. Míguez Bonino, *Faces*, 138.

calling for "justice, mercy, God's peace (*shalom*) [as] embodied in good law, good government, [and] a faithful community" as creatures of, and responses to, God's reign.[43] The story of Jesus is the center of our proclamation, and both trinitarian doctrine and the hermeneutical insights of liberation theologians make this story intelligible. Yet, read in these ways, Jesus's story necessarily calls and enables us to struggle against violence and injustice in church and world as part of our participation in God's active life. If we only see and proclaim what God has done for us without putting it into practice, we are like the rich man who knew Israel's God but couldn't follow the one who confronted him with the promise and challenge of eternal life (Mark 10:17–27).

Conclusion

I hope that this account of participation in God's mission, which is trinitarian in structure, liberationist in content, and evangelical in its sense of kerygmatic urgency, suggests attractive possibilities for the terms *evangelical* and *mission* in our day. Such possibilities depend to a great extent on our willingness to listen to voices evangelicals often reject or ignore. I believe that we can and must give these old words new life, wresting them from people who have put them to such offensive uses. As another of my teachers, Willie J. Jennings, once said to me, "'Evangelical' is a good word. We can't let the right-wingers have it." I suspect that, at the end of the day, Okholm would agree.

Bibliography

Barber, Daniel Colucciello. *On Diaspora: Christianity, Religion, and Secularity*. Eugene: Cascade, 2011.

Barth, Karl. *Church Dogmatics 4/1: The Doctrine of Reconciliation*. Translated by Geoffrey Bromiley et al. Edinburgh: T. & T. Clark, 1956.

———. *Church Dogmatics 4/2: The Doctrine of Reconciliation*. Translated by Geoffrey Bromiley et al. Edinburgh: T. & T. Clark, 1959.

Center for Religion and Civic Culture. "The Varieties of American Evangelicalism." https://crcc.usc.edu/report/the-varieties-of-american-evangelicalism/.

43. Míguez Bonino, *Faces*, 141. That is, God makes peace and calls us to do the same.

Collins Winn, Christian T. "Kingdom." In *Prophetic Evangelicals: Envisioning a Just and Peaceable Kingdom*, edited by Bruce Ellis Benson et al., 86–99. Grand Rapids: Eerdmans, 2012.

Cone, James H. *A Black Theology of Liberation*. Maryknoll: Orbis, 1986.

Emery, Gilles. *The Trinity: An Introduction to Catholic Doctrine on the Triune God*. Washington, DC: Catholic University of America Press, 2011.

Flett, John G. *The Witness of God: The Trinity, Missio Dei, Karl Barth, and the Nature of Christian Community*. Grand Rapids: Eerdmans, 2010.

Green, Joel B. "Kingdom of God/Heaven." In *The Dictionary of Jesus and the Gospels*, edited by Joel B. Green, 468–81. Downers Grove: IVP Academic, 2014.

Guder, Darrell L. *Called to Witness: Doing Missional Theology*. Grand Rapids: Eerdmans, 2015.

Gutiérrez, Gustavo. *A Theology of Liberation: History, Politics, and Salvation*. Translated and edited by Sister Caridad Inda and John Eagleson. Maryknoll: Orbis, 1988.

Jennings, Willie J. *The Christian Imagination: Theology and the Origins of Race*. New Haven: Yale University Press, 2010.

Jenson, Robert W. "The Church and the Sacraments." In *The Cambridge Companion to Christian Doctrine*, edited by Colin E. Gunton, 207–25. New York: Cambridge University Press, 1997.

Johnson, Keith L. "Reconsidering Barth's Rejection of Przywara's Analogia Entis." *Modern Theology* 26 (2010) 632–50.

Mays, James L. *The Lord Reigns: A Theological Handbook to the Psalms*. Louisville: Westminster John Knox, 1994.

Míguez Bonino, José. *Faces of Latin American Protestantism*. Translated by Eugene L. Stockwell. Grand Rapids: Eerdmans, 1997.

———. *Revolutionary Theology Comes of Age*. London: SPCK, 1975.

Moltmann, Jürgen. "On Latin American Liberation Theology: An Open Letter to José Míguez Bonino." *Christianity and Crisis* 36 (1976) 57–63.

Neder, Adam. *Participation in Christ: An Entry into Karl Barth's Church Dogmatics*. Louisville: Westminster John Knox, 2009.

Plantinga Pauw, Amy. *The Church in Ordinary Time: A Wisdom Ecclesiology*. Grand Rapids: Eerdmans, 2017.

Rivera, Luis N. *A Violent Evangelism: The Political and Religious Conquest of the Americas*. Louisville: Westminster John Knox, 1992.

Sobrino, Jon. "The Central Position of the Reign of God in Liberation Theology." In *Mysterium Liberationis: Fundamental Concepts in Liberation Theology*, edited by Ignacio Ellacuría et al., 350–87. Maryknoll: Orbis, 1993.

———. *Christ the Liberator: A View from the Victims*. Translated by Paul Burns. Maryknoll: Orbis, 2001.

Tanner, Kathryn. *Christ the Key*. New York: Cambridge University Press, 2009.

———. *Jesus, Humanity, and the Trinity: A Brief Systematic Theology*. Minneapolis: Fortress, 2001.

Webster, John. "The Church and the Perfections of God." In *The Community of the Word: Toward an Evangelical Ecclesiology*, edited by Mark Husbands et al., 75–95. Downers Grove: IVP Academic, 2005.

Wright, N. T. *Surprised by Hope: Rethinking Heaven, Resurrection, and the Mission of the Church*. New York: HarperOne, 2008.

4

Evangelicalism

A Home for All of Us

VINCENT BACOTE

"HAVE YOU HEARD ABOUT our Wheaton Theology Conference, Vince?" Rodney Clapp, working for InterVarsity Press at the time, handed me a flyer for the 1996 conference. The topic: The Gospel in Black and White. I politely took possession of the flyer and turned to Craig Keener (who I had accompanied to the InterVarsity Press display at the American Academy of Religion Conference) and said "I am not doing this."

Why was I so immediately adamant in my negative response? It was the first year of my doctoral program at Drew University, and I had vowed to myself that my academic pursuits would avoid "doing the Black thing." I did not want to do what I thought might be expected of me, which was to be an African-American evangelical whose work would produce a theologically conservative response to the work of James Cone and others identified with Black Theology. At that moment, I felt giving a paper at the conference would be a doorway leading to a career as the kind of person who mainly discusses race and does not give much attention to "mainstream" theological issues.

"It's just a single paper. It doesn't have to define your career," Craig gently replied. Persuaded, I eventually submitted a proposal which was accepted and presented "Theological Method in Black and White: Does Race Matter at All?" in April 1996. It was at this conference where I first

61

met Dennis Okholm, who was conference director, and by 2000 a colleague when I joined the Wheaton College faculty. His vision for the conference reflected his desire to see an evangelicalism that was more ethnically inclusive in thought and deed as much as in appearance. As he wrote in the volume produced from the conference, "The underlying assumption of this book is that the achievements in racial reconciliation we celebrate are not widespread realities even in the church because we have not addressed the issues at more fundamental levels."[1]

My Vexation

I begin with this anecdote not only because it conveys how I met Dennis, but also provides a window into my personal vexation at the time within evangelicalism. Back then I did not see it as vexation, but in hindsight I can see that I was contending with a complicated challenge. While I have never thought of myself as "not quite belonging" to the evangelical world, this anecdote is an indicator that there have been dissonant experiences that reveal some ways evangelicalism is movement with a "work in progress" sign when it comes to truly being "home" for everyone who generally seems to share its central biblical and theological commitments. While many would say they completely trust the Bible, emphasize Christ's saving work on the cross, believe in the need for a personal conversion to salvation, and agree that this faith should be actively shared with others, they also like myself encounter(ed) subtle to explicit discomfort related to questions of justice, race, and other social concerns. For me, this has not been mainly a matter of explicit experiences of racism but more of vexation about the demographics of evangelical institutions, the relationship between theology and ethics, and the inner workings of the approach to and construction of theology. All of these elements were at work in my vexation at the time, especially the latter.

Why at that time did I have such a fervent commitment to avoiding questions of race in theology, and why would I now say that I was amid an experience of vexation? Perhaps the answer comes by considering why I had reached a conclusion that giving attention to questions of race was a path to a form of confinement. No one had told me that it was a bad idea to give attention to questions of race as part of my scholarly expertise, but my experience within evangelical parachurch ministries, churches, and

1. Okholm, *The Gospel in Black and White*, 7.

institutions had led me to a place where I felt like a path to legitimacy as a theologian required demonstrating that I could write, preach, and teach about theology in an idiom with little to no connection to race. Put another way, I perceived that the way to do evangelical theology with a strong emphasis on biblicism was to convey questions of doctrine untethered to the particularities of context, especially when those particularities raised questions (often matters of Christian ethics) about social, political, and other life circumstances of those contending with matters of social concern. To do truly evangelical theology meant confinement within methods that excluded some context-rooted questions I saw as important biblical and theological inquiries.

Full disclosure: I had taken a hermeneutics class with Dr. Grant Osborne where he told us "theology always needs to be written" (because of our perpetual engagement with matters of context—his "hermeneutical spiral"), and I had taken courses related to urban ministry that strongly emphasized the need to give attention to context (particularly engagement in cultural exegesis). Yet, at that time I had a frame of mind where I thought the goal of writing evangelical theology was to give a kind of clear articulation of the doctrines that emerge directly from the Bible, a mode of theological discourse that would be readily accessible within and across most contexts. I now know that this aim, no matter how virtuous, was based in fantasy or skewed vision because of what was hiding in plain sight: the "pure" evangelical theology I wanted to pursue was itself an exercise in contextualization, even with the strong commitment to biblical integrity and clear understanding of the message of Scripture.

How did this pursuit of a pure evangelical theology catalyze vexation and a commitment to avoid the prison of being the person who attends to the questions of race? First, it is important to note that I was not opposed to giving attention to questions of race. In fact, I had often wondered what it took to have attention given to the topic because it was rarely present in theological discussion. In my exposure to evangelicalism it even seemed to be a challenge to get white evangelicals to see that racism was a sin—and that one could make this case from the Bible.[2] While I often felt very much at home in evangelical contexts because of my cultural fluidity and genuine friendships, I was concerned by the fact

---

2. Even if people thought racial injustice was bad, it seemed to me that for many evangelicals there was not the weight given to it in a manner similar to other forms of sin that were explicitly identified by a specific verse or set of verses.

there was little attention to race, or that there was much left unsaid when it was mentioned.

That said, while I wanted attention given to the concerns of non-whites, my desire for evangelical theological legitimacy was putting me into a bind I did not recognize at the time; the limits and boundaries of what I understood as the standard mode of evangelical theology required a "biblical" approach that required me to set aside contextual dimensions (such as race or politics) if my work was to have a positive reception. If I was to one day be a professor, a participant in the guild of evangelical theology, my work had to pass the test. My spiritual and theological formation in evangelical settings (for which I am immensely thankful) and my perception of evangelical theological discourse led me to conclude that I had to present my work in a particular idiom if I was to be a proper evangelical theologian. Because of my commitments to the truthfulness of Scripture and its primacy in evangelical theology, this all made sense to me.

For certain, no one sat me down prior to my pursuit of doctoral work and said "you have two choices: you can either write legitimate biblicist evangelical theology or you can merge that work with a focus on questions of race and become known as an evangelical respondent to James Cone." Yet, this is essentially what I thought was before me when I thought about my prospects for a career, and I did not want to be confined to matters of race. I wanted to be known as someone with expertise in the broad sweep of Christian doctrine,[3] a person whose work was known for its attention to standard questions about God, Jesus, Holy Spirit, Church, Eschatology, and others found in works of systematic theology.

While this aspiration was straightforward on the surface, it was a career trajectory envisioned amid vexation. The vexation could be expressed by this question: "Why are only some questions valid for evangelical theology and others are set aside to a kind of special interest domain?" Though I did not pose this question to myself or others as I began my doctoral studies, in truth it was hovering in my consciousness. The vexation could be put another way: "If I am to be at home as an evangelical theologian, does it require me to set aside questions of race?" "Is leaving these questions at the door the price of admission to the domain

---

3. Some might ask, "But weren't you always interested in faith and politics and that Dutchman Abraham Kuyper?" While the answer is "for certain," I also had a strong desire to be known as someone with expertise in evangelical systematic theology untethered from questions of race.

of *legitimate* evangelical theology?" Looking back to that conversation at the InterVarsity booth with which I opened this chapter, why did I feel I needed to be so clearly on a path to a non-racialized theology? While it is not problematic to consider the parameters of one's scholarly community, why was I so vexed that I thought the best strategy for my career included a dedicated avoidance of questions of race? How could it be the case that a theology centered on the Bible seemed to demand the marginalization of questions often unasked by those writing in the evangelical guild? One answer to these questions: in spite of many good intentions, evangelicalism has not always been "home" for all who share its core commitments.

A Broader Evangelicalism

Attending and participating in the 1996 Wheaton Theology Conference required me to contend with my vexation. From the opening address to the conclusion, the presentations covered multiple dimensions and facets of questions related to race (largely with attention to African-American concerns); my contribution considered the role of race in theological method.[4] Since that time, I have continued to contend with this circumstance with an eye toward the emergence of an evangelical movement characterized by its longstanding attention to the centrality of the Bible and historic Christian doctrines along with an expanded theological discourse that invites and engages the kinds of questions I thought I must leave at the door.[5] How might we get to this kind of evangelicalism, a new "home base"?[6]

To move forward, it is important to consider what gives the evangelical movement its distinctive character. I have come to regard evangelicalism as a "conservative Protestant ecumenism" because it is a movement in which significant unity is found among theologically diverse Christians

4. Bacote, "Theological Method in Black and White," 49–57.

5. Heltzel's *Jesus and Justice*, presents a similar vision, influenced by trends among younger evangelicals at the time. Many other trends since that time reveal we are still waiting.

6. Here I note that many might regard this vision as quixotic because of the challenges of race in the history of evangelicalism. There are many books and articles highlighting the complicity of the traditions that comprise evangelicalism in active racial division. Two examples: Noll, *The Civil War as a Theological Crisis*, and Tisby, *The Color of Compromise*. The point of my vision for a broader evangelicalism is not to deny the challenges of white supremacy in its history but to make the case for what the movement could be if it lived up to its central theological commitments.

who identify with the four markers of David Bebbington[7] (or the five of Timothy Larsen[8]). The denominational diversity of the evangelical movement is an indicator of its potential for bringing Christians together around "fundamental" matters such as the primary source of authority and the basics of salvation and mission. In a sense it is not unlike the view of those Christians of various traditions (Protestants and sometimes including Roman Catholics) who regard themselves compatriots with those committed to the affirmations found in the Apostles' or Nicene Creed (of course there are differences; here the emphasis is on the pursuit of a form of unity). Among evangelicals, the emphasis on the authority of Scripture is one of the unifying dimensions that creates a perpetual possibility for the changes that can yield a less vexing, more hospitable home environment in evangelicalism.

At this point some may protest that there are and have been proponents of biblical authority who are/were well entrenched in cultural and political commitments that contribute to the type of "not quite at home" vexation I describe above. While not denying this reality, the fact that those within the evangelical movement maintain a fierce commitment to the total truthfulness of the Bible means that there is always the opportunity to keep returning to Scripture and presenting biblical texts that call for responses of Christian fidelity and practice that can lead to a better evangelical abode. It may take a long time, but the question "do you really believe the Bible and are you really willing to submit to God and His word?" can be asked repeatedly as we strive for the goal. This trajectory can be pursued with sustained attention to biblical emphases such as openness to transformation (Rom 12:2), love of God and neighbor (Matt 22:28), suffering with others (1 Cor 12:26), and a community comprised of ethnic diversity (Rev 7:9). There are many other biblical texts, themes, and emphases that together could orient the evangelical community toward becoming broader, more genuinely hospitable, and more expansive in theological conversation. For certain, a naïve idealism assumes the mere presentation of Scripture will yield the intended effect; along with the presentation of Scripture I express a belief in the often

7. These four markers are Biblicism, Crucicentrism, Conversionism, and Activism. See Bebbington, *Evangelicalism in Modern Britain*.

8. Larsen, "Defining and Locating Evangelicalism," 1–14. Larsen adds an emphasis on an encounter with the Holy Spirit in his definition. In contrast to Bebbington, Larsen is not inclined to include Roman Catholics within the definition of those identified as "evangelical."

slow and steady work of the Holy Spirit that opens blind eyes and orients Christians toward the reception and performance of God's truth. At the most basic level, a path toward a more hospitable and ethnically inclusive evangelicalism requires and presumes the prominence of biblical authority. Put it this way: you can always put a Bible in the face of an evangelical and ask "do you believe this?"

In addition to what we might call a "responsive Biblicism," the path toward a broader evangelicalism requires reckoning and repentance. I write in 2020, four years after the election of Donald Trump, whose greatest support came from white evangelicals. While racial fault lines in evangelicalism are nothing new (and some would say these fault lines are part of the DNA of the movement), there has been a great intensification of the dissonance felt by minorities who inhabit evangelical spaces— from churches and educational institutions to parachurch ministries and publishing houses.[9] In many cases (long past as well as present) there are reports of emotional exhaustion, subtle and explicit expressions of disrespect, and (for some) perpetual frustration at a refusal to consider (much less respond to) concerns related to ethnic diversity.[10] These concerns are not new, and it would be false to suggest that there have not been persons and institutions that have attempted to begin seriously addressing these challenges. While here and there efforts are being made (including institutional and denominational acknowledgements of past racism), there is a need for a more large scale reckoning with the factors that have made the evangelical movement a challenging environment for many minorities.[11] Just as the evangelical movement has a strong emphasis on the authority of the Bible, the highly personal dimension of salvation includes a strong belief that life with God involves regular repentance for sin. This is not a new revivalism where there are public meetings that specifically encourage repentance and renewal around the conditions that have made the evangelical movement less like home. Rather, I mean approaches to

9. It is possible that social media has led to greater exposure of the difficulties for minorities in evangelicalism, but it is also possible that the heightened intensity is related to the greater attention to racial divisions after the deaths of Travyon Martin and Michael Brown (and others) along with a generally agitated public.

10. See Gilbreath, *Reconciliation Blues*, for one chronicle of these challenges.

11. I say "many" because not everyone has had the same difficulties. In my case, for example, I have high cultural fluidity that has helped me to thrive in various cultural settings, and some of my experience is unique. I do not have as many complaints or concerns as many others, but I am aware of various factors that make my experience exceptional. There are many other stories that are distressing.

evangelical Christian formation in churches and parachurch settings that lead to discipleship practices that cultivate a reflective and repentant disposition on matters beyond typical concerns of evangelical piety. This could be a disposition of reckoning where there is an ongoing openness to discovering and acknowledging the real problems with race and ethnicity along with the subsequent pursuit of embodied repentance from the personal to institutional level. This is necessary if evangelicalism is to be a home—a place of rest, renewal, and joyful service.

A final dimension has already been mentioned but requires more attention: the role of institutions in creating an evangelicalism that is truly "home" for non-whites. One major part of this is a commitment to cultural enrichment. This enrichment is not of the simplistic variety that might be characterized by extremes of tokenism or political correctness. Instead, this is an ongoing process where the histories and traditions of institutions and organizations are not jettisoned but enhanced by thoughtful and skillful incorporation of cultural elements that help the institution live up to its identity and mission with a more diverse population in mind. This is far from an easy task, and the goal is not the creation of a mélange that attends to special interests while refusing to broaden what "we" or "us" means. Institutions and organizations need to ask: "Are we a place to which all people want to come?" "Are we a place where people know they are at home and not merely welcomed as visitors?"

Some other questions: "Do they know their contributions are valued and capable of helping make the institution become its best self?" "Are we the kind of place/organization where we account for the extra and often uncompensated work sometimes required to help others navigate and (hopefully) flourish here?" In theological settings, institutions can work against the vexation I felt by inviting and welcoming theological discourse stemming from ethnic concerns as ways to more fully and deeply articulate the "evangel" that is at the root of the movement's name. Imagine: evangelical institutions developing a reputation as one of the primary places where there is openness about failures past and present amid an ethos where there is a constant pursuit of discerning and imagining an evangelicalism that many are proud to call "home." This type of evangelicalism would exemplify a perpetual aspiration to live up its primary theological commitments; it would be a movement more likely to be known for its proclamation *and practice* of the good news of the gospel.

My participation in the 1996 Wheaton Theology conference and encounter with Dennis Okholm is one of the most prominent factors in encouraging me to imagine and believe that the evangelical movement could become its better self. As I write this, we are still waiting for this version of evangelicalism to arrive, but even amid the frustrations there are signs that it could arrive. Thank you, Dennis, for creating one of those signs years ago.

Bibliography

Bacote, Vincent. "Theological Method in Black and White: Does Race Matter at All?" In *The Gospel in Black and White: Theological Resources for Racial Reconciliation*. Edited by Dennis L. Okholm, 49–57. Downers Grove: InterVarsity, 1996.

Bebbington, David W. *Evangelicalism in Modern Britain: A History from the 1730s to the 1980s*. London: Unwin Hyman, 1989.

Gilbreath, Edward. *Reconciliation Blues: A Black Evangelical's Inside View of White Chirstianity*. Downers Grove: InterVarsity, 2006.

Heltzel, Peter G. *Jesus and Justice: Evangelicals, Race, and American Politics*. New Haven: Yale University Press, 2009.

Larsen, Timothy. "Defining and Locating Evangelicalism." In *The Cambridge Companion to Evangelical Theology*, edited by Timothy Larsen et al., 1. Cambridge: Cambridge University Press, 2007.

Noll, Mark A. *The Civil War as a Theological Crisis (The Steven and Janice Brose Lectures in the Civil War Era)*. Chapel Hill: The University of North Carolina Press, 2015.

Okholm, Dennis L., ed. *The Gospel in Black and White: Theological Resources for Racial Reconciliation*. Downers Grove: InterVarsity, 1996.

Tisby, Jemar. *The Color of Compromise: The Truth About the American Church's Complicity in Racism*. Grand Rapids: Zondervan, 2019.

5

Herstory

Reclaiming Women's Voices for the Evangelical Tradition

JENNIFER M. BUCK

THROUGH HIS WRITING, TEACHING, and embodied life, Dennis Okholm has helped draw the church into a more expansive and inclusive land-scape. In my own life, he has helped me find a place within evangeli-calism—specifically within the evangelical Quaker tradition—in part by introducing me to the voices of neglected women in church history as well as strong, egalitarian evangelical theology. My own theological scholarship seeks to continue in the footsteps of Okholm by focusing on elevating the stories and voices of women that have been excluded from mainstream Christian theology despite their significant impact on the body of Christ as a whole and the evangelical tradition in particular.

This chapter will examine women in the Christian tradition begin-ning with their illumination in Scripture, then in church history, and concluding with examples from the modern evangelical tradition. Only a select example of stories will be included here, and only told briefly, as each merit not only a full chapter themselves but illuminate the dire need for the greater inclusion of women in order for the evangelical tradition to become its best self.

Female Imagery for God in Scripture

God

Centering women in the evangelical tradition begins with centering their identity in the biblical narrative. As a starting point, let us consider the gendered nature of God. If God is our Father, could God also be our Mother? As recorded in Matthew and Luke's Gospel, Jesus teaches us to pray "Our Father, who is in heaven," giving gendered language to God as a male parent. And like this, Scripture contains numerous other masculine metaphors for God—not only as Father, but also as Lord, Warrior, and King. But a warrior and a ruler are not necessarily male roles—neither is a parent. The Psalmist reminds us:

> As the eyes of servants look to the hand of their master,
> as the eyes of a maid to the hand of her mistress,
> so our eyes look to the Lord our God,
> until he has mercy upon us. (Ps 123:2)

The master can be both female and male, as can many other feminine-centered images in Scripture. God is identified through female animal metaphors such as mother bear (Hosea 13:8), mother eagle (Deut 32:11–12), and a mother hen (Matt 23:37; Luke 13:34). The book of Isaiah harnesses embodied female imagery for God repeatedly, describing God as a woman in labor (42:14), a nursing mother (49:15), and a mother comforting her child (66:13). Hosea 11:3–4 gives vivid imagery of a mother caring deeply for her child, saying:

> Yet it was I who taught Ephraim to walk,
> I took them up in my arms;
> but they did not know that I healed them.
> I led them
> with cords of human kindness,
> with bands of love.
> I was to them like those
> who lift infants to their cheeks.
> I bent down to them and fed them.

This imagery paints a picture of a mother who cares for scraped knees, scooping up little ones and snuggling them to her face. This familiarity and comfortability demonstrate a deep level of tenderness, telling of a nurturing God who is both mother and father.

God is both body and not body, existing beyond socially constructed gender roles yet also connecting with all humanity through relationships we can understand. God is identified to Moses as "I AM WHO I AM" in Exodus 3:14, in one of the most profound and mysterious definitions of God we are given in Scripture. Yet later in Deuteronomy 32:18, Moses gives this God a more direct human identifier: "You were unmindful of the Rock that bore you; you forgot the God who gave you birth." This cosmic entity also exists as intimately with humanity as a mother who grows a child in her womb.

In Luke 15, we are given a trio of stories on lost things: a shepherd searching for a lost sheep, a woman searching for a lost coin, and a father with two lost sons. God in these parables serves as the shepherd, the woman, and the father. This set of stories—intended to teach about the Kingdom of God realistically—presents metaphors of two genders. The result is a rich picture of God's relationship to humanity which transcends the boundaries of gender.

Women in Scripture

Now let us consider the examples of women throughout the biblical narrative. As a woman reading Scripture in the twenty-first century, I find myself torn over the Bible's portrayal of women. Certain passages tell stories of agency, valor, and hope in the inclusion of brave women, while others lament over the abuse and neglect over the treatment of the women in the community of the people of God. In the same book that tells of the prophet Deborah—the counselor, warrior, and only female judge mentioned in the Bible (Judg 4—5)—we have the story of the unnamed Levite woman's dismemberment (Judg 19). In 2 Samuel, we have an unnamed woman from Tekoa serving as a counselor to King David (2 Sam 14) appearing right after the rape of Tamar. These victims cannot be ignored, some of whom are not even given the dignity of a name, and their lives are to be remembered and grieved in our reading of Scripture. Yet Deborah and the woman from Tekoa are two of numerous examples of strong women leading and influencing the people of God. They exist right alongside Ruth, Hannah, Miriam, Huldah, Esther, and others whose stories emerge despite their patriarchal contexts.

In the New Testament, nine of Paul's twenty-eight greetings are to women who serve as prophets, apostles, and deacons in the early church.

Women lead house churches (Acts 12:12; Col 4:15) and Mary Magdalene, Joanna, and Mary the Mother of James serve as the first evangelists after Jesus's resurrection (Luke 24). And yet some of the Pauline teachings in 1 Corinthians 11 and 14, 1 Timothy 2, and Ephesians 5 appear to subjugate women when read outside of their historical context. Early churches shared leadership between women and men, but they also encountered the problem of early converts teaching without the proper training, causing disruption in worship (1 Tim 2:8–15). All are instructed to submit to one another out of reverence for Christ (Eph 5:21); all are told they have a hymn, lesson, revelation, tongue, or interpretation to share in worship (1 Cor 14:26); and all are now one in Christ Jesus, with divisions such as male and female no longer separating those within the Body of Christ (Gal 3:28).

The Witness of Dorcas

The previous survey highlights the paradoxes and tensions surrounding the lives of women in Scripture. One other example from the New Testament will be given special attention here: Dorcas. Acts 9:36–42 is one of only three places where a female disciple is named in Scripture. Both the Greek and Aramaic versions of her name, Dorcas and Tabitha, are included in the narrative, likely encompassing her ministry to both Jewish and Greek believers and demonstrating how well she was known in both contexts. Through examples like helping mother her church in Joppa and dressing the widows there, Dorcas is clearly beloved and essential to the life of her community. Her actions not only exude charity—a virtue characteristic of women and men in the early church—but also obedience to following Jesus's words about clothing the naked and poor and Scripture's repeated commands about caring for widows. When looking at Scripture, it often helps to note the silences: her family is not mentioned as she might even be a widow herself. It is likely she had means (she had the financial ability to practice charity and her home had an upper room) but we do not know how or why. Her trade as a seamstress might have provided her wealth, but that is not significant enough to include. Her legacy is not her wealth or her family, but her charity.

Jesus commanded his disciples to witness to all corners of the earth and Dorcas serves as an early, faithful example of that witness. She both loved her work and the people in this passage from Acts, as is evidenced by how they mourn her death. Her true legacy becomes clear when these widows all come to mourn her and show up in her home, a place where her hospitality is evident as they all seem familiar with the space. Luke honors her legacy by including her in the book of Acts, and in just these seven verses we get a glimpse into a woman who followed Jesus's teachings and mothered the vulnerable.

The more one reflects on the pictures of women in Scripture, the more one realizes that this context is not as far from our context today as one might think. Women today, like the Levite woman and Tamar, still fall victim to male violence and abuse. Women today still struggle to find their place as leaders and influencers in a patriarchal society. And yet women do serve as teachers and preachers in churches today, just like Deborah and the woman from Tekoa. Women do partner with men in leading in worship. And as followers of Jesus today, women and men are to understand themselves as all God's children, baptized in Christ, and equal to one another (Gal 3:26–29). There is still much work to be done in women and men "honoring Christ and putting others first" (Eph 5:21 CEV), but this is our calling if we are to be a people faithful to Scripture.

Women in Early and Medieval Church History

Numerous examples of women in the Christian tradition helped shape the theology and ministry of the church. In the middle of the second century, teachers of the faith are named who worked alongside and taught Jerome and Ambrose: Paula, Eustochium, Marcella.[12] To have a role as an educator—and to be educated and equipped to do so—would have been revolutionary for women during this time. Surveying chronologically from the sixth century through the fourteenth century, the ministries of Ita of Kileedy, Hilda of Whitby, Leoba, Liutberga, Heloise, Mechthild of Magdeberg, Hadewijch of Antwerp, and Birgitta of Sweden resound as well.[13]

Multiple medieval women served as examples of the mysticism and divine encounters early and medieval church women became known for, and their contributions deeply developed the spirituality of the church. Hildegard of Bingen described through dictation and illustrated visions her encounters with God while living at her convent. Her *Scivitas* details

12. Dray, "Women in Church History," 23.
13. Dray, "Women in Church History," 23.

a direct, unmediated encounter with God, accompanied by powerful emotions. Theresa of Avila, known for her public ministry and teaching, is also known for her spiritual writing. Catherine of Siena, sought after as a church leader, teacher, and public speaker, wrote of her meditations as a result of prayer, asceticism, and eucharistic encounters with Christ, directly bypassing the male priesthood. Beyond her writings, Catherine took on a public mission for the most vulnerable in Siena, carrying out a letter-writing campaign to Pope Gregory XI with the goal of ending war in Italy, returning to Rome, and working to reunify the church.[14] That such women would write and speak with divine, autonomous agency gave them a role as female prophets in the medieval church. Though un-educated in formal theology, these women boldly wrote and lived as a direct response to God's commands. As they found themselves filled with the Holy Spirit, and in support of the teachings of the church, their words taught and shaped their fellow Christian sisters and brothers.

Julian of Norwich

One final example, Julian of Norwich, deserves special attention for her feminine imagery of God as well as her contributions to Christian spiri-tuality. The Englishwoman born in 1342, well-known for her teaching, spiritual writings, and wisdom, spent her life in service to the Church of St. Julian and St. Edward in Norwich. Her most influential work, *Revela-tions of Divine Love,* is a guidebook in Christian spirituality.[15] As an an-chorite, it was during an isolated illness that she describes sixteen visions and revelations of God. After six hours of meditations on the crucifix, her revelations came upon her and she wrote extensively on the love of God, the passion of Christ, and the perichoretic nature of the Trinity. Significantly, Julian focuses on the feminine aspects of God through Jesus as nurturing, feeding, and caring for the believers. As she describes, "And though, possibly, an earthly mother may suffer her child to perish, our heavenly Mother Jesus can never suffer us who are his children to perish. For he is almighty, all-wisdom, and all-love."[16] This God who suffers with us, embodying aspects of both genders, echoes of the Biblical proph-ets and serves as a powerful metaphor for the individual's bonded

14. MacHaffie, *Her Story,* 72.

15. Julian, *Revelations of Divine Love.*

16. Julian, *Revelations of Divine Love,* 166–67.

relationship with Jesus. "God is nearer to us than our own souls," she writes, and her most well-known words speak of the depths of closeness with God: "Jesus answered with these words, saying: 'All shall be well, and all shall be well, and all manner of thing shall be well.'"[17] These words have given spiritual direction and clarity to Christians over the ages, and Julian's example is one of the more memorable in church history. Her writings developed the church's spirituality as well as its understanding of God's mothering nature.

Quaker Women in Contemporary Church History

Margaret Fell Fox and Lucretia Mott play central roles in my own Quaker tradition and serve as two early examples of women leaders in the Protestant tradition after the Reformation. These two examples embody several aspects of the true spirit of evangelicalism: (1) Activism on behalf of the most vulnerable as a direct result of their study of Scripture, and (2) Encounters with the living Jesus.

Margaret Fell Fox

Margaret Fell Fox (1614–1702), often referred to as the "nursing mother of Quakerism," served as one of the original leaders of the Quaker movement and became a significant advocate for the role of women both in the church and in society. Through her marriage to George Fox, the two worked for the cause of conversions as well as social justice throughout England. In Fell's important tract, "Women's Speaking Justified," she persuasively argues for the integral role of women in church leadership based on themes she found in the Bible. In it, she supports her case for gender equality by relying upon the basic treatise of spiritual equality in Quakerism: that of God in everyone. Her belief was that God created all people, therefore both women and men were capable of not only possessing the Inner Light but also of speaking, teaching, and prophesying for edification of the community of faith.

Fell is remembered as one who managed the Swarthmore Manor, her home, as a center of peace and hospitality. Her house served ministers, runaway slaves, and any who needed a place to find refuge or respite.[18]

17. Julian, *Revelations of Divine Love*, 124.
18. Trueblood, *The People Called Quakers*, 192.

Her work alongside her husband brought organization and structure to the entire Quaker movement, especially during times of state-sponsored persecution.

Fell serves as a wonderful example of early Quaker peacemaking through her work with the Quaker church. At the genesis of its movement—of which Fell was an integral part—when the continued existence of Quakerism was an open question, their call to justice was often on behalf of other Friends. Fell wrote numerous tracts and worked to raise money and consciousness about those in prison for religious persecution or otherwise. George Fox recalls in his journal that Fell "went to the King [Charles II of England] and told him what sad work there was in the city, and in the nation, and shewed [sic] him, that we were an innocent peaceable people."[19] Fell peaceably confronted the King of England for the sake of the Quaker movement and the king's threats of imprisonment. She preached peace among the Quakers, in spite of threats from the monarchy. Fell became a courageous voice for justice, a model that sparked the Friends work in later years as a voice of justice on behalf of others.

Lucretia Mott

Nearly one hundred years after Fell, Lucretia Mott (1793–1880) continued the legacy of the peacemaking which was emblematic of Fell's life and the Quaker tradition at large. She devoted her life to the abolition of slavery, women's rights, school and prison reforms, temperance, peace, and religious tolerance. Mott became a Quaker minister—one of the only denominations allowing such a role for women at that time—and she used her gift of preaching to speak to the Quaker distinctive of the equality of all people and the presence of the divine light in every individual. Within the Quaker movement, she married James Mott and together the couple worked against the evil of slavery by giving speeches, founding women's abolitionist societies such as the Pennsylvania Anti-Slavery Society, and housing runaway slaves. Her own home became a stop on the Underground Railroad. Her founding of abolitionists societies was especially significant since other organizations within the anti-slavery movement refused to admit women. In her work for the anti-slavery movement, she advocated for pacifism and boycotting goods made or harvested by slaves as a part of her Quaker convictions.

19. Trueblood, *The People Called Quakers*, 194.

In 1837, Mott helped organize the First Anti-Slavery Convention of American Women—an event she worked on with her colleagues, the sisters Angelina and Sarah Grimké. Her vision for reform consisted primarily of connecting the causes of antislavery and feminism and she advocated for equal pay for equal work. She believed in the equal treatment of all people, and that work for women's equality must also go hand-in-hand with anti-slavery work. Years after the Anti-Slavery Convention, Mott channeled that energy into the Seneca Falls Convention in 1845—the first annual women's rights convention. One byproduct of this convention was a revision modeled after the United States Declaration of Independence titled, "The Declaration of Sentiments." It boldly declared, "We hold these truths to be self-evident: That all men and women are created equal," leaving in its wake a host of controversy.[20]

Another one of Mott's controversial but important actions was the passage of the Fugitive Slave Act of 1850, after which her home became a station for the Underground Railroad. This work was part of her commitment to pacifism as well as to aid the plight of slaves and seek equality for all. Mott frequently spoke about the value of all people, a position that led her to advocate for the entrance of women into higher education, equal property rights, and the right for women to vote. Her work for all the disenfranchised—women, freed and enslaved Africans, and Native Americans—stemmed from her deep Quaker convictions of peace and equality. Both Fell and Mott engaged God's word as a result of their encounters with Jesus through Scripture. Their engagement with the world modeled a public witness to action for those on the margins and was a direct outworking of their Christian faith.

Evangelical Women in Contemporary Church History

The landscape of evangelicalism has continued to evolve over the last two centuries. A variety of women will be briefly sketched here to represent the female embodiment of the modern evangelical movement. The examples of the women chosen will speak to the profound stream of activism within certain strands of evangelicalism—activism which has specifically focused on addressing issues such as slavery, education, homelessness, and income inequality.

20. Barbor and Frost, *The Quakers*, 46.

Harriet Beecher Stowe

Harriet Beecher Stowe (1811–1896) is known for helping fugitive slaves escape and find freedom and also as the author of the novel *Uncle Tom's Cabin*. After studying and then teaching at Hartford Female Seminary, she moved to Lane Theological Seminary where her father was appointed President. It was there that Stowe married a theology professor and the two became deeply involved in critiquing slavery and supporting the Underground Railroad. Her actions and writings helped motivate many to act against slavery, influencing President Lincoln and the Civil War.[21]

Fanny Crosby

Fanny Crosby (1820–1915), the famous blind hymnwriter, is known for penning "Blessed Assurance," "To God Be The Glory," as well as eight thousand other hymns. Known as the "Queen of Gospel Song Writers," her true commitment was to serve the poor doing home missionary labor. Alongside her hymnody work, she should also be remembered for her work in countless rescue missions, frequently giving the majority of her proceeds from her poetry and music to the poor and often refusing payment altogether. She had written that the lines, "blessed assurance, Jesus is mine," were inspired by an interpretation of Philippians 1:21, "For me to live is Christ and to die is gain."[22]

Emma Whittemore

One of the city missions where Fanny Crosby worked was run by Emma Whittemore (1850–1931). As the founder of over one hundred "Doors of Hope" missions, Whittemore saw that women under her care received "refuge, food, clothing, medical care, occupational training as well as the Gospel."[23] Whittemore describes her calling to ministry in this way: "It became evident that something more than an occasional visit or a kind word was required. If ultimate results in reclamation were to be attained, there must be a loving nurture and care that were impossible when

---

21. Phillips and Okholm, *Welcome to the Family*, 216.
22. Morgan, *Then Sings My Soul*, 183.
23. Phillips and Okholm, *Welcome to the Family*, 247.

contacts were only occasional."[24] She spoke of how God gave her a heart for vulnerable populations and she was able to see the stigma society placed on lower-class women. She opened her first home in 1890 in New York City, and her model offered women trade and banking skills which helped them rebuild their lives. The women were free to leave the home whenever they chose, as "the only restraint was that of Christ's love."[25]

Corrie ten Boom

The Dutch Christian Corrie ten Boom (1892–1983) actively resisted Nazis during the Holocaust, and, along with her family, began hiding Jews from the Gestapo in her family's watch shop. She was responsible for creating a network of safe houses in the Netherlands which saved upwards of eight hundred Jews during the Holocaust. She was imprisoned for these efforts at the Ravensbrück Concentration Camp where she ministered to others in the camp. It was in this camp where even her own sister died. Ten Boom later tracked down one of the prison guards to forgive him.[26] Her life is a profound example that illuminates the story of God's faithfulness even in the midst of the darkest corners of life on earth. Her famous work, *The Hiding Place*, tells her story and launched a ministry that took her around the world telling the story of Jesus's hope and the power of forgiveness. In her own words, "We must tell them that there is no pit so deep that He is not deeper still."[27]

Elizabeth Cady Stanton

Elizabeth Cady Stanton (1815–1902) came to view the Bible as the greatest hindrance to women's liberation so she organized a committee of women to write commentaries on portions of the Bible that deal with women. *The Woman's Bible*, published in two parts in 1895 and 1898 respectively, drew attention to both the feminist, liberating aspects of the Bible as well as honestly confronting portions typically interpreted patriarchally. The Seneca Falls Convention, which her writings and activism

---

24. Whittemore, *Mother Whittemore's Records*, 48.

25. Whittemore, *Mother Whittemore's Records*, 236.

26. Phillips and Okholm, *Welcome to the Family*, 84.

27. Ten Boom, *Hiding Place*, 210.

helped convene, is regarded today as one of the first women's rights gatherings in the United States.

Henrietta Mears

Henrietta Mears (1890–1963) served as the director of Christian Education at First Presbyterian Church in Hollywood, CA, and left a tremendous legacy as a Christian educator, author, and evangelist. During her lifetime she helped grow a Sunday School from four hundred to six thousand—the same Sunday school which shaped the likes of Bill Bright and Billy Graham. Her ideas helped develop the landscape of modern evangelical theology in the twentieth century, particularly in regards to conversion and discipleship. She founded Forest Home Conference Center and Gospel Light Publishing Company, and her writings and teachings have made a lasting influence on the evangelical movement to the present.[28]

Fannie Lou Hamer

Fannie Lou Hamer (1917–1977) serves as a strong example of advocacy and activism in the evangelical tradition. Born in Mississippi as the child of a minister and sharecropper, she fought tirelessly for black women's suffrage. Her faith gave her the resilience to continually stand against forces seeking to keep her and her community from full participation in society and the democratic process. In her own words: "Ain't no such of a thing as I can hate and hope to see God's face."[29] She worked for the Student Nonviolent Coordinating Committee leading voter registration campaigns and was falsely arrested and imprisoned as a part of her activism. She ran (unsuccessfully) for congress in Mississippi and helped found the Mississippi Freedom Democratic Party through which she went on to become the first African American since the Reconstruction era and the first woman from Mississippi to take a seat as an official delegate at a national party convention.[30] She later pioneered the Freedom Farm Cooperative, making it her mission to make land more accessible to African Americans through financial counseling, scholarship funds,

28. Phillips and Okholm, *Welcome to the Family,* 258.
29. DeRuscha, *50 Women Every Christian Should Know,* 329.
30. DeRuscha, *50 Women Every Christian Should Know,* 332.

and FHA subsidized housing. Her faith informed her activism work, and in commenting on her understanding of Scripture, civil rights activist Lawrence Guyot admired the manner in which she "connected the biblical exhortations for liberation and the struggle for civil rights any time that she wanted to."[31] Her work on racial, gender, and economic justice continues to inspire the evangelical church today.

The activist faith of these women in modern evangelical history does not stand alone. Many of the women included here may be familiar, but many are unknown or forgotten and will never remembered by Christian history books. Through their humble service and sacrifices of time, money, and prayer, evangelical women have shaped and sustained the movement. This legacy reaches into the present day including women such as Rachel Held Evans, Beth Moore, Austin Channing Brown, Brenda Salter-McNeil, Elizabeth Conde-Frazier, Karen Swallow Prior, and Lisa Sharon Harper deserve recognition as well as a combination of both academics, authors, activists, and pastors. The Fuller Theological Seminary essay volume, *Still Evangelical?*, highlights a number of these diverse contemporary voices as well, and serves as a valuable contribution critiquing some of the more troubling varieties of evangelicalism today which ignore, hamper, or reject the contributions women can and have made in formal and informal leadership positions to the body of Christ.

Conclusion

The women highlighted in this chapter created a way for me when there was no way and served as my foremothers in Scripture, church history, and the evangelical tradition. Significant work still needs to be done in order to make the evangelical tradition a more expansive and inclusive home for women and men alike. My own commitment to helping evangelicalism in particular and Christianity as a whole become its best self has its roots in Okholm's influence on my life and scholarship. I write out of the legacy of the lives, ministries, and theologies of women who have come before me in order to continue their work of shaping the evangelical tradition. May their *herstory* continue to embolden future generations and may they no longer be viewed as an alternative or marginalized tradition, but reclaimed as some of the true architects and leaders of the evangelical tradition and the Christian faith as we know it today.

31. Chappell, *A Stone of Hope*, 312.

Bibliography

Barbor, Hugh, and J. William Frost. *The Quakers.* New York: Greenwood, 1988.

Chappell, David L. *A Stone of Hope: Prophetic Religion and the Death of Jim Crow.* Chapel Hill: University of North Carolina Press, 2004.

DeRusha, Michelle. *50 Women Every Christian Should Know: Learning from Heroines of the Faith.* Grand Rapids: Baker, 2014.

Dray, Stephen. "Women in Church History: An Examination of Pre-Reformation Convictions and Practice." *Evangel* 21:1 (2003) 22–25.

Julian of Norwich. *Revelations of Divine Love.* Edited by Halcyon Backhouse et al. London: Hodder & Stoughton, 1987.

Labberton, Mark, ed. *Still Evangelical?: Insiders Reconsider Political, Social, and Theological Meaning.* Downers Grove: InterVarsity, 2018.

MacHaffie, Barbara J. *Her Story: Women in Christian Tradition.* Minneapolis: Fortress, 2006.

Morgan, Robert J. *Then Sings My Soul: 150 of the World's Greatest Hymn Stories.* Nashville: Thomas Nelson, 2003.

Okholm, Dennis L. *Learning Theology Through the Church's Worship: An Introduction to Christian Belief.* Grand Rapids: Baker Academic, 2018.

Phillips, Timothy R., and Dennis L. Okholm. *A Family of Faith: An Introduction to Evangelical Christianity.* Grand Rapids: Baker Academic, 2001.

———, eds. *The Nature of Confession: Evangelicals and Postliberals in Conversation.* Downers Grove: InterVarsity, 1996.

ten Boom, Corrie. *The Hiding Place.* Uhrichsville: Barbour, 1971.

Trueblood, D. Elton. *The People Called Quakers.* Richmond: Friends United, 1967.

Webber, Robert E. *The Younger Evangelicals: Facing the Challenges of the New World.* Grand Rapids: Baker, 2002.

Whittemore, Emma M. *Mother Whittemore's Records of Modern Miracles.* Toronto: Missions of Biblical Education, 1931.

6

Thinking Theologically about
Interfaith Dialogue

RICHARD J. MOUW

IN 1983 LEONARD SWIDLER published "The Dialogue Decalogue," a set of guiding principles for effective interfaith engagement.[1] Swidler's Decalogue has become a classic text for people engaged in interfaith dialogue, as it sets forth the basic qualities for facilitating interfaith understanding. Swidler's document focuses on the importance of approaching other perspectives with a genuine desire to learn, as well as on the need to cultivate the humility that allows one to engage in self-critique.

It would be hard to fault Swidler's principles as providing an account of what goes into effective dialogue. Indeed, his efforts can be seen as providing a kind of phenomenology of actual dialogues that have gone well. Swidler stresses, for example, the need for each group to define their own perspective. In order for a dialogue partner to grasp properly the other person's belief it is necessary to formulate that belief in a way that the person himself/herself would endorse. Swidler rightly insists that people enter dialogues with a willingness to set aside preconceived notions about what the other party believes.

All of that seems right and helpful. Swidler's guidelines have shaped my own efforts in interfaith engagement. In the evangelical world, however, dialogic efforts have not been without opposition. Why would

1. Swidler, "The Dialogue Decalogue," 1–4.

Christians be opposed to sincere efforts to engage in dialogue with persons of other faith communities? Is there some part of, say, Swidler's characterization of the necessary ingredients for dialogue that they reject? Not likely. There might be a quibble over this or that principle, but the opposition is not focused primarily on the elements of effective interfaith engagement. The real objection has to do with the *very project* of engaging in sincere dialogue with those with whom we nurture serious disagreements.

Nor is it difficult to see what direction the objection might take. Suppose, for example, that someone were to set out a list of "ten commandments for a successful bank robbery." I might agree that if one is going to rob a bank these are exactly the guidelines one should follow if one wants to pull off a successful heist. But I could also make it clear that I firmly believe that one should not rob banks. Similarly, a Christian could see Swidler's principles as a good account of what interfaith dialogue should look like, while still insisting that such engagements are wrongheaded.

Evangelicals who oppose interfaith dialogues often deny the possibility of the factor that is basic to the whole scheme Swidler sets forth: the element of trust. To enter into dialogue with persons representing another religious perspective requires that the parties trust each other to a significant degree. We have to assume that each party is sincere in an expressed desire to learn from the other, and that they are honestly setting forth their own convictions.

Distrust of Mormons, for example, has been a dominant theme in "counter-cult" depictions of Mormon life and thought. This has been obvious in the criticisms of the Mormon-Evangelical dialogue which I have co-moderated with my good friend Robert Millet, and in which Dennis Okholm—whom we honor in these pages—has also been an active participant. And a similar pattern of distrust characterizes opposition to dialogue with Muslims. In each case, the basic objection takes the form of: "You can't trust what they say." Mormonism and Islam are deceptive religions, it is thought, and their representatives deliberately mislead in order to disguise their true convictions and designs.

Christians who take this kind of stance can point to biblical mandates that they see as supporting their posture of distrust. We must be on guard against the machinations of those who would "deceive the very elect" (Matt 24:24 KJV). And we are urged to "test the spirits" (1 John 4:1). Fair enough—but the emphasis on "testing" must also be taken seriously.

The prophet not only proclaims God's judgment on "those who call evil good" but also those who label that which is good as evil (Isa 5:29).

Bearing false witness against our neighbors—and this includes our Mormon and Muslim neighbors—is a serious violation of God's will for human beings. Testing the spirits is an exercise in discernment, which in turn requires asking questions—and with a desire to engage in the kind of spirit of mutual learning that Swidler insists is essential for engaging in genuine dialogue.

The Theological Dimension

The Swidler approach to interfaith dialogue rightly emphasizes the importance of what we might think of as a spirituality of interfaith engagement. Genuine dialogue with folks whose fundamental beliefs are very different from our own requires such things as humility, self-awareness, a learning posture, and trust. In my own dialogue engagements, I have regularly been aware of the need for cultivating these spiritual dispositions.

For Christians, however, there also needs to be *theological* preparation for dialogue. And this is particularly true for evangelicals. Even if we make considerable progress on the spiritual level, we still face important theological questions about interfaith dialogue.

One major concern in this area for evangelicals stems from our strong commitment to evangelism. This has meant that our theological thinking about interfaith matters has been dominated by soteriological and apologetic concerns. We have wanted to convince people of other faiths that their religious beliefs and practices cannot deliver on what they are designed to deliver, and that the abundant life can only be found by putting their trust in Christ as Savior and Lord.

Evangelicals have often been nervous, therefore, about any focus on other religions that wanders too far from an intentional focus on the evangelistic mandate. To study other religions simply out of intellectual curiosity, then, has been seen as a dangerous business. It can lead us into versions of universalism and relativism. Or we can be lured into accepting religious counterfeits. We need to keep our spiritual guard up, then, by constantly reminding ourselves of the evangelistic mandate.

I sense the power of those concerns. I share the evangelical conviction that a commitment to evangelism is non-negotiable for the Christian community. Certainly one criterion, then, for the adequacy of an evangelical theology of interfaith engagement is whether our formulations comport well with our attempts to bring the Gospel to those who have not yet accepted Christ.

However, while evangelism is one important task for the Christian community, it is not the only task. Promoting good scholarship, engaging in works of justice, promoting peace-making, doing our daily work in a way that brings glory to God—all of this has value for the Christian life, even when such things are not directly connected to evangelistic goals.

I think interfaith dialogue has this kind of value. It is doing a good thing, even if it does not directly aim at bringing about conversions. Discussing important topics with persons of other faith communities is a way of getting clearer about God's creation. It gives us insights into the human condition, informing us of the diverse ways in which people wrestle with the deep issues of life.

What I have just said about learning from other religions seems obvious to me. But even when I make those points to many evangelicals they seem to be nervous about the case I am making. Directly engaging in friendly dialogue with persons of other faiths seems to be different from other modes of learning about the views of other faiths.

Suppose, for example, I were to tell my evangelical friends that I was embarking on a serious study of Freudian psychology, and that in addition to reading the works of Sigmund Freud and his disciples, I was going to engage in extensive conversations with actual Freudians, posing questions about their views concerning the human condition—all of this simply to understand Freudianism better, given its impact on the world of psychotherapy. I think that many evangelicals would see this as a legitimate project—nor would they be disturbed if I made it clear that I was not engaging in my conversations with Freudians with any intention of trying to convert them to Christianity.

I don't see any real difference between this project and a serious attempt to understand, say, Mormonism or Islam. But many evangelicals would treat the interfaith version differently. They would wonder—and some would even express their misgivings with passion—how I could go about such a project without at least having an evangelistic motive, even if I did not make that motive explicit with the Mormons or Muslims with whom I would be engaging.

Here is how I want to reply to such an insistence: Interfaith dialogue is not evangelism. We should not see the point of such engagements as a subtle evangelistic strategy. It has its own value. It is one of the things that the Christian community should see as valuable in its own right.

Of course, we are talking about *dialogue* here. And that means not only our learning from others but also hoping that others will learn from us. In explaining our own convictions to persons of other faiths, then, we will naturally want to give expression to our convictions so as to put them in the best possible light. As my Mormon dialogue partner Robert Millet has often observed, while those of us who are convinced about what we believe will not be disappointed if someone with whom we are engaging in dialogue actually comes to accept our viewpoint, that is not the point of the dialogue. We have not failed in our dialogic efforts when that does not happen.

Openness to Truths

The example that I cited about studying Freudianism has to do in large part with satisfying scholarly interests. It is important for Christian scholars to understand schools of thought that have had a profound influence on contemporary cultural life, and Freud's thought certainly is one of those influences. But there are also broader intellectual modes of curiosity. For example, I will never write a scholarly study of—or even give a class lecture about—folks in our present-day culture who believe in "a flat earth." I am curious about their views, however. How can people who have been raised with photos of the earth taken from the moon still believe that the earth is shaped like a flat saucer? And since many of them deny that those photos are authentic—the moon landings were faked, they say—how can they seriously sustain that elaborate set of convictions? I am intrigued by the attraction for many people of what I consider to be outlandish conspiracy theories. Attempts to understand those patterns of thought do reveal, I am convinced, something about the complexities of the human condition.

My intellectual curiosity about flat earth beliefs is driven mainly by an interest in understanding better why people believe things that I take to be patently false. In listening carefully to the explanations of flat earth advocates I do not expect to gain any insights from them about the laws of geophysics or astronomy. For some Christians, this might also serve as a compelling rationale for engaging in dialogue with, say, Buddhists or

Hindus. We engage in conversations with them so we may better understand religious error.

However, the understanding-error motive for dialogue is not adequate in the case of interfaith dialogue. It might be the right motive in some cases, of course—I have a difficult time imagining another reason to have conversations with "Church of Satan" types. But there is much to be gained by approaching interfaith dialogue more generally with a genuine desire to learn from others. And this is what should move us beyond thinking about interfaith dialogue in exclusively soteriological-apologetic terms. It is one thing to ask, for example, whether a person can attain eternal salvation by relying solely on Buddhist beliefs and practices. My firm answer to this question is: No. It is another thing to ask, however, whether we can learn true things from Buddhists about spiritual-philosophical matters. Here I want to answer firmly in the positive.

There is much room, of course, for considering diverse theological grounds for explaining how and why we can rightly expect to gain positive insights from other religions. In my own case I can draw directly upon Reformed sources. Indeed, I do not have to look any further than John Calvin himself. Before his evangelical conversion, the Reformer had studied law, and he had been particularly fond of the writings of ancient Roman jurists and rhetoricians—Seneca in particular. When he began writing about theological matters, Calvin remained indebted to those writers. He testified that he found in them "admirable light of truth shining." This is the case, he argues, because "the mind of man, though fallen and perverted from its wholeness," can still be "clothed and ornamented with God's excellent gifts." To refuse to accept, then, the truth produced by such minds is "to dishonor the Spirit of God."[2] Herman Bavinck, following Calvin, applies this directly to views found in other religions: in Muhammad and others, he writes, "there is a revelation of God, an illumination by the Logos, a working of God's Spirit."[3]

Bavinck's pneumatological reference in this observation points to the importance of taking with utmost seriousness the uniqueness of each religious perspective. A dialogue is a conversation between actual people representing their own unique convictions and perspectives. Stephen Neill makes this point nicely, based on his longtime engagement with diverse religious groups in India. He notes that the "comparative

2. Calvin, *Institutes*, 2.3.
3. Bavinck, *Reformed Dogmatics*, 318.

method" approach to the study of religions often treats "all religions as commensurables."[4] Thus, scholars will lay various conceptions of the divine alongside each other and discuss the similarities and differences among them, thereby ignoring the ways that they are abstracting those ideas from other ideas with which they are interconnected. In doing this, Neill says they detach the ideas in question "from the living experiences which has given rise to them. In so doing we rob them of their life," thus ignoring "the living fabric of the religion from which the idea has been somewhat violently dissevered."[5]

The "Abrahamic" Issue

We do well to heed Neill's warning against the presumption of commensurability among faith traditions. There are some legitimate questions regarding commonness, however, with regard to the so-called "Abrahamic" faiths: Judaism, Islam, and Christianity. The Vatican II document *Lumen Gentium* takes an expansive position on the salvation of persons in non-Christian religions "who, through no fault of their own, do not know the Gospel of Christ or his Church, but who nevertheless seek God with a sincere heart, and, moved by grace, try in their actions to do his will as they know it through the dictates of their conscience." But the bishops grant a special status to Islam: "[T]he plan of salvation," they declare, "also includes those who acknowledge the Creator, in the first place amongst whom are the Moslems: these profess to hold the faith of Abraham, and together with us they adore the one, merciful God, mankind's judge on the last day."[6]

The French historian Alain Besancon, himself a Catholic, takes a less charitable view. "The Abraham of Genesis," he writes, simply "is not the Ibrahim of the Qur'an." Furthermore, he argues, Islam's Moussa does not function in the same way as Israel's Moses. Nor does the Qur'an's Issa have anything in common with the Jesus whom Christians worship. What all of this means, for Besancon, is that Islam must be relegated, from the point of view of Jews and Christians, to the status of a "natural theology."[7] And in offering this assessment it is clear that Besancon

---

4. Neill, *Christian Faith and Other Faiths*, 3.

5. Neill, *Christian Faith and Other Faiths*, 3.

6. Second Vatican Council, "Dogmatic Constitution on the Church," sec 16.

7. Besancon, "What Kind of Religion is Islam?"

means to minimizing any impression of commonality that Islam has with either Christian or Jewish thought.

Obviously it would be difficult to make the same case regarding Judaism, where there is clearly a direct "Abrahamic" historical link between the religion of ancient Israel and present-day Christianity. What *is* debated by Christians regarding Judaism, however, is the theological significance of that historical link for contemporary Jewish-Christian relations. A straightforward supersessionism would take the view that because Judaism does not acknowledge Jesus as the promised Messiah, it has forfeited its "chosen people" status, replaced now by the church established in the New Testament and presently has the status of a "false religion." This is a view that has some currency in my own Reformed community, and I will soon say something about my own journey in wrestling with this issue.

In the broader evangelical community, a theological understanding of the present status of Jewish beliefs and practices has been strongly influenced by dispensational thought—a theological perspective that continues to shape much of evangelicalism's support of the modern nation-state of Israel.

The dispensationalist view holds that God's relationship to Abraham and his physical descendants is very different from the divine plan for the New Testament church. God's promises to Israel—as both an ancient and a contemporary people—are linked to a divine calling that has an "earthly" character, as spelled out in various political and economic blessings promised by God to Israel in ancient times. The Christian church, on the other hand, has been given a very different divine assignment, linked to a "heavenly" destiny which is to be pursued in the context of a purely "spiritual" mission. To confuse or mix these two very different assignments can only lead to a violation of God's intentions in calling these two distinct communal entities into existence.[8]

While dispensationalism insists on this divinely ordained distinction between Judaism and Christianity, it is certainly not of a "separate but equal" sort of relationship. Judaism as it presently exists is, for dispensationalism, a defective religious perspective. Jewish people will only come to see things correctly when in the end-time they accept Jesus as their Messiah. And in the meantime, dispensationalists advocate programs of "Jewish evangelism." While in the broader Christian community there is

8. Chafer, *Dispensationalism*, 41.

considerable opposition to efforts to convert Jews to Christianity, these perspectives seldom simply treat Christianity and Judaism as equally valid modes of redemption.

A 2015 document issued by the Vatican's Commission for Religious Relations with the Jews, commemorating the fiftieth anniversary of the Vatican II encyclical *Nostra Aetate*, is instructive in this regard. "From the Christian confession," it states, "there can be only one path to salvation." But that does not mean, it quickly adds, "that the Jews are excluded from God's salvation because they do not believe in Jesus Christ as the Messiah of Israel and the Son of God."[9] Recognizing that it has not exactly clarified things in what it has just set forth, the document goes on to admit that it has not answered adequately "the highly complex theological question of how Christian belief in the universal salvific significance of Jesus Christ can be combined in a coherent way with the equally clear statement of faith in the never-revoked covenant of God with Israel." But the Church cannot deny "that Christ is the Saviour for all. There cannot be two ways of salvation." All we can do, then, is "confront the mystery of God's work, which is not a matter of missionary efforts to convert Jews, but rather the expectation that the Lord will bring about the hour"—and here the document quotes *Nostra Aetate*—when all peoples will call on God with one voice and "serve him shoulder to shoulder."[10]

Before describing my own struggles with this set of issues, I need to point out that even if we do insist upon some version of "Abrahamic" commonalities—which I am inclined to—we still need to pay close attention to the "living fabric" realities of these distinct religious communities. Cornelis van der Kooi, who has been actively engaged in Christian encounters with Jews and Muslims, rightly reminds us that there are still some deep differences that can easily be hidden when we treat Christianity, Judaism, and Islam as sharing a common Abrahamic pattern of belief. The "Abrahamic religions" rubric can then function as "a systematic theological proposal which . . . does not do justice to the various traditions in their self-understandings." Is it really plausible to think, van der Kooi asks, that "our basic [Christian] ideas of incarnation, kenosis and substitution still receive the key position if we theologically return

---

9. Commission for Religious Relations with the Jews, "The Gifts and the Calling of God," sec 36.

10. Commission for Religious Relations with the Jews, "The Gifts and the Calling of God," sec 37.

to Abraham?" Christians have to be focused instead, he insists, on "going forward to Jesus Christ and to thinking and living out of Him."[11]

Nothing in van der Kooi's insightful warning rules out using our common professions, with Jews and Muslims, regarding the worship of the God of Abraham. Finding some common reference points for our dialogues can be a helpful way of entering into respectful conversations with each other about what it means for us today to continue the journey that Abraham began when, as the writer to the Hebrews tells us, he set out with a strong faith in the divine promise that he was heading to "the city that has foundations, whose architect and builder is God" (Heb 11:10 NRSV).

Wrestling with "Replacement" Theology

Here I will inject some comments about my own personal theological journey in attempting to get clear theologically about the present status of the Jewish people.[12] I was raised in a dispensationalist environment, where the notes appended to the biblical text in the Scofield Bible were treated as having their own canonical status. In my undergraduate college days, however, I rejected that perspective and embraced Reformed theology. For me, this meant giving up on the idea of two distinct salvific economies, one for the Jews and another for Gentile Christians. Instead, I came to accept the notion that the promises made by God to ancient Israel have now been transferred to the Christian community.

In adopting this replacement notion, I was especially impressed by the imagery set forth in Peter's First Epistle. There the apostle, in addressing a group of Christians that obviously included Gentiles, begins by greeting them as "the exiles of the Dispersion" (1 Pet 1:1). He then continues to allude to ancient Israel in his second chapter, where he addresses the Christian community as "a chosen race, a royal priesthood, a holy nation, God's own people," adding a quotation from one of the prophets: "Once you were not a people, but now you are God's people" (2:9-10). The implication of this seemed clear to me: the New Testament church has exclusively taken on the identity of "Israel" in God's eyes.

11. Van der Kooi, "Towards an Abrahamic Ecumenism?", 7.

12. I offer an expanded version of these autobiographical reflections in my book, *The Smell of Sawdust*, 77-93.

I no longer take this passage to be grounds for a simple replacement view. I do not believe that the status and calling of being "a chosen race, a royal priesthood, a holy nation, God's own people" have now been straightforwardly and exclusively transferred to the church. Instead, I see the church as now being incorporated—grafted onto, to use Paul's image in Romans 11—an *expanded* version of the Israel that was called into being when God announced the covenant with Abraham.

I say all of this, not only as a Calvinist, but as a Calvinist evangelical. It will always be awkward for people of my theological bent to talk with Jewish friends about our basic disagreements without getting into extremely sensitive issues. We cannot in good conscience avoid those issues. But I have come to sense an obligation to place those convictions in a larger context that is characterized by two themes that I constantly stress with my evangelical compatriots. One theme is the importance of allowing room for considerable messiness in one's theology, especially on the relationship between ancient Israel and the church. The other theme is the need for forming personal friendships with our Jewish dialogue partners.

Theological Messiness

I was first forced to address the issue of messiness on the relationship between ancient Israel and the church because of a serious academic struggle. The only failing grade I ever received for a course during my years of formal academic study was while I was a seminary student. The course was on the Epistle to the Romans, and much of the grade depended on the writing of a ten-page exegetical paper. I chose to write on Romans 11, where Paul discusses the theological status of the Jews since the coming of Christ. I eagerly set about to complete the assignment, reading commentators who set forth a variety of interpretations. I also worked through the chapter in the Greek, reading it over many times.

I never wrote the paper, and my "Incomplete" became an "F" on my record. It is one of the few times in my life when I simply could not put my thoughts on paper. The more I read the Apostle Paul on the subject, the more I was convinced that he was not setting forth a clear step-by-step case for a coherent perspective on the subject. This awareness was deeply distressing for me. I *wanted* him to be absolutely clear about the status of the Jews. I was committed to being orthodox in my theology, and I had no room for messiness in what I saw as the Bible's teaching on an important topic. Furthermore, I was studying in a Reformed seminary, and I was eager to demonstrate that the promises associated with God's Old Covenant with ethnic Israel have now been transferred to the church of Jesus Christ, the people of the New Covenant. But I did not know how to make the case confidently, so I never wrote the paper.

In subsequent years I developed my views about the church as the new Israel as a basis for Christian social ethics. In doing so, as I have already reported, I made much use of Peter's First Epistle, and other passages that gave support to such a view. But I always had a nagging sense that I was cheating a bit—that I had no right to state my case so boldly unless I could make my peace with Romans 11.

I have now made my peace with the messiness—after a fashion, at least. I can now read Romans 11 with an easy conscience, because I have come to see the Apostle Paul himself as incapable of making a perfectly coherent case on the subject of the Jews who did not believe that Jesus was the promised Messiah. He goes back and forth: their rejection of Jesus as the heaven-sent Messiah is seriously displeasing to God; they are branches that have been broken off and a wild shoot has been grafted in their place (v. 17); but Gentiles should not take this as cause for pride, since the Jews are still the "natural branches" who will eventually be grafted back onto the tree (v. 25). Does this mean, then, that Israel as a people will be saved? Well, "God has imprisoned them all in disobedience so that he may be merciful to all" (v. 32). Having read Paul thus far on the subject, I want desperately to have him answer a few more important questions for clarification, since I cannot put all of this together into a coherent package. But instead he starts singing a hymn about the mystery of God's ways. And I have learned at this stage of my theological journey to set my questions aside and simply sing along with him:

> O the depth of the riches and wisdom and knowledge of God!
> How unsearchable are his judgments and how inscrutable his
> ways!
>   "For who has known the mind of the Lord?
>   Or who has been his counselor?"
>   "Or who has given a gift to him,
>   to receive a gift in return?"
> For from him and through him and to him are all things. To him
> be the glory forever. Amen. (Rom 11:33–36)

The Dynamic Dimension

My second theme is the importance of finding common ground and building trust as an important preparation for taking on the important differences between us. In a 1987 volume of essays devoted to evangelical-Jewish dialogue, both Jewish and evangelical writers regularly called for the forming of friendships between persons in their two communities, in order that conversations about significant differences can take place in an atmosphere of trust. Here, for example, is a plea from an evangelical historian, David A. Rausch:

> I strongly recommend that dialogue be maintained and that evangelicals and Jews continue to get to know one another personally. This should occur not only at the leadership level but also on the grass roots level (and it is occurring!). Friendship does dispel caricature, stereotype, and distorted views. Such interaction should be nurtured and misperceptions as to its efficacy should be laid to rest by a more knowledgeable evangelical leadership.[13]

This emphasis on the importance of friendship in interfaith engagements may come across simply as a commendable reminder that difficult theological discussions often go better when people treat each other amicably. I want to argue, though, that the friendship dimension is not just an "affective" supplement to theological dialogue—it is itself integral to the theological task that we pursue in interfaith engagement.

What the friendship element points us to is the fact that in the very entering into an interfaith conversation we are already influenced by theological factors. John Calvin gets at this point in his observation about the obligation to love our neighbors:

> It is the common habit of mankind that the more closely men are bound together by the ties of kinship, of acquaintanceship, or of neighborhood, the more responsibilities for one another they share. This does not offend God; for his providence, as it were, leads us to it. But I say: we ought to embrace the whole human race without exception in a single feeling of love; here there is no distinction between barbarian and Greek, worthy and unworthy, friend and enemy, since all should be contemplated in God, not in themselves.[14]

13. Rausch, "What and How Evangelicals Teach about Judaism," 89.

14. Calvin, *Institutes*, 2.8.

Calvin is insisting here that our engagements with neighbors must be shaped at the outset by a theological contemplation. In our interfaith encounters, for example, it isn't that we try to start off with a friendly disposition and then hope that some good theological insights emerge someplace along the way. We bring theological insights *to* the encounter. At the very outset of our encounters with non-Christian dialogue partners we must see them "in God, not in themselves."

There are some obvious aspects of seeing people "in God" that influence us in our encounters—not the least being that each person whom we meet is created in the image of the God of the Scriptures. But I have come to see the "in God" factor as highlighting the presence of the dynamic character of each interfaith encounter. Calvin himself did not, of course, engage in—or discuss theologically—interfaith dialogue as we know that kind of encounter today. The closest he came is the kind of thing I referred to earlier, when he observed that if we refuse to accept truths from ancient Greco-Roman writers we "dishonor the Spirit of God."[15] The fact that Calvin does refer to the Holy Spirit in this context, however, is at least a hint that the Reformer might have been getting at the kind of emphasis that is being explored actively these days by advocates of what Amos Yong has labeled "a pneumatological theology of religion."[16]

Several Reformed theologians have been exploring the relation of the work of the Holy Spirit in other religions, and I see this as an important advance. Benno van den Toren has pointed out, for example, that in approaching interfaith encounters it is not enough "simply [to] look for a more or less distorted recognition of God's general revelation in his creation" along with a "universal presence of the Logos through which God created the universe." Those two emphases, long associated with the first two Persons of the Trinity, while theologically appropriate, need to be supplemented by the important conviction that "the Spirit has been present" in the lives of the persons whom we are encountering.[17] Herman Bavinck had made a similar point in his *Reformed Dogmatics*. In Islam and other faith communities, Bavinck observed, "there is a revelation of God, an illumination by the Logos, a working of God's Spirit."[18]

---

15. Calvin, *Institutes*, 2.3.

16. Yong, *Beyond the Impasse*, 20.

17. Van den Toren, "The Relationship between Christ and the Spirit," 268–69.

18. Bavinck, *Reformed Dogmatics*, 318.

It is the sense of the active presence of the Holy Spirit in the lives of persons of other faiths that introduces a key dynamic element in our engagements with them. We can ask how the Spirit is at work in the religious community we are engaging. But even more concretely, we can ask the question: How is the Holy Spirit at work in the life of *this* Muslim, *this* Buddhist? Asking the questions in this way adds the dynamic dimension to our interfaith encounters. Gijsbert van den Brink and Cornelis van der Kooi spell out the implications of this pneumatological dimension nicely. In all of our interfaith encounters, they say, we can proceed with the conviction that "God may present himself in his freedom and love through the open relationships that followers of Christ enter into with those who believe differently," and in the awareness of "the hidden but never-ceasing work of the Spirit of God, who does not leave people alone and who can also reach people who are closed."[19]

As Amos Yong puts it, a pneumatological approach to interfaith engagement requires a commitment to "discerning the religions," which means that it is necessary "to proceed empirically" in our relationships with persons of other faiths.[20] Earlier I mentioned Stephen Neill's insistence that we take seriously the "living fabric" of another religion. Here we can take this a step further and insist that we take seriously the "living fabric" of another religious perspective as it is uniquely embodied in the life of this *individual*—this very real human being—with whom I am engaging at this stage of each of our journeys. What can I discern about how the Holy Spirit is at work in *this* conversation?

Complex Discernings

Since we are honoring Dennis Okholm's leadership in these essays, it is appropriate to illustrate some of the themes I have been discussing with specific reference to the Mormon-evangelical dialogue in which he and I have been actively involved. In the following chapter, Robert Millet provides an extensive account of this dialogue. Here I will only briefly add some evangelical perspectives as they bear on the themes I have been discussing in this essay.

In my own dialogic efforts I have concentrated exclusively on faith communities with close historical ties with my own brand of

19. Van der Kooi and van den Brink, *Christian Dogmatics*, 197.

20. Yong, *Beyond the Impasse*, 185.

Protestantism—the folks whom we have left and those who have left us: Judaism, Islam, Catholicism, and Mormonism.

I could have included others in this broad category. In the past three years I have been contacted separately by representatives of both the Christian Science church and the Jehovah's Witnesses, inquiring whether I was willing to help organize a dialogue between evangelicals and leaders of their movements. In each case the representative referred to the Mormon dialogue. Since I have been willing to foster friendly discussions between evangelicals and Mormons, would I also do the same with their groups?

I respectfully declined these invitations, not because I think those dialogues ought not to occur, but because any given dialogue requires sustained focus—focus that I am not able to provide at this point in my life. My own dialogue efforts have concentrated primarily on Judaism and Mormonism, and the latter has been my most sustained project.

The reasons why Mormon-evangelical dialogue has been able to bear fruit has been the willingness of the participants to take our assignments with intense seriousness. Millet, for example, has certainly read more books on evangelical life and thought than many scholars in the evangelical community. In my own case, even though I am not a historian of American religion by training, I have developed over the past two decades a good working knowledge of nineteenth-century Mormonism.

To say that interfaith dialogue requires working at friendships, trust, intellectual curiosity, and humility is not to utter truisms. My own experience of almost two decades of participation in this specific dialogue makes me suspicious of folks who claim to specialize in "interfaith dialogue" as such. For some of us, at least, we need to attend to the challenges posed by particularities of a specific interfaith engagement. Each dialogue relationship requires its own unique kind of hard work.

Forming trusting friendships in our Mormon-evangelical group has required significant investments of time and the nurturing of relationships. Those of us on both "sides" of the dialogue have had to endure attacks by persons in our own communities who have been convinced that the dialogue as such constituted a betrayal of our distinctive convictions. For the evangelicals in the dialogue, we have even had to face serious differences among ourselves about the aims and purposes of our engagement with Mormons and Mormonism.

Most importantly—given the overall theme of my comments here— we have learned that serious dialogue requires hard theological work.

We decided early on that we would avoid the topics associated with past evangelical-Mormon polemics, particularly questions about the origins of the Book of Mormon and the motives of Joseph Smith. Instead, we would concentrate specifically on questions related to what constitutes a proper relationship with the divine. What does it mean to "get right with God"? What are we "saved" *from*? What are we "saved" *for*? What would have to happen on God's part in order for the likes of us to be restored to what we were created to be and do? And where do we find authoritative guidance on such matters?

In discussing those important questions together we evangelicals and Mormons have discovered that we actually agree on some key topics where we thought we had serious disagreements. On other matters, we came to see that we continue to have profound theological disagreements. In all of that, however, we found it increasingly natural to pray, and to sing "How Great Thou Art," together. That, in spite of serious theological differences. And that reality too has taught us some important theological lessons!

Bibliography

Bavinck, Herman. *Reformed Dogmatics, Vol. One: Prologomena.* Translated by John Vriend. Grand Rapids: Baker Academic, 2003.

Besancon, Alain. "What Kind of Religion is Islam?" *Commentary.* May, 2004. https://www.commentarymagazine.com/articles/what-kind-of-religion-is-islam/.

Calvin, John. *Institutes of the Christian Religion.* The Library of Christian Classics 20. Translated by Ford Lewis Battles. Philadelphia: Westminster, 1960.

Chafer, Lewis Sperry. *Dispensationalism.* Dallas: Dallas Seminary Press, 1936.

Commission for Religious Relations with the Jews. "'The Gifts and the Calling of God are Irrevocable' (Rom 11:29): A Reflection on Theological Questions Pertaining to Catholic-Jewish Relations on the Occasion of the 50th Anniversary of 'Nostra Aetate' (No. 4)." Vatican. December 10, 2015. http://www.vatican.va/roman_curia/pontifical_councils/chrstuni/relations-jews-docs/rc_pc_chrstuni_doc_20151210_ebraismo-nostra-aetate_en.html.

Mouw, Richard J. *The Smell of Sawdust: What Evangelicals Can Learn from Their Fundamentalist Heritage.* Grand Rapids: Zondervan, 2000.

Neill, Stephen. *Christian Faith and Other Faiths: The Christian Dialogue with Other Religions.* New York: Oxford University Press, 1961.

Rausch, David A. "What and How Evangelicals Teach about Judaism." In *A Time to Speak: The Evangelical Jewish Encounter,* edited by A. James Rudin et al. Grand Rapids: Eerdmans, 1987.

Second Vatican Council. "Dogmatic Constitution on the Church: Vatican II, *Lumen Gentium,* 21 November, 1964." In *Vatican Council II: The Conciliar and Post*

Conciliar Documents, edited by Austin Flannery, 350–426. New Revised ed. Grand Rapids: Eerdmans, 1992.

Swidler, Leonard. "The Dialogue Decalogue: Ground Rules for Interreligious Dialogue." *Journal of Ecumenical Studies* 20.1 (1983) 1–4.

van den Toren, Benno. "The Relationship between Christ and the Spirit in a Christian Theology of Religions." *Missiology: An International Review* 40.3 (2012) 263–80.

van der Kooi, Cornelis. "Towards an Abrahamic Ecumenism? The Search for the Universality of the Divine Mystery." *Acta Theologica* 32 (2012) 240–53.

van der Kooi, Cornelis, and Gijsbert van den Brink. *Christian Dogmatics: An Introduction.* Translated by Reinder Bruinsma et al. Grand Rapids: Eerdmans, 2017.

Yong, Amos. *Beyond the Impasse: Toward a Pneumatological Theoloy of Religion.* Eugene: Wipf and Stock, 2014.

7

Talking with Evangelicals

The Latter-day Saint-Evangelical Dialogue in Retrospect

ROBERT L. MILLET

IN 1998 I RECEIVED in the mail a "call for papers" for the Wheaton Theology Conference. The conference was to focus on the life and work of C. S. Lewis, since that year was a centennial celebration of Lewis's birth (1898). I was shocked. I assumed that there had to be a major mistake that the call for papers was sent to me, a Professor and Dean of Religious Education at Brigham Young University (BYU). To be completely honest, Evangelicals and Latter-day Saints had not exactly been on the best of terms since Joseph Smith walked out of a grove of trees in 1820. The fact is, however, that C. S. Lewis was then and is now amazingly popular among Latter-day Saints and has been so for at least fifty years. I had been a fan for at least forty of those years and even now try to read *Mere Christianity*, *The Problem of Pain*, and at least one other Lewis volume during the year (either *Miracles*, *The Weight of Glory*, or *A Grief Observed*).

I sent in a proposal and, even more startling, my proposal—"The Theology of C. S. Lewis: A Latter-day Saint Perspective"—was accepted. A colleague and I travelled out to the conference several months later and enjoyed ourselves immensely. We were treated warmly and enjoyed stimulating conversations with a number of the Wheaton faculty, including Christopher Mitchell, curator of the Wade Center, that contained a large collection of Lewis's papers and memorabilia. Students and others asked excellent questions following my presentation and couldn't have been more respectful. My colleague and I were so impressed with the entire experience that on returning to Utah we began plans for a similar conference at BYU, which we held in early December of 1998. The two keynote speakers were Chris Mitchell and Elder Neal A. Maxwell, one of the senior Latter-day Saint leaders, who was a huge fan of Lewis.

The organizers of the Wheaton conference were Professors Tim Phillips and Dennis Okholm. My faculty associate and I became well acquainted with Okholm during our time at Wheaton, and he has over the years become an admired, valued, and treasured friend. Okholm has been a crucial and contributing member of the Latter-day Saint-Evangelical dialogue since the early 2000s. I am honored and pleased to be invited to participate in this well-deserved festschrift.

The Beginnings

Let me share a bit about my own religious background. I was born and raised in Baton Rouge, Louisiana, and so most of my friends were Roman Catholic or Southern Baptist. Although I was brought up in The Church of Jesus Christ of Latter-day Saints, I didn't know many members of my church beyond those in our little congregation. There was a season of a few years when my family was not active participants in the Church, and I can remember very well during that time attending a Vacation Bible School one summer when we lived in Nashville, Tennessee. As I grew up, I discovered that quite a few of my cousins were Baptists and one set of relatives was Pentecostal. And so a life embedded in religious diversity is one I have known over the years. I have felt something deep down for persons of other faiths for a long time. Further, I know what it's like to be a part of a religious minority, and so I tend to be a bit more sensitive to those outside my own faith who live in Utah, where my wife and I have resided since 1983.

The year I started the sixth grade, our family moved to a small town in southern Louisiana, a tiny Cajun community made up almost exclusively of Roman Catholics. On the first day of class, my teacher, Mrs. Templet, asked the question: "Is there anyone here who is not Catholic? If so, I need to know." My heart raced, and my blood pressure rose. I looked about the class in a frightened and terribly shy way. I saw one boy across the room lift his hand slowly. "What are you?" Mrs. Templet asked. "I'm a Baptist," he responded, in a voice that was just above a whisper. I sat there, clearly realizing that there was not one human being in the room besides myself who knew anything at all about my religious persuasion, including the teacher. My temptation was to sit still and be quiet. In a twinge of conscience, however, I slowly lifted my hand into the air. "And you, what church do you attend?" the teacher asked sternly. My faith failed and my strength went down the drain as I replied timidly, "I'm a Baptist too." (I should add here that some of my beloved evangelical friends who have, over the years, heard me relate that story have commented: "Do you see, Bob? The Lord has had his hand on you for a long time!")

Not long after I was appointed Dean of Religious Education at BYU in January 1991, one of the senior leaders of our church said to me, "Bob, you need to find ways to reach out. You must begin to build bridges of friendship and understanding with persons of other faiths." He said a number of other things to me, but that particular charge weighed upon me for months. Some of my colleagues and I began a series of visits to other religious campuses—Notre Dame, Catholic University, Baylor, and Wheaton.

In April 1997 one of the members of our religion faculty invited Professor Bruce Demarest of Denver Seminary to visit Provo and speak to us. His topic was the man Melchizedek, an enigmatic Old Testament figure whose ministry is a matter of some interest to Latter-day Saints. Demarest had done his doctoral research on Melchizedek under the direction of the great F. F. Bruce. Besides our own faculty, two local ministers were in attendance, one of which was Pastor Gregory Johnson, who was then shepherding a small flock of Baptists in Huntsville, Utah, about two hours northeast of Provo. Greg introduced himself to me after the meeting and we made our way into my office. I should insert here that in the mid-80s I had discovered an evangelical radio station in Provo and found myself listening on my way to work in the mornings and then again in the late afternoon as I headed home. I became "acquainted" with John MacArthur, Charles Stanley, Ravi Zacharias, Chuck Swindoll, Tony Evans, James Dobson, David Jeremiah. I began reading their books, and eventually read works by John Stott, J. I. Packer, Philip Yancey, John Stackhouse, Randall Balmer, Mark Noll, George Marsden, and, of course, Billy Graham. During that time I also began a major reading program in Christian history and theology. I showed Greg the section of my library on evangelical writings and he was stunned.

Greg and I began to have lunch together about once each month to discuss our respective faiths and belief systems. We spoke of God,

Christ, Trinity/Godhead, salvation, agency and predestination, and other doctrinally stimulating topics. We compared and contrasted, we asked questions, and we answered them. I should add here that one major factor adding to the dynamic of our conversations was that Greg had been brought up in The Church of Jesus Christ of Latter-day Saints. He had, however, joined an evangelical church at the age of fourteen as a result of having a "born again" experience at a Bible camp. Importantly, our discussions were characterized by a mood of openness, candor, and a general lack of defensiveness. We knew what we believed, and we were committed to our own religious tradition. Neither was trying to convert the other; rather, we were making an effort to better understand one another. In a rather informal manner, Pastor Johnson and I sought to acquire the skills and art of what our friend Richard Mouw has called "convicted civility."[1]

Pastor Johnson likes to tell the story of his encounter with a BYU religion faculty member. This particular professor became quite intrigued with the relationship Greg and I had developed over a few years, and he invited Greg to lunch just off the BYU campus. They sat down, had a little spaghetti, and the professor said: "Tell me what's going on with you and Bob Millet." Greg shared a little bit more about our friendship and some of the interactions we were having. My faculty friend said, "Well, let me get to the point, Greg. I think you are aware that Robert Millet is the dean of our religion faculty." Greg said, "Of course." "Surely you don't think he's going to convert to the evangelical Christian way of life, do you?" he inquired. Greg said, "You know, to be honest with you, I'm pretty sure he doesn't plan to do that." The professor continued: "Well, I'm assuming that as an evangelical pastor you're not considering becoming Latter-day Saint." Greg replied, "No, I'm not." In a moment of frustration, the professor shook his head and blurted out, "Well what's the point?"

That comment characterizes the sentiments of many who suppose that there is no compelling reason to associate with a person of another faith unless conversion is the intention and the result. Greg and I have repeatedly explained that there is tremendous value in having serious interactions with persons who see and believe things differently than you do. Such engagements build friendships, broaden one's perspective, and inevitably allow a person to jettison misconceptions that he or she may have learned in the past. Being willing to reach out and understand

---

1. Mouw, *Uncommon Decency*, 13–14.

others is not easy, but it is immensely rewarding. It requires, first of all, an unquestioned allegiance and devotion to one's own faith tradition, and at the same time a mind and heart that are open to truth and light, a belief that the God and Father of us all is working in his mysterious ways through good people throughout the earth. It requires us to love people, even those who make it so difficult to love them (see John 13:34–35). In the words of John Stackhouse, "God cares about people more than he cares about 'truth' in the abstract. *Jesus didn't die on the cross to make a point. He died on the cross to save people whom he loves.* We, too, must represent our Lord with love to God and our neighbor always foremost in our concerns."[2]

Greg and I were invited on many occasions to meet with religious groups, describe the nature of our relationship, and model for those in attendance how we had over the years been able to discuss our doctrinal differences in an amicable, peaceful, and productive manner. These two-hour programs came to be known as "A Mormon and an Evangelical in Conversation," a presentation we were invited to make over sixty times throughout the United States, Canada, and Great Britain. Our venues were mostly universities (to students at their respective schools), Protestant chapels, Latter-day Saint meetinghouses, and convention halls.

Expanding the Discussion

As our friendship developed over time, Greg and I began to wonder if there might be some merit in enlarging our small interfaith circle. A formal gathering of scholars took place in the spring of 2000 at Brigham Young University in Provo, Utah. The Evangelical participants included Greg Johnson; Richard Mouw of Fuller Theological Seminary; Craig Blomberg of Denver Seminary; Craig Hazen of Biola University; David Neff of *Christianity Today*; and Carl Moser, who was at the time a doctoral student in Scotland. On the Latter-day Saint side, participants included myself, Stephen Robinson, Roger Keller, David Paulsen, Daniel Judd, and Andrew Skinner, all from BYU. Names and faces have changed somewhat, but the dialogue has continued since that first gathering. We met every six months at either Provo or Pasadena, California (the main campus of Fuller Seminary). Each of the participants came prepared

---

2. Stackhouse, *Humble Apologetics*, 142. Emphasis added.

(through prior readings of articles and books) to discuss a particular doctrinal subject.

In the early sessions, it was not uncommon to sense a bit of tension, a subtle uncertainty as to where this was going, a slight uneasiness among the participants. As the dialogue began to take shape, it was apparent that we were searching for an identity—was this to be a confrontation? An argument? A debate? Was it to produce a winner and a loser? Just how candid and earnest and forthright were we expected to be? Some of the Latter-day Saints wondered: Do the "other guys" see this encounter as a grand effort to set our denomination straight, to make it more traditionally Christian, more acceptable to skeptical onlookers? Some of the evangelicals wondered: Are those "other guys" for real? Is what they are saying an accurate expression of their church's teachings? Can a person be a genuine Christian and yet not be a part of the historic Christian Church? A question that continued to come up—an important one, in many ways—was: Just how much "incorrect theology" can the grace of God compensate for? Before too long, those kinds of issues became part of the dialogue itself, and in the process, much of the tension began to dissipate.

The meetings have been more than conversations. We have visited key historical sites, eaten and socialized, sang hymns and prayed, mourned together over the passing of members of our group, and shared ideas, books, and articles throughout the year. The initial feeling of formality has given way to a sweet informality, a brother-and-sisterhood, a kindness in disagreement, a respect for opposing views, and a feeling of responsibility toward those not of our faith—a responsibility to represent their doctrines and practices accurately to folks of our own faith. No one has compromised or diluted his or her own theological convictions, but everyone has sought to demonstrate the kind of civility that ought to characterize a mature exchange of ideas among a body of believers who have discarded defensiveness. There have been those times, as well, when many of us have felt what Krister Stendahl has described as "holy envy"—something stronger and more satisfying than tolerance, something definitely more heartwarming and even compelling than ideological indifference. No dialogue of this type is worth its salt unless the participants gradually begin to realize that there is much to be learned from others.

Topics of Discussion

The first dialogue, held at Brigham Young University in the spring of 2000 was, as suggested earlier, as much an effort to test the waters as to dialogue on a specific topic. But the group did agree to do some reading prior to the gathering. The evangelicals asked that we all read or re-read John Stott's classic work, *Basic Christianity* (1958) and some of my LDS colleagues recommended that we read a book I had written entitled *The Mormon Faith* (1998). We spent much of a day discussing *The Mormon Faith*, concluding that there were a number of theological topics deserving of extended conversation. When it came time to discuss *Basic Christianity*, however, we had a most unusual and unexpected experience. Richard Mouw asked, "Well, what concerns or questions do you have about this book?" There was a long and somewhat uncomfortable pause. Mouw followed up after about a minute: "Isn't there anything you have to say? Did we all read the book?" Everyone nodded affirmatively that they had indeed read it but no one seemed to have any questions. Finally, one of the Latter-day Saint participants responded: "Stott is essentially writing of New Testament Christianity, with which we have no quarrel. He does not wander into the creedal formulations that came from Nicaea, Constantinople, or Chalcedon. We agree with his assessment of Jesus Christ as presented in the New Testament. Good book." That comment was an important one, as it signaled where we would eventually lock our theological horns: Nicaea.

Our second gathering took place at Fuller Seminary in Pasadena. After our initial dinner together, each participant spoke of what they had done since the last meeting, what articles or books they had published, their current research thrust, and any newsworthy issues the group might find worthwhile (a procedure that has continued to the present). In the second dialogue we chose to discuss the matter of soteriology (a study of salvation), and much of the conversation was taken up with the relation between divine grace, faithful obedience (good works), and salvation. The evangelicals insisted that our theology did not contain a provision for grace, and that we seemed to be obsessed with a kind of works righteousness. This is a matter that had come up many times before in my conversations with evangelicals—namely that Latter-day Saints tend to be so focused on doing the right thing, doing *enough* of the right thing, and laboring tenaciously to accomplish the "work of the kingdom" that it appeared that the Saints felt that they could somehow save themselves, that in fact divine grace was not necessary.

One of the first things the Latter-day Saints in the dialogue did was to return to our own scriptural texts to demonstrate how often and consistent the grace of God is emphasized, for example, in the Book of Mormon. One member of our group, Stephen Robinson, asked the group to turn to several passages in the Book of Mormon in which the text stressed the fact that we are saved only through the merits, mercy, and grace of the Holy Messiah. After an extended silence, I remember hearing one of the evangelicals say, almost in a whisper, "Sounds pretty Christian to me."

The Latter-day Saint participants pointed out that what they had observed quite often among evangelicals was what Dietrich Bonhoeffer had warned of—"cheap grace"—a kind of easy believism that frequently resulted in spiritually unfazed and unchanged people. I added that there were a surprising number of books by evangelical scholars that cautioned their own people about separating justification from sanctification, that is, driving a wedge between one's conversion or salvation experience and the requisite faithfulness that ought to characterize true faith. One of my group indicated that from his perspective evangelicals tend to have a high view of forgiveness but a low view of repentance; many sermons stress the goodness of God and the forgiveness of Jesus Christ; congregants were reminded repeatedly of the good news while receiving precious little counsel on how to repent of their sins and, further, of the need to demonstrate the depth of one's faith through dedicated discipleship (Jas 2:19–20).

In some ways, this topic—grace and works—is seldom referred to any longer among the dialogists. While both groups acknowledge that there will probably always be differences in how salvation in Christ is described between the two faith traditions, in reality we were on the same page and thus to some extent this particular issue became a theological straw man to which no one felt the need to strike a match. This dialogue was a breakthrough that we often refer to when we are in the middle of a doctrinal log jam: we ought to be just as eager to celebrate similarities as we are to define differences.

One of our dialogues took place in 2004 at the meetings of the American Academy of Religion and the Society of Biblical Literature. We had agreed as a large group to discuss the person and work of Joseph Smith. We extended an invitation to Richard Bushman, professor of history at Columbia University and a practicing Latter-day Saint, to discuss with us his biography of Joseph Smith.[3] Bushman quickly got everyone's attention as he turned to the evangelical element of the group and asked simply, "Is Joseph Smith an impossibility for you?" After a long delay, he restated the question. This time someone replied: "No, Dick, it's not an impossibility. God can speak to us and certain individuals can have the gift of prophecy and revelation. We just do not believe God appeared or spoke to Joseph Smith."

The dialogue proceeded from there, discussing true and false prophets, whether Joseph Smith was a prophet with a large or small P (as someone put it), and whether The Church of Jesus Christ of Latter-day Saints could be an expression of something good or Christian if Joseph Smith did not really see God (the matter of historicity). As a follow-up, Mouw spoke at our next gathering on "The Possibility of Joseph Smith: An Evangelical Perspective," posing the question: Isn't there a way for us to examine Joseph Smith without resorting to such labels as liar or lunatic? How can Evangelicals understand Joseph Smith properly without considering the context of nineteenth-century Restorationism?

One of the most memorable of all our discussions centered around the concept of *theosis* or divinization, the doctrine espoused by Latter-day Saints and also a vital facet of Eastern Orthodoxy. For this dialogue we invited Veli-Matti Kärkkäinen, professor of theology at Fuller Seminary, to lead our discussion. In preparation for the dialogue we read his book, *One With God: Salvation As Deification and Justification*, as well as Latter-day Saint writings on the topic. It seemed to me that in this particular exchange there was much less effort on the part of evangelicals to "fix Mormonism" or continue another round of "tryouts for true Christianity." Instead, there was much reflection and introspection among the entire group. Latter-day Saints commented on how little work they had done on this subject. They found themselves fascinated with such expressions as *participation* in God, *union* with God, *assimilation* into God, receiving of God's *energies and not his essence*, and *divine-human synergy*. More than one of the evangelicals asked how they could basically have ignored a matter that was a part of the discourse of Athanasius, Augustine, Irenaeus, Gregory of Nazianzus, and even Martin Luther. There was much less said about "you and your faith," and far more emphasis on

3. Bushman and Woodworth, *Joseph Smith*.

"we" as professing Christians, when addressing divinization and related themes.

Not long after our dialogue on deification, Richard Mouw suggested that we meet next time not in Provo, but rather in Nauvoo, Illinois. Nauvoo was the site of a major historical moment (1839–1846) within our church, the place where the Saints were able to establish a significant presence, where some of Joseph Smith's deepest and most controversial doctrines were delivered to his people, and the site from which Brigham Young and the Mormon pioneers began the long exodus to the Salt Lake Basin in February 1846. Because a large percentage of the original dwellings, meetinghouses, places of business, and even the temple have been restored in modern Nauvoo, our dialogue was framed by the historical setting and resulted in perhaps the greatest blending of hearts of any of our dialogues. Two years later, we met in Palmyra, New York and once again focused much of our attention on historical sites, from the Sacred Grove (where Joseph Smith claimed to have received his first vision) to Fayette, where the church was formally organized on April 6, 1830. We had reaffirmed what we had come to know quite well in Nauvoo—that there is in fact something very real about "sacred space." Following the Palmyra exchange, the participants of my faith insisted that Mouw plan similar experiences for us in Wittenberg and Geneva. Needless to say, those recommendations did not receive much follow up! Over the years, however, we have studied and conversed at Wheaton College, in Chicago (to discuss Billy Sunday and Dwight Moody), and in Los Angeles (to converse about the rise of Pentecostalism on Azusa Street, as well as the ministry and influence of Amy Semple McPherson).

Interesting Challenges

Progress has not come easily. This is tough sledding, hard work. In my own life it has entailed a tremendous amount of reading. Early on, it seemed to me that one of the best compliments I could make to my new friends was to come to know who they were, what they believed, who their key spokespersons were, what the hot topics of the day were. I soon realized that I could not very well enter into their world and their way of thinking unless I immersed myself in their literature. This is particularly difficult when such efforts come out of your own hide, that is, when you must do it above and beyond everything else you are required to do as a university professor (teaching classes, researching and writing). It takes a significant investment of time, energy, and money.

Second, it soon became clear that the kinds of persons that should be invited to participate in the dialogue were not necessarily those with sheer brilliance or intellectual acumen, but a non-defensive, clear-headed, thick-skinned, persistent but pleasant personality. Kindness works really well. Those steeped in apologetics, whether Latter-day Saint or evangelical, face a particular hurdle, since such a person is obsessed with proving the other person wrong. For example, the evangelicals decided early in our encounters that they would not devote time in the dialogue trying to disprove Joseph Smith's first vision or the historical veracity of the Book of Mormon. These were sacred Latter-day Saint historical moments and our holy book. Mouw insisted upon this guideline, just as in a Christian-Muslim dialogue (of which he has been a part) there was never an inclination to spend appreciable time evaluating proofs or evidences of whether Muhammad had actually entertained the angel Gabriel.

Third, as close as we have become, as warm and congenial as the dialogues have proven to be, some of the Latter-day Saints have perceived a continuing and underlying but unstated premise that guided most of the evangelical participants: that The Church of Jesus Christ of Latter-day Saints is the tradition that needs to be tweaked and to do the theological "adjusting" in order for the larger Christian world to feel more comfortable with us. To be sure, the Latter-day Saint participants have become well aware that many of our theological positions have been grossly misunderstood. A number of my cohort have voiced this concern openly and suggested that it just might be a healthy exercise for the evangelicals to open themselves to a bit more introspection, to consider that this enterprise is in fact a *dialogue*, a mutual conversation, one where long-term progress will come only as both sides are convinced that there is much to be learned from one another, including doctrine. As one of the Latter-day Saint participants, Spencer Fluhman, put it, on too many occasions it seemed as though the dialogue tended to slip into a mode best described as "Latter-day Saint tryouts for Christianity."

Early in our conversations, one of the evangelical dialogists remarked to one of the senior leaders of our church that one of the great discoveries he had made was how well versed the Latter-day Saints were in the Bible. He commented: "This is an important point. I'm convinced that if your people could focus more and more attention on the Bible and less and less on the Book of Mormon, many of your problems would be solved." Our church leader smiled and said: "Well, we certainly would like people to feel better toward us, and we would be excited to have our people even more Biblically literate than they are, but you need to understand that we will be dragging those golden plates with us wherever we go!"

A fourth challenge is one we did not anticipate. In evangelicalism there is no organizational structure, no priestly hierarchy, no living prophet or magisterium to declare the "final word" on doctrine or practice, although there are supporting organizations like the National Association of Evangelicals and the Evangelical Theological Society. On the other hand, The Church of Jesus Christ of Latter-day Saints is clearly a hierarchical organization, the final word resting with the First Presidency and the Quorum of the Twelve Apostles (analogous, I suppose, to the Roman Catholic magisterium or teaching office). In that sense, it is easier for us to explain the church's position on this or that matter, whereas there is no final doctrinal arbiter on theological interpretation within evangelicalism.

This is not unlike the challenge faced by the evangelical team involved in the ecumenical effort called "Evangelicals and Catholics Together." ECT has issued several joint declarations such as "The Christian Mission in the Third Millennium" (1994), "The Gift of Salvation" (1997), "Your Word Is Truth" (2002), "The Communion of Saints" (2003), "The Call to Holiness" (2005), "That They May Have Life" (2006), and "The Blessed Virgin Mary in Christian Faith and Life" (2009). Unfortunately, the results of the interactions seem still to be questioned by individual Catholics and institutional Catholicism. On the other hand, recent Latter-day Saint Official Declarations, such as "The Family, A Proclamation to the World" (1997) and "The Living Christ" (2000) were prepared and issued by the First Presidency and Quorum of the Twelve Apostles, upon whom the responsibility rests for the determination of doctrine and policy, and these two documents enjoy near-canonical status among Latter-day Saints.

Retrospect and Prospect

From the beginning we chose to ignore the question of where these dialogues were headed or exactly what the final product of our investigation would look like. Through it all, including the ups and downs, many of us have felt a superintending Presence brooding over our halting but sincere efforts. We have gained a greater appreciation for the words of Jesus to his disciples that "where two or three are gathered together in my name, there am I in the midst of them" (Matt 18:20). I have learned that I cannot take another religious tradition seriously without (1) coming to appreciate beauty, truth, and conviction within its adherents, and recognizing in their lifestyle something commendable and even praiseworthy; (2) delving deeper into my own tradition, including its theological consistency and relevance in the modern world; and (3) recognizing that God is in fact moving in the hearts and lives of men and women throughout the world in ways not easily perceived.

In reflecting back on his visit to Salt Lake City and a major message he delivered in the Tabernacle on Temple Square in Salt Lake City in 2004, evangelical teacher and author Ravi Zacharias observed:

> The last time an Evangelical Christian was invited to speak there was 1899, when D. L. Moody spoke . . . I accepted the invitation . . . and I spoke on the exclusivity and sufficiency of Jesus Christ. I also asked if I could bring my own music, to which they also graciously agreed. So Michael Card joined us to share his music. He did a marvelous job, and one of the pieces he sang brought a predictable smile to all present. It was based on Peter's visit to Cornelius' home and was entitled, "I'm Not Supposed to Be Here." He couldn't have picked a better piece! I can truly say that I sensed the anointing of the Lord as I preached and still marvel that the event happened. The power of God's presence, even amid some opposition, was something to experience. As the one closing the meeting said, "I don't want this evening to end." Only time will tell the true impact. Who knows what the future will bring? Our faith is foundationally and theologically very different from the Mormon faith, but maybe the Lord is doing something far beyond what we can see.[4]

"If I esteem mankind to be in error," Joseph Smith observed in 1843, less than a year before his death, "shall I bear them down? No. I will lift them up, and in their own way too, if I cannot persuade them my way is better; and I will not seek to compel any man to believe as I do, only by the force of reasoning, for truth will cut its own way. Do you believe in Jesus Christ and the Gospel of salvation which he revealed? So do I. Christians should cease wrangling and contending with each other, and

---

4. Zacharias, *Ravi Zacharias International Ministry Newsletter*, 2.

cultivate the principles of union and friendship in their midst; and they will do it before the millennium can be ushered in and Christ takes possession of His kingdom."[5]

Jesus the Christ has commanded us to love other people, even those we would consider to be our enemies—and to pray for them (Matt 5:43–44). Few things are more needed in this tense and troubled world than understanding. Rarely if ever before in the history of our world has there been a greater need for courtesy, for kindness, for civility, and for assuming the best about others who may differ from us. My dear friend Richard Mouw wrote: "One way in which Satan tries to get at us, I'm convinced, is by getting us to go all out in attacking others. G. K. Chesterton offered wise counsel when he wrote, 'Idolatry is committed, not merely by setting up false gods, but also by setting up false devils.' Wrongly to demonize a person who is not a demon is itself a terrible thing."[6] Surely it is time for those of us who profess Christian discipleship to cease name-calling, avoid categorizing, and eschew demonizing. This is especially the case among those of us who profess to be followers of the Prince of Peace. My sincere hope is that we may do more talking and more listening—and in the process gain more understanding.

Bibliography

Bushman, Richard L., and Jed Woodworth. *Joseph Smith: Rough Stone Rolling*. New York: Knopf, 2005.

Mouw, Richard J. *Talking with Mormons: An Invitation to Evangelicals*. Grand Rapids: Eerdmans, 2012.

———. *Uncommon Decency: Christian Civility in an Uncivil World*. Revised and Expanded ed. Downers Grove: InterVarsity, 2010.

Kärkkäinen, Veli-Matti. *One with God: Salvation As Deification and Justification*. Collegeville: Liturgical, 2004.

Smith, Joseph. *History of the Church of Jesus Christ of Latter-day Saints*. Vol. 5. Edited by Dean C. Jessee. Salt Lake City: Deseret, 2002.

Stackhouse, John G., Jr. *Humble Apologetics: Defending the Faith Today*. New York: Oxford University Press, 2002.

Zacharias, Ravi. *Ravi Zacharias International Ministry Newsletter* 3 (Winter 2004).

5. Smith, *History of the Church*, 498–99.

6. Mouw, *Talking with Mormons*, 18.

8

The Monkhood of All Believers

On Monasticism Old and New

RODNEY CLAPP

IN AUGUST OF 1988, I published an unsigned editorial in *Christianity Today*. It began by citing three evangelical stalwarts, all striking a surprising common note.

> John R. W. Stott, the elder statesman of British evangelicalism, has stated recently that if he were young and beginning his Christian discipleship over, he would establish a kind of evangelical monastic order. Joining it would be men vowed to celibacy, poverty, and peaceableness.
>
> Senate Chaplain Richard Halverson, speaking last April to the Anabaptist Hutterian Brethren, said something "cataclysmic" is in the air. Perhaps it is the return of Christ or, less dramatically, a "mighty visitation of God upon the Earth, upon the church." When it happens, "people in the evangelical community will have to move a lot more in the direction you [the Hutterians] are, more toward simplicity, away from the materialism that I believe now has really infected badly the whole evangelical community."
>
> Fuller Seminary philosopher Richard Mouw, speaking a few months back at Wheaton College, suggested that the church, and its evangelical sector in particular, would benefit from "remonasticization"—the clear and radical witness of a

smaller body within the church, calling the entire church to a
clearer and more radical witness.

The editorial mused on what forms such remonasticization, within
Protestant confines, might take. Young single Christians might live in
community, committed to nonviolence, poverty, and celibacy. Families might buy up homes in the same neighborhood, "enabling them to
meet daily for common worship and mutual discipleship." And, "Given
increased longevity, Christians at retirement might form their own communities, devoting themselves to intensive worship and study of the
Scripture, and to service in the world."[1]

In 1988, the same year the editorial was published, evangelical theologian Dennis Okholm became an oblate in the Order of St. Benedict.[2]
Soon thereafter he joined the American Benedictine Academy for its
scholarly meetings, and a few years later he became the first non-monas-
tic and non-Catholic board member of the Academy.[3] Okholm's immersion in Benedictine monasticism has resulted in a series of classes at his
successive university locations, multiple teachings in various Protestant
churches, and winsome book-length expositions of monastic wisdom for
the wider church.[4]

Something was in the air. The sense of a need for remonasticization
gained momentum through the 1990s, and in 1998 theologian Jonathan
Wilson published *Living Faithfully in a Fragmented World*. There he
coined the phrase *new monasticism* to designate, within Protestantism,
an embodied and communal reclamation of distinctly Christoform practices that set the church apart from the world (but for the sake of the
world). Scant years later, Wilson's daughter, Leah, and son-in-law, Jonathan Wilson-Hartgrove, established the Rutba House, a new monastic
community in Durham, North Carolina. Concurrently, Wilson-Hartgrove's former classmate at Eastern University, Shane Claiborne, par-
ticipated in the birthing of the Simple Way, a new monastic community
in Philadelphia. By 2005, the Wilson-Hartgroves, Claiborne, and others

1. "Remonking the Church," *Christianity Today*.

2. See Brother Benet Tvedten's appendix in this volume for a personal account of
Okholm's journey into Benedictine spirituality: "At the Advice of a Sister," 213–19.

3. Okholm, *Monk Habits*, 19.

4. Besides Okholm's *Monk Habits*, see his *Dangerous Passions*.

published *School(s) for Conversion*, which promulgated "12 Marks of a New Monasticism."[5]

Thus from the late 1980s onward, Protestants have intensely re-engaged an ancient tradition of the church, monasticism. Now, thirty years later, I intend to take stock. More specifically, and in the Okholmian spirit, I want to focus on "remonking" as a practice crucially aimed at all Christians, and avoiding the formation of a new elite apart from the church as a whole.

Antecedents

Taking account of Protestant remonasticization entails first remembering that it did not happen in a vacuum, and without roots. Original or traditional monasticism may be understood as a renewal movement within and on behalf of the church. The fourth-century Desert Fathers and Mothers who withdrew to the Egyptian wilderness were responding to the tepidness and even corruption of a Constantinian church grown lax, worldly, and indistinct from the surrounding society. The early monks simply wanted to preserve and practice Christian discipleship. Like Jesus at his temptation in the wilderness, they went to the desert not so much to escape evil as to confront it at its heart: in the wastelands that were understood as the special haunt of demons (Isa 13:21–22; 34:1–5; Rev 18:2). Heeding the Apostle Paul, they trained and buffeted their appetites like athletes, but in pursuit of an imperishable rather than perishable wreath (1 Cor 9:25).

Withal, the original monks did not set themselves to be insular or inaccessible from the surrounding church. In his considered remarks on the Desert Fathers, Thomas Merton writes that for them, "Charity and hospitality were matters of top priority, and took precedence over fasting and personal ascetic routines."[6] A few pages on, Merton observes that the early monks owned responsibility to the world.

> The simple men who lived their lives out to a good old age among the rocks and sands only did so because they had come into the desert to be themselves, their *ordinary* selves, and to forget a world that divided them from themselves. There can be no other valid reason for seeking solitude or for leaving the

5. The "12 Marks" will be engaged below.

6. Merton, *The Wisdom of the Desert*, 16–17.

world. And thus to leave the world is, in fact, to help save it in saving oneself. This is the final point, and it is an important one. The Coptic hermits who left the world as though escaping from a wreck, did not merely intend to save themselves. They knew that they were helpless to do any good for others as long as they floundered about in the wreckage. But once they got a foothold on solid ground, things were different. Then they had not only the power but even the obligation to pull the whole world to safety after them.[7]

We find a similar spirit if we skip ahead to the sixth century and St. Benedict, the founder of Western monasticism. The first verse of chapter 53 of Benedict's famous *Rule* exhorts, "All guests who present themselves are to be welcomed as Christ." (And verse 15 movingly adds, "Great care and concern are to be shown in receiving poor people and pilgrims, because in them particularly Christ is received; our very awe of the rich guarantees them special respect.")[8] Besides their caring and open practice of hospitality, Western monastics preserved classical as well as specifically Christian learning, trained clergy, and operated hospitals. And they did all this theocentrically or "doxocentrically," serving or flowing from their worship and prayer. The "pagan" classics, for example, were seen as essential to learning grammar, the better to read and engage Scripture; mathematics had to be mastered to accurately calculate liturgical holidays and seasons.[9] So the monks, even though (or because) they majored on service to God, made significant contributions to the wider church. Indeed, as Jean Leclercq summarizes it, "Without a doubt, the monasteries had at times exerted such great influence that all Christian society lived, more or less, in the light they diffused. Curtius' conclusion is as true of the Middle Ages as of the patristic period: 'Much of what we call Christian is purely and simply monastic.'"[10]

---

7. Merton, *The Wisdom of the Desert*, 22–23.

8. Benedict, *The Rule*, 73–74.

9. See Leclercq, *The Love of Learning*. Similarly, Okholm observes, "Most impressively, Benedictine monasteries preserved ancient literature that helped to make possible the cultural and religious achievements of the thirteenth century and the Renaissance of the fifteenth. But such achievements were byproducts of a deep interior life, cultivated by the legacy of a man who was intent on seeking God and who taught his followers how it should done" (*Monk Habits*, 26).

10. Leclercq, *The Love of Learning*, 256.

Protestant Critiques

How, then, did the earliest Protestants respond to monasticism?

Luther, characteristically, was sweeping and vehement in his critique. He dismissed the institution *in toto*: "To become a monk (unless one is saved by a miracle) is to become an apostate from faith, to deny Christ, and to become a Jew, and, as Peter prophesied, to return to one's heathen vomit."[11]

Calvin reacted more temperately and discerningly. Rather than dismissing monasticism wholesale, he distinguishes between an earlier monasticism (which Augustine approved) and the abuses of the monasticism of his day.[12] The Genevan excerpts a long passage from Augustine, in which Augustine praises the monks for their commitment and holiness, emphasizing that they are "not swollen by pride" and "counsel [one another] without pride."[13] Such monasticism, Calvin avers, did not set itself above or beyond the rest of the church. Indeed, the monastic "colleges" served as "seminaries of the ecclesiastical order," faithfully training and supplying clergy for the body of Christ.[14]

By contrast, Calvin saw the monks of his time accruing a long list of rigid requirements concerning "those things left free to us by the Lord's Word." To wit, "they count it an unforgivable crime for anyone to depart even in the slightest degree from what is prescribed in color or appearance of clothing, in kinds of food, or in other trifling and cold ceremonies." Furthermore, "Our present-day monks find in idleness the chief part of their sanctity. For if you take idleness away from them, where will that contemplative life be, in which they boast they excel all others and draw nigh to the angels?" Finally, says Calvin, "Augustine requires a kind of monasticism which is but an exercise and aid to those duties of piety enjoined upon *all* Christians."[15]

It is this last point that preoccupies Calvin, spurring him to devote the remainder of a long paragraph and four more chapters to it. A monasticism acceptable to Calvin is non-elitist, free of pride, and centered

---

11. Quoted in Okholm, *Monk Habits*, 120. In a post-Holocaust age, we can only cringe at the ugly anti-Semitism in these remarks. Thank God for the New Perspective on Paul.

12. Calvin, *Institutes* 4.9–10.

13. Calvin, *Institutes* 4.9.

14. Calvin, *Institutes* 4.8.

15. All citations in this paragraph are at Calvin, *Institutes* 4.10. Emphasis added.

on commitments and practices available to every Christian. Matthew Boulton neatly encapsulates it: "For Calvin, monastics are mistaken only insofar as they make elite, difficult, and rare what should be ordinary, accessible, and common in Christian communities: namely, whole human lives formed in and through the church's distinctive repertoire of disciplines, from singing psalms to daily prayer to communing with Christ at the sacred supper."[16]

For a final, and modern, Protestant critique of monasticism, I turn to Karl Barth. In his *Church Dogmatics,* Barth devotes a small-print, eight-page excursus to monasticism. He begins by noting that the monastic impulse for renewal and radical discipleship "has asserted itself almost from the very beginnings of the Christian Church." As if anticipating new monasticism, Barth says that this impulse "not only is . . . still with us to-day, but we can say with tolerable certainty that either in its traditional forms or in new ones it will be so in the future."[17]

He zeroes in on the hermetic or solitary monk as representative of monasticism. Right here we may quibble. The earliest ones called "monks" were solitaries. But very soon coenobitic or communal monasticism developed. Is this not at least equally representative of monasticism? However that may be, Barth observes that the impulse to a lone pursuit of sanctity is found at many points in the history of the church, and not just within Roman Catholicism. Barth thrusts the English Baptist John Bunyan into the dock, with his fictional pilgrim who flees the wife and children that weep after him. "But he sticks his fingers in his ears and runs on with the cry: Life, life, everlasting life, not looking behind him, but taking a straight course across the plain."[18]

Barth worries that this can be self-seeking escapism, plain and simple, and there is nothing distinctively Christian about it. "The question that we have to put to this mode of conduct is the obvious one that one does not have to be a Christian to be sated with the world and man, to wish to have done with the turmoil of earth, to hurry away as fast as one's feet can carry one. And to become and be a Christian one does not need to be up and off into the desert. A flight from the world is not in any sense identical with the flight to God."[19]

16. Quoted in Smith, *Imagining the Kingdom,* 155. Boulton also suggestively refers to "the monkhood of all believers."

17. Barth, *Church Dogmatics* 4/2:11.

18. Barth, *CD* 4/2:12.

19. Barth, *CD* 4/2:12.

Having said this, Barth allows that monastic forays are not necessarily self-seeking and escapist. After all, there are "notable precedents in the Bible" for a proactive and positive withdrawal, undertaken ultimately not to reject world and church, but to serve them more effectively and faithfully (see in this regard our earlier quotes from Thomas Merton). Such instances, in Barth's view, represent "a highly responsible and effective protest and opposition to the world, and not least to a worldly Church, a new and specific way of combating it, and therefore a direct address to it—a retreat, in fact, for the purpose of a more effective attack."[20] Indeed, "Can there be either for the Church or for individuals any genuine approach to the world or men unless there is any equally genuine retreat?"[21]

Further, Barth sees the service monasticism at its best can offer in an eschatological light. "With its principle of asceticism both Eastern and Western asceticism has in fact rendered one obvious service to the Church—that of bringing and keeping vividly before it (by way of analogy and example) the passing of this world and its lusts (1 Cor. 7:31, 1 Jn. 2:17) and the existence of a new man and the direction which he gives." In this regard monasticism has resisted the "de-eschatologising and secularising" of the church's "life and message."[22] Such monastic, ascetic witnesses ought not to have been made into acontextual principles or laws. And, echoing Calvin, they "ought not to have been interpreted as distinctions between perfect and imperfect, or gradations of calling." Nor should they succumb to a realized eschatology, imagining that in this life or age there can be perfect fulfillment.[23]

In short, Barth allows that "the desire and aim of monasticism was to achieve in its own distinctive a form of that discipleship of the Lord which is not only commanded generally in the Gospels but partially at least, and by way of illustration, more specifically outlined." Though he ends with halting and cumbersome qualifications,[24] Barth finds an important place for monasticism—especially if it is not escapist, individualistic, exclusively introverted, legalistic, perfectionistic, or presented as a unique higher calling. Monasticism at its best is an eschatological witness or sign to the wider church and to the world, answering the gospel call

20. Barth, *CD* 4/2:13.

21. Barth, *CD* 4/2:14.

22. Barth, *CD* 4/2:15.

23. Barth, *CD* 4/2:15.

24. Barth, *CD* 4/2:18.

to discipleship, spurring all Christians to answer the same call in their stations and status.

Taking Account: Traditional Monasticism

With the telling concerns of Calvin and Barth in mind, we may then wonder how modern monasticism fares. Okholm, after decades of exposure to contemporary Benedictines, argues convincingly that they are not perfectionistic, that they are not escapist, that they do not consider themselves as elite among an otherwise mediocre church, and that they freely offer their way of life to be adapted by Christians outside monasteries.

Noting that Calvin worried about monasticism setting up a sectarian "double Christianity" that separates monks from the rest of the church, Okholm responds, "Benedictine monks today would deplore such a division of divine expectations and Christian caste system. In fact, they just might be the first to admit they fall far short of many Christians who live daily lives in the secular arena."[25]

As for the charge of escapism, Okholm has only to point to the record. Benedictines are intensely involved with "meeting the needs of the dispossessed, the marginalized, and the impoverished." They have established monasteries amid and served Native Americans, "have supported the arts, administered successful inner-city schools, cared for the elderly—and the list goes on."[26]

Okholm does not imply that monastics are above criticism, or romanticize monasticism. Instead, he insists on the mundanity of monastic life.

> In fact, Benedictine spirituality is not glamorous. It is *extraordinarily ordinary.* A few years ago, shortly after Kathleen Norris's second bestseller appeared (*The Cloister Walk*), I asked a monk who was traveling with me what he thought of her writing. He commended it, with one caveat: "She makes our life sound so interesting, but it's so d—n tedious." Benedict surely would have applauded, for his conception of monastic life rejected the goal of forming spiritual gold medalists or religious superstars. With no pun intended, it is a life of habits that, in turn, develop virtues (character traits) and muscles of the soul.[27]

25. Okholm, *Monk Habits,* 119–20, quotation from 120.

26. Okholm, *Monk Habits,* 127–28.

27. Okholm, *Monk Habits,* 21. From the start, monks encountered empty boredom

Finally, Okholm finds it significant that Benedictines vigorously counsel non-monastics on how they might adapt Benedictine spirituality in their daily, "secular" lives. Consider these fifteen guidelines on "How to Take Benedictine Spirituality Home with You":

1. Pray at least two Offices daily.

2. Read and meditate on sacred scripture at least once a day.

3. Practice times of silence.

4. Practice a contemplative type of daily prayer.

5. Remember that every moment of our lives is lived in the Divine Presence.

6. Do a partial or full fast (or abstain from meat) at least once a week.

7. Attend church services and/or receive the Holy Eucharist at least once weekly.

8. Care for those you live with, work with, and worship with.

9. Treat your family and your daily work/profession as your main Christian ministry.

10. Refrain from judging others and pray for them instead.

11. Be consistently involved in at least one ministry/program of your parish.

12. Treat all physical objects in your environment with care and reverence.

13. Remember [*Rule of Benedict*] 4: "The love of Christ must come before all else."

14. Be faithful (stable) in your family, employment, parish responsibilities.

15. Serve others with consistent patience and care.[28]

Such guidelines, though demanding, require no spiritual super-heroism.[29] They contextualize discipleship and spiritual practice in the

---

and apparent, enervating stasis in their praying. This condition was closely analyzed and engaged as what, under the rubric of the seven deadly sins, came to be called *acedia* (sloth). For a penetrating and precise overview, with recourse to Gregory the Great, John Cassian, and modern psychology, see Okholm, *Dangerous Passions*, 135–56.

28. See Okholm, *Monk Habits,* 134–35.

29. The late Phyllis Tickle, an Episcopalian, though busy as a writer and popular

lives of typical non-monastics, with jobs, families, and daily involvement in the marketplace. They assume that the Christian life will be embedded in the worship and service endeavors of the church.

All told, we find here a monasticism that does not envision anything like a "second baptism," that shuns elitism and sectarianism, that engages the wider church and the world, and is more self-deprecating than prideful. It is Christocentric, deeply practical, and commonsensical, recognizing the ineluctable importance of habits in developing (or, in the case of bad habits, eroding) character. It does not attempt salvation by works. Rather, it dives into participation in the body and life of the Christ who alone saves, and through that faithful participation expects virtue and "muscles of the soul" to grow stronger. I conclude that, like all human practices and institutions, traditional monasticism must remain vulnerable to criticism and scrutiny, but it has been and continues to be a boon to the church.

Taking Account: New Monasticism

In assessing new monasticism, it is first important to recognize that what we may now call "new monasticism," though so named in the 1990s, was well preceded within Protestantism itself. We may trace it to the earliest Anabaptists, who saw the Sermon on the Mount as a guide not only to traditional monastics, but to all Christians. (In this regard, it bears mentioning that Michael Sattler, a founder of Anabaptism, was a former Benedictine.) Thus it has been a consistent impulse, right into modern times, for Anabaptists to form intentional communities centered on Christian discipleship. The Bruderhof ("place of brothers" in German) was founded in 1920 in Germany, and now has communities throughout the world.

Alluding still to Germany but moving outside Anabaptism, it is worthwhile to note that the Lutheran Dietrich Bonhoeffer instituted monastic practices at his short-lived seminary in Finkenwalde.[30] The book eventuating from this experience, *Life Together*, remains profitable for

---

speaker, regularly prayed the offices and encouraged other laypersons to do likewise. For a biography, see Sweeney, *Phyllis Tickle*, esp. chapter 12. For Tickle's guidance in praying the offices, see her *The Divine Hours*.

30. Another Protestant movement to be noted is English early Methodism, which with its cells, prayer, Scripture reading, and other "methods" is well interpreted as a monastic phenomenon.

guidance on discipleship and the necessity of Christian community. Ever astute, Bonhoeffer warns against romanticized Christian community, and even counsels that every member of such a community needs to pass through a disillusionment with dreamy confusion "of Christian community with some wishful image of pious community." Christian community with limited, sinful human beings is constantly challenging and demanding. Bonhoeffer hopes that, "By sheer grace God will not permit us to live in a dream world even for a few weeks and to abandon ourselves to those blissful experiences and exalted moods that sweep over us like a wave of rapture. For God is not a God of emotionalism, but of truth."[31]

Turning to a focus on the United States, it is significant that in the twentieth century, waves of Protestant intentional Christian communities were founded, many of which still function. To take but two examples, Clarence and Florence Jordan's still vital Koinonia Farm was birthed in 1942, in Americus, Georgia. And in 1957, Reba Place Fellowship, which continues to the present, was founded in Evanston, Illinois.[32]

So new monasticism has its immediate as well as its ancient antecedents. The original, 2004 meeting of what would be dubbed new monasticism, in fact included several representatives from older communities. The new monastics agreed on twelve "marks" that characterize their communities, both those long and those more recently established. So we are within bounds to assess new monasticism in light of the twelve marks, which follow.

1. Relocation to the abandoned places of Empire.

2. Sharing economic resources with fellow community members and the needy among us.

3. Hospitality to the stranger.

---

31. Bonhoeffer, *Life Together/Prayerbook of the Bible*, 34–35. For a candid account of such disillusionment within contemporary new monastic community, see Lee, *Deconstructed Do-Gooder*.

32. Countless such communities have followed. Sojourners in Washington, DC, in 1971 initiated publication of the famous magazine that later went by that name. Other communities I have visited and appreciated include the Bruderhof in Woodcrest and Pleasant View, New York; Rutba House; Antioch in Jackson, Mississippi; the Jesus People USA in Chicago; and the Church of Servant King in Portland and Eugene, Oregon. Though I am here concentrating on Protestant communities, Dorothy Day's and Peter Maurin's Catholic Worker movement, founded in 1933, should be noted. Some 240 Catholic Worker houses, comprised mostly of laypersons, operate today.

4. Lament for racial divisions within the church and our communities combined with active pursuit of just reconciliation.

5. Humble submission to Christ's body, the church.

6. Intentional formation in the way of Christ and the rule of the community along the lines of the old novitiate.

7. Nurturing common life among members of intentional community.

8. Support for celibate singles alongside monogamous married couples and their children.

9. Geographical proximity to community members who share a common rule of life.

10. Care for the plot of God's earth given to us along with support of our local economies.

11. Peacemaking in the midst of violence and conflict resolution within communities along the lines of Matthew 18.

12. Commitment to a disciplined contemplative life.[33]

I note first that the new monastics locate themselves solidly within and as responsible to the church (mark five, "Humble submission to Christ's body, the church"). They heed the early counsel of theologian Jonathan Wilson that new monasticism should be aimed at "the whole people of God," with no distinction between sacred and secular vocations.[34] New monastics insist not on their perfection, but their ordinariness. Thus Shane Claiborne's *Irresistible Revolution* is subtitled *Living as an Ordinary Radical* and dedicated to "all the hypocrites, cowards, and fools . . . like me."[35] They foreground openness to the visitor (mark three, "Hospitality to the stranger"). They pledge "Commitment to a disciplined contemplative life" (mark twelve). In his commentary on mark twelve, Jonathan Wilson-Hartgrove looks directly to the ancient contemplative practice enacted by Catholics such as Jim Douglass.[36] It is a relief that the new monastics have a sense of history, and do not seek to reinvent the wheel. They pursue formation "in the way of Christ and the rule of

33. The Rutba House, *School(s) for Conversion*, xii–xiii.

34. Wilson, *Living Faithfully*, 72–75.

35. Claiborne, *Irresistible Revolution*. See also Claiborne et al., *Common Prayer: A Liturgy for Ordinary Radicals*.

36. Wilson-Hartgrove, "Commitment to a Disciplined Contemplative Life," 168–69.

community along the lines of the old novitiate" (mark six), that is, the initiatory disciplines of traditional monasticism. In his commentary, Reba Place's David Janzen avers, "Renewal movements have a historical ministry, to preserve in a new setting what has been tested and proven of worth."[37] Accordingly, new monastic communities often have rules of life modeled on Benedict's *Rule*.

One thing the new monastics cannot be accused of is escapism. The desert many (though not all) "flee" to is the deserted inner city. With "Relocation to the abandoned places of Empire" (mark one), new monastics stand with the impoverished and usually neglected citizens of a nation hellbent on getting and staying ahead. Sensitive to poverty, new monastics strive to share economic resources (mark two) and resist the systematic oppression of the poor. As Sr. Margaret McKenna writes in her shrewd commentary on mark one,

> We will not allow ourselves to be intimidated by the "Powers" of Empire We will employ the organic (yeast-like), grassroots model that starts with oneself and reaches to ever-widening circles, rather than the top-down approach to social transformation. We will live and witness from the inside out. With the early Christians and the desert hermits of the fourth century, we will invite the Holy Spirit to reveal possibilities of creative non-participation in Empire's oppressive self-glorification. What we promote, we will begin by practicing. Ordinariness rather than impressiveness will mark the style. The pursuit of a healthy reciprocity of receiving as well as giving will be a practice of humility, respect, and justice.[38]

New monastics pledge peaceableness (mark eleven, "Peacemaking in the midst of violence") and are vocal in resisting war, the arms race, gun culture, and the death penalty.[39] They recognize at the same time that disagreement is inevitable in all communities and strive to activate Christocentric conflict resolution within their own (mark eleven).

The new monastics, furthermore, are woke to America's original and ongoing sin, racism. They both lament racial divisions within the church and society, and pledge "active pursuit of a just reconciliation" (mark four). Here we do well to admit that Western monasticism has long been a predominantly white affair. New monasticism is no different.

37. Janzen, "Intentional Formation in the Way of Christ," 81.
38. McKenna, "Relocation to the Abandoned Places of Empire," 21.
39. See Claiborne and Martin, *Beating Guns*; Claiborne, *Executing Grace*.

In his insightful commentary on mark four, Chris Rice, a veteran of interracial Christian community, notes, "From Sojourners in Washington D.C. to Reba Place in Chicago to Koinonia in rural Georgia, these communities tried very hard, and largely failed, to recruit members of color." He suspects, citing the hypothesis of his African-American partner-in-community Spencer Perkins, that whites and (especially) blacks were simply headed in different directions. "[E]ducated whites who came from family histories of social privilege, and had come to see the dead end of materialism and the 'rat race,' were now willing to mobilize downward. But African American life was on a very different trajectory, coming from the margins into new educational and economic possibilities, mobilizing upward."[40] For new monastics as well as the church and society as a whole, interracial reconciliation remains a profoundly knotty and pressing concern. The new monastics are aware and engaged.

Finally, taking a cue from Barth, we may note that new monasticism has an eschatological tenor. New monasticism's founding theologian, Jonathan Wilson, called the new monastics to focus not on the penultimate but the ultimate, the ultimate being "participation in the coming kingdom" of Christ. New monasticism would serve "not by concentrating on its own survival but by devoting its life to the eschaton revealed, established and consummated by Jesus Christ."[41] In light of the all-encompassing, apocalyptic effects of Christ's eschaton, new monastics are holistically engaged, bringing realms including the social, political, economic, and ecological (mark ten, "Care for the plot of God's earth given to us") to Christ's feet for examination and transformation.

All this said, I should not ignore criticisms of new monasticism, most of which I have encountered in conversation. There is a worry that some new monastics are publicity hounds and aggrandize themselves with the telling of others' stories. One university chaplain told me he disinvited a popular new monastic speaker when it became clear one of the requirements was buying and hustling t-shirts promoting the event. And I notice that Shane Claiborne's visage adorns the cover of his latest edition of the bestselling *Irresistible Revolution*. Have Claiborne and others overstepped? Observers' judgments will differ, but negotiating the fine line between self-aggrandizement and legitimate publicization to get a

40. Rice, "Lament for Racial Divisions," 65. For the considerable fruits of Perkins's and Rice's determined wrestlings with racism, see their *More Than Equals*.

41. Wilson, "Introduction," 7.

hearing will require ongoing discernment and discretion for any blessed (if that is the word) with some degree of fame.

Finally, others criticize Claiborne for not stepping far and clearly enough. Some progressive Christians believe he should not be invited back as a main speaker at the leftish Wild Goose Festival until he unequivocally affirms same-sex marriages. The argument, considerable enough, is that Claiborne is entrapped in a flat, prooftexty reading of the Bible that will not allow or empower him to truly embrace his LGBT brethren.[42] As with race, we here enter an entangled arena that ties into vexatious knots the whole church and society. Negotiating it gracefully is an issue for all of us, and not just new monastics.[43]

The Impulse for Renewal

Concluding, I reiterate that monasticism is best understood as a recurring renewal impulse and movement spanning the history of Christianity.[44] Inasmuch as, qua Barth, Jesus Christ is an Event constantly disrupting, reawakening, and redirecting the people of God, such renewal is the very lifeblood and heartbeat of the church. Monasticism, old and new, will have to remain alert to the temptations of escapism, perfectionism, and elitism. Above all, it must always remember that we do not seek Christ, but Christ first seeks us. He handed himself into human hands at the cross, and still commits himself into grubby, fallible human hands at our regular eucharistic celebrations. As such, in the words of Matthew Boulton, "the church's practices are fundamentally divine works of descent and accommodation, not human works of ascent and transcendence."[45] Christ comes to us in many guises, and one of the most persistent is in the faces of imperfect monks. Like Dennis Okholm, I receive this gift with great gratitude.

---

42. See Clark, "Progressive Proof-Texting."

43. In airing these criticisms particularly of Claiborne, I risk my own hypocrisy, since I asked and he generously agreed to endorse my latest book. I am afraid Shane's pithy, notable eloquence and subsequent fame have made him into something of a lightning rod. Suffice to say that, despite the bolts crashing around him, I deeply respect his work and person. For a deft and honest accounting of same-sex issues from a new monastic perspective, see Otto, *Oriented to Faith*.

44. Indeed, as Acts 21:26 possibly suggests Paul took a Nazirite vow, it may date nearly to the birth of the church.

45. Quoted in Smith, *Imagining the Kingdom,* 15.

Bibliography

Barth, Karl. *Church Dogmatics 4/2: The Doctrine of Reconciliation.* Translated by G. W. Bromiley et al. Edinburgh: T. & T. Clark, 1958.

Benedict. *The Rule of St. Benedict.* Edited by Timothy Fry. Collegeville: Liturgical, 1981.

Bonhoeffer, Dietrich. *Life Together/Prayerbook of the Church.* Dietrich Bonhoeffer Works 5. Translated by Daniel W. Bloesch and James H. Burtness. Minneapolis: Fortress, 1996.

Calvin, John. *Institutes of the Christian Religion.* The Library of Christian Classics 20. Translated by Ford Lewis Battles. Philadelphia: Westminster, 1960.

Claiborne, Shane. *Executing Grace: How the Death Penalty Killed Jesus and Why It's Killing Us.* New York: HarperOne, 2016.

———. *Irresistible Grace: Living as an Ordinary Radical.* Updated and Expanded ed. Grand Rapids: Zondervan, 2016.

Claiborne, Shane, and Michael Martin. *Beating Guns: Hope for People Weary of Violence.* Grand Rapids: Brazos, 2019.

Claiborne, Shane, et al., eds. *Common Prayer: A Liturgy for Ordinary Radicals.* Grand Rapids: Zondervan, 2010.

Clark, Fred. "Progressive Proof-Texting." *Slacktivist.* https://www.patheos.com/blogs/slacktivist/2018/02/121/progressive-proof-texting/.

Janzen, David. "Intentional Formation in the Way of Christ and the Rule of the Community Along the Lines of the Old Novitiate." In *School(s) for Conversion: 12 Marks of a New Monasticism,* edited by the Rutba House, 80–96. Eugene: Cascade, 2005.

Leclercq, Jean, OSB. *The Love of Learning and the Desire for God: A Study of Monastic Culture.* New York: Fordham University Press, 1982.

Lee, Britney Winn. *Deconstructed Do-Gooder: A Memoir About Learning Mercy the Hard Way.* Missional Wisdom Library. Eugene: Cascade, 2019.

McKenna, Margaret M., Sr. "Relocation to the Abandoned Places of Empire." In *School(s) for Conversion: 12 Marks of a New Monasticism,* edited by the Rutba House, 10–25. Eugene: Cascade, 2005.

Merton, Thomas. *The Wisdom of the Desert.* New York: New Directions, 1960.

Okholm, Dennis. *Dangerous Passions, Deadly Sins: Learning from the Psychology of Ancient Monks.* Grand Rapids: Baker Academic, 2014.

———. *Monk Habits for Everyday People: Benedictine Spirituality for Protestants.* Grand Rapids: Brazos, 2007.

Otto, Tim. *Oriented to Faith: Transforming the Conflict over Gay Relationships.* Eugene: Cascade, 2014.

Perkins, Spencer, and Chris Rice. *More Than Equals: Racial Healing for the Sake of the Gospel.* Revised and Expanded ed. Downers Grove: InterVarsity, 2000.

"Remonking the Church." *Christianity Today,* August 12, 1988. https://www.christianitytoday.com/ct/2005/septemberweb-only/52.0.html.

Rice, Chris. "Lament for Racial Divisions Within the Church and Our Communities Combined with Active Pursuit of a Just Reconciliation." In *School(s) for Conversion: 12 Marks of a New Monasticism,* edited by the Rutba House, 55–67. Eugene: Cascade, 2005.

The Rutba House. *School(s) for Conversion: 12 Marks of a New Monasticism.* Eugene: Cascade, 2005.

Smith, James K. A. *Imagining the Kingdom: How Worship Works*. Cultural Liturgies 3. Grand Rapids: Baker Academic, 2013.

Sweeney, Jon M. *Phyllis Tickle: A Life*. New York: Church, 2018.

Tickle, Phyllis. *The Divine Hours: Pocket Edition*. Oxford: Oxford University Press, 2007.

Wilson, Jonathan R. "Introduction." In *School(s) for Conversion: 12 Marks of a New Monasticism*, edited by the Rutba House, 1–9. Eugene: Cascade, 2005.

———. *Living Faithfully in a Fragmented World: Lessons for the Church from MacIntyre's After Virtue*. Harrisburg: Trinity, 1998.

Wilson-Hartgrove, Jonathan. "Commitment to a Disciplined Contemplative Life." In *School(s) for Conversion: 12 Marks of a New Monasticism*, edited by the Rutba House, 162–72. Eugene: Cascade, 2005.

9

When Friends Become Siblings

A Pauline Theology of Friendship

Scot McKnight

In her delightful essay on Ralph Waldo Emerson, Mary Oliver describes what appears to be Emerson's common experience of friendship:

> If he tried to be at home among the stars, so, too, he strove to be comfortable in his own living room. Mentor to Thoreau and neighbor to Hawthorne, the idiosyncratic Bronson Alcott, the passionate Margaret Fuller, the talkative Ellery Channing, and the excitable Jones Very, he adorned his society with friendliness and participation. His house was often full of friends, and talk. Julian Hawthorne, then a young boy, remembers him sitting in the parlor, legs crossed, and—such was their flexibility— with one foot hitched behind the other ankle. Leaning forward, elbow on one knee, he faced his guests and held converse.[1]

There was only one Emerson, and that Concord gathering of friends was a one-of-a-kind, but many of us have friends, including Jesus and the apostle Paul whose ideas are simultaneously rooted in the Hebrew Bible (here, Old Testament) and in their ordered experiences with other humans.

A noteworthy statement from the Bible is the famous description of Israel's God, YHWH, speaking with Moses: "Thus the Lord used to speak

---

1. Oliver, *Upstream*, 70.

to Moses face to face, as one speaks to a friend" (Exod 33:11). To be sure, the term behind "friend" (*rea*) can be translated "neighbor" but in this instance the two English terms are indistinguishable. Commentaries get lost in discussions about whether one can see God or speak "face to face" with God while ignoring the surprising intimacy, if not casualness, of such a description of God speaking to a human as to a friend. One would have to say that YHWH and Moses are in some sense friends, and the same is true of Abraham (Isa 41:8; also Jas 2:23). Most of us are aware, too, that Job has a set of friends (e.g., Job 2:11). Friendship in the Old Testament would then have been a resource for Jesus and Paul.[2]

Friendship and Jesus

Some accuse Jesus of being "a friend of tax collectors and sinners" (Matt 11:19), Jesus speaks of his listeners as having friends (Luke 11:5, 8; 14:10, 12; 15:6, 9, 29; John 3:29), and urges his followers to make friends (Luke 16:9). Jesus calls Lazarus a friend (John 11:11). But the singularly most significant lines in the Gospels about friendship appear in Luke and John.

> I tell you, my friends, do not fear those who kill the body, and after that can do nothing more. (Luke 12:4)

> No one has greater love than this, to lay down one's life for one's friends. You are my friends if you do what I command you. I do not call you servants any longer, because the servant does not know what the master is doing; but I have called you friends, because I have made known to you everything that I have heard from my Father. (John 15:13–15)

Jesus' disciples are his friends and he speaks to them as his friends. The supreme example of love of friends is to die for them, but friendship with Jesus entails allegiance to him. Such allegiance, however, now moves beyond that of a slave (the Greek term in John 15 is *doulos*) because Jesus has revealed to them "everything that I have heard from my Father." Friendship, and the Greek term is *philos*, is rooted in love (*agape, agapao*), and Jesus loves his disciples and they love him in return. This means they are friends. Marianne Meye Thompson wisely ties together obedience, love, and being chosen by Jesus:

2. For a wonderful analysis, see Olyan, *Friendship in the Hebrew Bible*.

> From all that Jesus has said, one might conclude that it is by keeping Jesus' commands and doing as he does that one stands among his circle of friends or becomes a part of the flock for which he has given his life. Yet Jesus makes it clear that the disciples belong to him, not by virtue of what they have done, but by virtue of his love for them and the fact that he chose them. . . . Jesus' assertion that he has chosen his disciples recalls the biblical notion that God has chosen certain persons, including Abraham and David, and has chosen the people of Israel to be his holy people because he has loved them. In this sense "chosen" refers to a call to service, a vocation. Jesus' command to his disciples that they are to love one another indicates that he has chosen them all and that they belong, not only to him, but also to each other. Jesus' words here are the Johannine development of the Old Testament picture of Israel as a people bound in covenant to God and to each other, now applied to Jesus' disciples as those who love God and their neighbors as themselves.[3]

The occasional explicitness of friendship between God and a human found in the Old Testament is matched by the occasional use of friendship for Jesus' relationship with his followers. But the importance of friendship for Paul is by no means occasional. Before we can see the Pauline conversion of friendship into siblingship we need to pause to look at some of the greatest sources on friendship in the history of the discussion.[4]

Friendship in the Classical World

Many today don't read the classical studies on friendship nor have many read about friendship since that period, so a brief mention of my favorite treatments may prove worthwhile. Aristotle's *Nicomachean Ethics* contains the fundamental Greek treatment while Cicero's *Letters to Friends* along with Plutarch's "How to Tell a Flatterer from a Friend" are enduring studies, while among modern studies I'm a huge fan of Joseph Epstein's *Friendship: An Exposé*. Along with them one can find much joy in *The Oxford Book of Friendship* collected by D. J. Enright and David Rawlinson. Pastors and prominent leaders, if I may, are perhaps those most in

---

3. Thompson, *John*, 329–30.

4. The following two sections draw upon, with revisions, my chapter on friendship, "A Culture of Friendship," 31–56. The textual evidence, however, is what it is.

need of reading about and forming friendships, but I leave that discussion to the book mentioned in footnote four.

Aristotle *defined* friendship as follows:

> To be friends therefore, persons must feel goodwill for each other, that is, wish each other's good, and be aware of each other's goodwill, and the cause of their goodwill must be one of the lovable qualities mentioned above [namely, what is useful and good and pleasant].[5]

Notice how Aristotle's definition implies the communication of one's love and friendship with the others. Cicero improved Aristotle's theory in these words:

> For friendship is nothing else than an accord in all things, human and divine, conjoined with mutual goodwill and affection, and I am inclined to think that, with the exception of wisdom, no better thing has been given to man by the immortal gods.[6]

Friendship in the classical world, and this summary is one I regularly use in lectures, is a consensual, committed, caring, and conversational relationship in which persons both think well of one another and say as much to one another.

We will get to the apostle Paul soon but it is perhaps worth observing here that Paul grew up in a classical world approach to friendship. He grew up in nothing less than a major university city, Tarsus, where he was publicly exposed to both a rich banquet of public lectures and leading figures who emulated Aristotelian and Ciceronian approaches to friendship. What was the purpose of friendship in the classical world? The answer unequivocally and uniformly was *growth in virtue by emulation*. The classical world framed friendship in terms of morality. Plutarch puts it this way:

> Indeed a peculiar symptom of true progress is found in this feeling of love and affection for the disposition shown by those *whose deeds we try to emulate*, and in the fact that our efforts to *make ourselves like them* are always attended by a goodwill which accords to them a fair meed of honour.[7]

---

5. Aristotle, *Nicomachean Ethics*, 8.2.4. All classical sources are cited in the Loeb Classical Library editions.

6. Cicero, *On Friendship*, 6.20.

7. Plutarch, "Progress in Virtue," 84.14.

Manuals of virtue were common and we still read the moral treatises of Plutarch's *Parallel Lives*, the study of *Characters* by Theophrastus and the biographies of Suetonius. Morality was about emulation and friendship was formed with those worthy of emulation.

Friendship in the classical world legitimated that world's categories, one of the most significant of which was male domination. Friendship was between males, at least as the literature survives. Classical friendship required people of virtue and such persons are almost entirely (in their opinions) male and elite. In striking contrast to our world, which was not "our world" until the twentieth century, it was conventional to believe that a man and his wife were not "friends" (*philoi*).[8] In our world husbands and wives want to see themselves as best friends, while in the ancient world friendship and spouse were mostly disjointed.

Cicero echoed Aristotle when he said this about friendship: "*good persons* love and join to themselves other *good persons*, in a union which is almost that of relationship and nature" (*On Friendship* 13.50; also 5.18).[9] Furthermore, friends must be equals (*isotes*; cf. *Nic. Eth.* 8.5) and even if their statuses are unequal, that friendship would make them equals (*On Friendship* 19.69). This permits a brief statement about sexual relations and friends: male friendship is non-erotic because sexual relations are about dominance and friendship about equality. Accordingly, same sex male erotic relationships, differing from same sex female relationships, are not friendships because they are erotic.

Perhaps the most influential theme of classical world friendship has to do with the types of friendship we all experience, and Aristotle presented three types: utility, pleasure, and virtue (*Nic. Eth.* 8.3.1–6): friendships that are rooted in what they give to us or to the other, friendships that bring joy and pleasure, and friendships—the deeper friendships—that are about growing together in virtue.[10] Cicero, ever on the heels of Aristotle, said: "for when persons have conceived a longing for this virtue they bend towards it and move closer to it; so that, by familiar association with that person whom they have begun to love [emulation], they may enjoy that person's character, equal that person in affection, become

8. Konstan, *Friendship in the Classical World*, 71–72.

9. There are parallels with the Jewish, elitist, male wisdom tradition: Blenkinsopp, *Sage, Priest, Prophet*, 32–37.

10. For a brief comparison of these three kinds of friends with similar classifications in the Old Testament, see Olyan, *Friendship in the Hebrew Bible*, 107.

readier to deserve rather than demand that person's approval, and vie with that person in a rivalry of virtue" (*On Friendship* 9.32).

There are three more elements of the classical theory of friendship, three traits that are as true now as they were then. Trust is first and I turn to the Stoic Seneca, tutor to Nero himself, in a letter of his to Lucilius that speaks of trust:

> You have sent a letter to me through the hand of a "friend" of yours, as you call him. And in your very next sentence you warn me not to discuss with him all the matters that concern you, saying that even you yourself are not accustomed to do this; in other words, you have in the same letter affirmed and denied that he is your friend. Now if you used this word of ours in the popular sense, and called him "friend" in the same way in which we speak of all candidates for election as "honorable gentlemen," and as we greet all men whom we meet casually, if their names slip us for a moment, with the salutation "my dear sir,"—so be it. *But if you consider any man a friend whom you do not trust as you trust yourself, you are mightily mistaken and you do not sufficiently understand what true friendship means.* . . .
>
> Those persons indeed put last first and confound their duties, who . . . judge a man after they made him their friend, instead of making him their friend after they have judged him. Ponder for a long time whether you shall admit a given person to your friendship; but when you have decided to admit him, welcome him with all your heart and soul. Speak as boldly with him as with yourself.[11]

Loyalty is second, and this from Dio Chrysostom's third oration on kings:

> *Friendship, moreover, the good king holds to be the fairest and most sacred of his possessions,* believing that the lack of means is not so shameful or perilous for a king as the lack of friends, and that he maintains his happy state, not so much by means of revenues and armies and his other sources of strength, as by the loyalty of his friends. For no one, of and by himself, is sufficient for a single one of even his own needs; and the more and greater the responsibilities of a king are, the greater is the number of co-workers that he needs, and the greater the loyalty required of them, since he is forced to entrust his greatest and most important interests to others or else to abandon them.

11. Seneca, "On True and False Friendship," 3.1–2; emphasis added.

Furthermore, the law protects the private individual from being easily wronged by men with whom he enters into business relations, either by entrusting them with money, or by making them agents of an estate, or by entering into partnership with them in some enterprise; and it does so by punishing the offender. *A king, however, cannot look to the law for protection against betrayal of a trust, but must depend upon loyalty. Naturally, those who stand near the king and help him rule the country are the strongest, and from them he has no other protection than their love.* Consequently, it is not a safe policy for him to share his power carelessly with the first men he meets; but *the stronger he makes his friends, the stronger he becomes himself.*[12]

Honesty, better yet, "frankness" (*parrhesia*) is our final element in classical friendship. One of the major issues for leaders, especially for those who score high on narcissism scales, is the flatterer. Friends must tell one another the truth. Plutarch knew the problem well so he wrote "How to Tell a Flatterer from a Friend." It could be quoted *ad nauseam* but the term "flatterer" evokes for most leaders all one needs to hear. Avoid them. In a letter to Antipater, Isocrates commends in glowing terms a man named Diodotus, and includes these important lines on his frankness:

> In addition to these good qualities he possesses frankness in the highest degree, not that outspokenness which is objectionable, but that which would rightly be regarded as the surest indication of devotion to his friends. This is the sort of frankness which princes, if they have worthy and fitting greatness of soul, honor as being useful, while those whose natural gifts are weaker than the powers they possess take such frankness ill, as if it forced them to act in some degree contrary to their desires—ignorant as they are that those who dare to speak out most fearlessly in opposition to measures in which expediency is the issue are the very persons who can provide them with more power than others to accomplish what they wish. For it stands to reason that it is because of those who always and by choice speak to please that not only monarchies cannot endure—since monarchies are liable to numerous inevitable dangers—but even constitutional governments as well, though they enjoy greater security: whereas it is owing to those who speak with absolute frankness in favor of what is best that many things are preserved even of those which seemed doomed to destruction. For these reasons

12. Chrysostom, *Discourses*, 3.86–90; emphasis added.

it is indeed fitting that in the courts of all monarchies those who declare the truth should be held in greater esteem than those who, though they aim to gratify in all they say, yet say naught that merits gratitude; in fact, however, the former find less favor with some princes.[13]

When one thinks of friendship in the world of Paul, then, these are the terms that shaped the world around him:

> males,
> elites,
> equality,
> virtue,
> goodwill,
> consensus,
> affection,
> trust,
> loyalty,
> and frankness or honesty.

Friendship in Paul

When I set out to write some lectures on Paul as a pastor, I planned to begin with friendship and to explain some of Paul's pastoral strategy in terms of friendship. One can speak here of echoes of terms drawn from the friendship register,[14] but one can more easily think of the long list of names of what had to be seen as friends by his contemporaries: Priscilla and Aquila, Urbanus, Timothy, Titus, Epaphroditus, Clement, Jesus called Justus, Philemon, Mark, Aristarchus, Demas, and Luke. Think, too, of the names mentioned by Paul in Romans 16:3–16.

Philos becomes Epaphras

I provide an example of someone—Epaphras—about whom all public figures in Colosse or Ephesus or Corinth would say, "That's Paul's friend." Friendship, as mentioned already, is learned in relationship more than by

13. Isocrates, "Letter 4: To Antipater," 4.4–6.

14. A leader in studying echoes of friendship is John Reumann, and I mention two items: Reumann, "Philippians, Especially Chapter 4, as a 'Letter of Friendship'"; Reumann, *Philippians*.

reading Aristotle or Cicero or Plutarch. Paul learned friendship in Tarsus, in Jerusalem, and on mission, and one of his friends was Epaphras, who is mentioned three times in Paul's letters: Colossians 1:7, 4:12 and Philemon 23.[15]

One could be excused for thinking he's not important, but quick-study conclusions on Paul's friends are often mistaken. Here's what we know: (1) When Paul says Epaphras "is one of you" (Col 4:12) he means he's from Colosse; (2) it appears Epaphras was converted to Jesus during Paul's second missionary trip as he emerges into Paul's letters as a result of that mission; (3) he was commissioned by Paul to gospel the Lycus Valley and three churches came into being during this commissioning: Laodicea, Hierapolis, and Colosse (cf. Col 4:13); (4) Epaphras was imprisoned along with Paul in what I think was Ephesus (not Rome) (Phlm 23),[16] and some have suggested it was a voluntary imprisonment in order to be of assistance to the apostle.[17] These basics, however, can be probed to unveil some facts about Epaphras' pastoral life and relationship to Paul.

First, if we date Epaphras' conversion in approximately 50 AD, and Paul's letter to the Colossians somewhere around 54–55 AD, then we have Epaphras being converted, discipled, sent, establishing three churches, and encountering problems all within the span of five years. Paul no doubt learned from Epaphras about problems at Colosse and wrote this letter to resolve Epaphras' questions. In writing to Colosse Paul affirms the ministry of Epaphras (Col 1:7). Paul had never been to Colosse: Colossians 2:1 reads "and for those in Laodicea, and for all who have not seen me face to face," a sure indicator he had not been there. Epaphras evidently conducted his mission as an extension of Paul's own mission work. It is most likely that he established house churches, one of which is that of Philemon (see Phlm 1–2), through synagogue teaching and preaching.

Noticeably, second, Epaphras encountered theological and philosophical tensions between the Pauline gospel and ideas gaining traction among the Colossian Christians. This letter corrects what I have called "halakhic mystics," that is, Jewish believers who believe in rigorous

15. The evidence for believing Epaphras is identical to Epaphraditus (Phil 2:25; 4:18) is possible but not persuasive.

16. McKnight, *Colossians*, 34–39.

17. Paul calls Aristarchus a "fellow prisoner" along with Epaphras and some infer from the "fellow" part that it was voluntary. For this theory, see Dunn, *The Epistles to the Colossians and to Philemon*, 275–76.

observance of the Torah but who also appear to be seeking mystical experiences through ascetic rigor.[18] Epaphras, I infer, was unable to meet their challenges. He high-tailed it to Ephesus where he met Paul in prison and got Paul to respond to them. That is, Paul said what we read in Colossians 1:15–20, 2:1–5, and especially 2:8–23.

Third, Epaphras learned somewhere—and surely his challenging ministry with the halakhic mystics contributed—that ministry needs to be bathed in prayer. What Paul says in Colossians 4:12–13 reveals this attribute of Epaphras: "He is always wrestling in his prayers on your behalf, so that you may stand mature and fully assured in everything that God wills. For I testify for him that he has worked hard for you and for those in Laodicea and in Hierapolis." It should further be observed that Paul seems to have chosen Epaphras for ministry in the Lycus Valley because he was a hometown boy (Col 4:12; Phlm 23). As a hometown missionary of the Pauline gospel, Epaphras was one who passed on "good gossip" to Paul about the maturity of the Christians in his mission locations. What we read in Colossians 1:4–8 about the Colossians—their faith, their love, their hope, and the growth of the gospel work there—is from Epaphras (though probably not only from him).

Finally, and touching now directly upon the Aristotelian and Ciceronian theories of friendship, Paul overtly affirms Epaphras in the letters to Colosse. Here are his terms for him: "our beloved fellow servant" and "faithful minister" (1:7) and "a servant [better: slave] of Christ Jesus" (4:12). He never calls him "friend" and this will be explored in the rest of this study.

What Paul means by friendship is best seen in Paul's own friends, but there's more to say about Paul's theology of friendship than what we see in this concrete example.

Philos becomes Agapetos

It is noticeable that Paul does not use the term *philos* for what others would call his friends. Paul used the term *agapetos*, and thus moves us to see his friends more in terms of "loved ones." Because I have written about this in other locations,[19] I will draw attention without defense to five terms characteristic of the Bible's sense of love and how Paul would

18. Discussed in McKnight, *Colossians*, 18–34.
19. See McKnight, "A Culture of Friendship," 31–56.

have learned what love is. Before anything is said we must grapple with the priority of defining love not by looking at a dictionary or at our own experience of love—though both may provide some insight—but with how God loves in the pages of Israel's history. First, love is a covenant commitment to another person. This focuses our attention on the term covenant. Second, love is about divine presence, and the theme of God's being "with us" or "with them" or they "with God" is a feature of biblical faith. Third, love means advocating for the one loved then reciprocating with advocacy for the one loving that person. Fourth, love in Israel's story—here we think of Aristotle's theory of friendship of virtue—is about direction: God loves us to transform us from sinners into saints and we are loved in order to be transformed, so we love others in a mutual direction of growing in Christlikeness. Finally, though at odds with some of the classic Christian teachings on friendship and love, love in the Christian Bible is about affection too: God's emotions, our emotions, and our emotions with others who love us emotionally.

While these themes about love are not unknown to the classical world they are the focus of Jesus and Paul and they are so emphatic for Paul that he renegotiates the "friendship register" (*philos*) to become a "love register" (*agapetos*). It's not simplistic to say Paul turned from *philos* to *agapetos*. The overlap is noticeable but just as noticeable is the shift to Christ as the paradigm of love, and that paradigm turns Paul's friends from friends to loved ones.

Agapetos becomes *Adelphos*

Thus, a noticeable element of Paul's obvious network of friends is that there is not one shred of evidence that Paul called his co-workers "friends." We argue that he saw them as *agapetoi*, loved ones. Yet, that is not enough in the conversion of registers for Paul. His concern was the church, and what Paul called people—his friends, his loved ones, his churches—is another register conversion.[20] Paul does not call his co-workers *philoi* and he used *agapetoi* only so often because he understands his friends and loved ones in another register altogether, that of *brothers*

---

20. See Minear, *Images of the Church*. Also, Trebilco, *Self-Designations and Group Identity*. P. 14 alone contains much of Minear. A wider study is Dulles, *Models of the Church*.

and sisters.[21] This stands in contrast to the Old Testament where, in the summary statement of Saul Olyan, "friends are rarely if ever referred to using familial terminology (e.g., 'brother'), another way in which friends are distinguished from relatives."[22]

The *heart of pastoral ministry for the apostle Paul* was to nurture friendships into siblingships.[23] The term *adelphos*, or "brother," occurs 127 times in Paul's letters and 317 times in the New Testament and, alongside this is also the term *adelphe*, or "sister," which appears twenty-six times in the New Testament but only six times in Paul. "Sister" always refers to a female but "brother" often is inclusive and means "brothers and sisters." Thus, "siblings" is a good translation of *adelphos.* We must conclude that *siblingship is the dominant image of the church for Paul.*[24] Metaphors guide us to think of one thing (diverse Christians) in terms of another (siblings). Paul's emphasis on "sibling" led his own church people to think of themselves far more often as siblings than as the "body of Christ" or the "saints" or a "fellowship" or, which surprises many, the "church."[25] Paul was not nurturing friendships in the classical model in his churches but rather sibling relationships. We are all more aware today of how words work and how metaphors matter.

Siblingship connects to "family" and "household" and all that conveys, not least love, support, and cultural formation. Since metaphors are never complete analogies, Paul's largely ignoring spiritual mothers and fathers does not mean he plays siblings off against family. Paul does not think of his churches exclusively in terms of siblings or families. It is commonly observed that in Paul's theology God is the Father. Yet, Paul thinks

21. The dominance of *adelphos*/sibling language for the Pauline mission churches in some ways reveals that Paul's churches are not simply to be identified as *collegia* or associations inasmuch as *adelphos*/sibling language there is much less present. But see Harland, *Associations, Synagogues, and Congregations*, 31–33.

22. Olyan, *Friendship in the Hebrew Bible*, 37.

23. For a broader but still useful sketch, see the discussion of body, fellowship, and siblingship in Best, *Paul and His Converts*, 125–37.

24. See Horrell, "From *Adelphoi* to *Oikos*"; Aasgaard, *My Beloved Brothers and Sisters!*; Clarke, "Equality or Mutuality?"; Trebilco, *Self-Designations and Group Identity*; Horrell, *Solidarity and Difference*, 121–26.

25. "Body," (*soma*) for the church some thirty times, with eighteen times in 1 Cor 12:12–27; "saints," again about thirty times; "fellowship," about a dozen times; and "church," about sixty times.

of himself as both father (1 Thess 2:11–12; 1 Cor 4:15; Phlm 10; Phil 2:22) and mother (Gal 4:19; 1 Thess 2:7; 1 Cor 3:1–2) to his siblings.[26]

Why choose siblings as his most important image for his churches? The most important text from the time of Paul on this topic comes from Plutarch, "On Brotherly Love," while Reidar Aarsgaard[27] and Paul Trebilco[28] are two contemporary scholars who have summarized siblingship in the ancient world.

Family relations are primary, if not primordial, and that means all relations derive from family relations. Plutarch said all non-family relations are "shadows and imitations and images" of family relations.[29] In his important study, Trebilco finds four major themes that describe family relations:

1. Love

2. Harmony, concord, and cooperation

3. Discord, conflict, leniency, and forgiveness

4. Hierarchy

If we assume the above as characteristic of the world in which Paul was nurtured in Tarsus, we can turn to a brief note now on why Paul shifts what appeared to be friends into siblings and what that would have meant for Pauline mission. I find in Paul five themes that mark sibling relations:

1. Love

2. Love for all siblings

3. Mutual growth into Christoformity

4. Recognizing the safety and security of boundaries

5. Knowing that sibling relations began with Jesus, our Brother

---

26. For now see Gaventa, *Our Mother Saint Paul*. Estimates for the ancient world are always a bit speculative, but experts contend eighty percent of children had a living father at birth, at twenty that number decreases to fifty percent, at thirty to twenty percent, at forty to ten percent, and by fifty most had no living father. See Aasgaard, *My Beloved Brothers and Sisters!*, 37.

27. Aasgaard, *My Beloved Brothers and Sisters!*, 61–106.

28. Trebilco, *Self-Designations and Group Identity*, 17–21.

29. Plutarch, "On Brotherly Love," 3.

Conclusion

I have already emphasized the importance and definition of love, but it is worth reminding ourselves that Paul thought love was the number one Christian virtue (Gal 5:14; Rom 13:10). One has to wonder if Paul's theology worked from the centrality of love to sibling as the central metaphor or if his experience with other believers as siblings led to the centrality of love. I suspect we'll never sort that one out with confidence. What is noticeable for sibling relations is that they are usually genetically-determined. What is then noticeable with Paul is that sibling relations are not genetically-determined. There is in Christ equality of all as siblings (Gal 3:28; 1 Cor 12:13; Col 3:11). The tensions in Rome between the Strong and the Weak (Rom 14:1—15:13) can be seen as a Pauline assault on status identity markers in the Roman world and a plea to learn to see themselves as siblings. The crucial observation is that sibling describes the relationship of *all* in the churches, and this all-ness reshaped what sibling meant. Paul's letters are formed with a purpose, and that purpose is not abstract theology. Rather, Paul's focus is a kind of lived theology.[30] Our tendency has often been to move from the abstract and theoretical to the concrete and practical, and thus we read Paul's letters as theology leading to application. But what if we actually thought backwards? What if we think of his letters as determined by the practice or *habitus* he envisions and letting that practice turn into theological or theoretical rationalization? That is, I am convinced we need to think more about how Paul's theology is shaped by, if not determined by, his practical aims. Even if one is not willing to enter that world of thinking with me, one cannot deny the practice Paul enjoins on the siblings. Romans 12—16 then is but one example, and Galatians 5—6 another. All his letters have practice as their aim, and this fits perfectly into the classical world's theory of friendship where sibling growth was in part the responsibility of fellow siblings in a family. Again, Plutarch, "On Brotherly Love."[31]

Two more observations and we can wrap this study up: siblings are a boundaried community. Married couples retained their sibling relationships and sibling relationships were ranked in the ancient world superior to all relationships (*Nic. Eth.* 8.12.1–6). One text from Paul, not mentioned often enough in discussions, is Galatians 6:10: "So then, whenever we have an opportunity, let us work for the good of all, and especially for

---

30. Marsh et al., *Lived Theology.*
31. Plutarch, "On Brotherly Love," 12, 14.

those of the family of faith." That term "especially" both shows the importance of sibling relations/family relations among Christians but it also effects a boundary between the siblings/family and the "all." I conclude with this: Matthew 23:8 reads, "But you are not to be called rabbi, for you have one teacher, and you are all students." Sometimes one wonders what is in the mind of translators. The NIV has "students" instead of "brothers" and this is slightly amended by the CEV's "brothers and sisters." The latter two are right: Jesus told his closest followers that they were all siblings. He had said something similar in Mark 3:31–35 and 10:29–30.

Paul may be responsible for turning friendships into siblingships, but he got it from Jesus. Legs crossed, facing his disciples, Jesus taught his followers to embody a new kind of living together, one characterized as siblings. Paul followed suit.

Bibliography

Aasgaard, Reidar. *'My Beloved Brothers and Sisters!' Christian Siblingship in Paul.* London: T. & T. Clark, 2004.

Aristotle. *Nicomachean Ethics.* Translated by H. Rackham. Loeb Classical Library 73. Cambridge: Harvard University Press, 1926.

Best, Ernest. *Paul and His Converts.* The Sprunt Lectures 1985. Edinburgh: T. & T. Clark, 1988.

Blenkinsopp, Joseph. *Sage, Priest, Prophet: Religious and Intellectual Leadership in Ancient Israel.* Louisville: Westminster John Knox, 1995.

Chrysostom, Dio. *Discourses 1–11.* Translated by J. W. Cohoon. Loeb Classical Library 257. Cambridge: Harvard University Press, 1932.

Cicero. *On Old Age. On Friendship. On Divination.* Translated by W. A. Falconer. Loeb Classical Library 154. Cambridge: Harvard University Press, 1923.

Clarke, Andrew D. "Equality or Mutuality? Paul's Use of 'Brother' Language." In *The New Testament in Its First Century Setting: Essays in Honour of B. W. Winter on His 65th Birthday*, edited by P. J. Williams et al., 151–64. Grand Rapids: Eerdmans, 2004.

Dulles, Avery. *Models of the Church.* Second ed. New York: Image, 1991.

Dunn, James D. G. *The Epistles to the Colossians and to Philemon.* Grand Rapids: Eerdmans, 1996.

Enright, D. J., and David Rawlinson, eds. *The Oxford Book of Friendship.* New York: Oxford University Press, 1991.

Epstein, Joseph. *Friendship: An Exposé.* Boston: Houghton Mifflin, 2006.

Gaventa, Beverly R. *Our Mother Saint Paul.* Louisville: Westminster John Knox, 2007.

Harland, Philip. *Associations, Synagogues, and Congregations: Claiming a Place in Ancient Mediterranean Society.* Minneapolis: Fortress, 2003.

Horrell, David G. "From *Adelphoi* to *Oikos*: Social Transformation in Pauline Christianity." *Journal of Biblical Literature* 120 (2001) 293–311.

————. *Solidarity and Difference: A Contemporary Reading of Paul's Ethics.* 2nd ed. London: Bloomsbury T. & T. Clark, 2015.

Isocrates. "Letter 4: To Antipater." In *Volume III*, 411–22. Translated by La Rue Van Hook. Loeb Classical Library 373. Cambridge: Harvard University Press, 1945.

Konstan, David. *Friendship in the Classical World.* New York: Cambridge University Press, 1997.

Marsh, Charles, et al., eds. *Lived Theology: New Perspectives on Method, Style, and Pedagogy.* New York: Oxford University Press, 2016.

McKnight, Scot. "A Culture of Friendship." In *Pastor Paul: Nurturing a Culture of Christoformity in the Church*, 31–56. Theological Explorations for the Church Catholic. Grand Rapids: Brazos, 2019.

————. *The Letter to Colossians.* Grand Rapids: Eerdmans, 2018.

Minear, Paul S. *Images of the Church in the New Testament.* Philadelphia: Westminster, 1960.

Oliver, Mary. *Upstream: Selected Essays.* New York: Penguin, 2016.

Olyan, Saul M. *Friendship in the Hebrew Bible.* New Haven: Yale University Press, 2017.

Plutarch. "How a Man May Become Aware of His Progress in Virtue." In *Moralia, Volume I*, 397–458. Translated by Frank Cole Babbitt. Loeb Classical Library 197. Cambridge: Harvard University Press, 1927.

————. "How to Tell a Flatterer from a Friend." In *Moralia, Volume I*, 261–395. Translated by Frank Cole Babbitt. Loeb Classical Library 197. Cambridge: Harvard University Press, 1927.

————. "On Brotherly Love." In *Moralia, Volume VI*, 243–325. Translated by W. C. Helmbold. Loeb Classical Library 337. Cambridge: Harvard University Press, 1939.

Reumann, John. *Philippians: A New Translation with Introduction and Commentary.* Anchor Yale Bible Commentary 33B. New Haven: Yale University Press, 2008.

————. "Philippians, Especially Chapter 4, as a 'Letter of Friendship': Observations on a Checkered History of Scholarship." In *Friendship, Flattery, and Frankness of Speech: Studies on Friendship in the New Testament World*, edited by J. T. Fitzgerald, 83–106. Leiden: Brill, 1996.

Seneca. "On True and False Friendship." In *Epistles, Volume I: Epistles 1–65*, 9–13. Translated by Richard M. Gummere. Loeb Classical Library 75. Cambridge: Harvard University Press, 1917.

Thompson, Marianne Meye. *John: A Commentary.* New Testament Library. Louisville: Westminster John Knox, 2015.

Trebilco, Paul. *Self-Designations and Group Identity in the New Testament.* Cambridge: Cambridge University Press, 2012.

10

Wiri Nina *in the Body of Christ*

Considering Friendship from an African Perspective

David Fugoyo-Baime

The body of Christ is composed of Christ's friends! If friendship is removed from the body of Christ, the body collapses. Practicing Christians are members of one church, united spiritually in what the Apostle's Creed refers to as the "holy catholic [or universal] Church." The church cannot be confined to a single location because friends gather together to worship Christ as Lord all over the world (1 Cor 12:13–14). The church consists of people from all tribes and nations; geographical differences and national borders do not constitute a boundary for Christians regardless of the land they inhabit. Nor, as Paul says, is the church confined to one generation over another (Eph 3:21). In short, friendship with Christ unites Christians across all times and across every land.

Although the global church consists of so much diversity of tribes and tongues, the given contexts in which Christians find themselves matter for how they understand their friendship with Christ and the members of Christ's body. From my own context as a South Sudanese Christian currently living in Uganda, I seek to highlight the indispensable role of friendship—or *Wiri Nina*[1]—in the universal body of Christ,

---

1. As I will explain later in this chapter, *Wiri Nina* is used by the Azande people of South Sudan and literally means "son or daughter of my mother." *Wiri Nina* has different forms and plurals such as *Awirina* and *Awirinina*. In this paper, I will use the word *Wiri Nina* as representative of all forms.

the church. I will do so by assessing the cultural values of friendship and community many Africans hold in common, highlighting some of the ways African Christians build upon those values as the community of Christ's friends. The *Wiri Nina* that forms among Christians is further strengthened by the African cultural concept of *Ubuntu*, which denotes togetherness and mutual support. It is through *Wiri Nina* and *Ubuntu* that the indispensable role of friendship in the body of Christ in my context can be understood.

The Body of Christ as One Family

For Christians, the expanded family that is the body of Christ consists of Christ's friends. The concept of friendship appears throughout the Christian Bible: Ruth and Naomi, David and Jonathan, Daniel and his three friends, Jesus and Lazarus and his sisters, etc.

Jesus was no stranger to friendship; the formation of friendships was central to the way he lived.. Consider the familiar yet striking passage in John 15:

> This is my commandment, that you love one another as I have loved you. No one has greater love than this, to lay down one's life for one's friends. *You are my friends if you do what I command you.* I do not call you servants any longer, because the servant does not know what the master is doing; but I have called you friends, because I have made known to you everything that I have heard from my Father. You did not choose me but I chose you. And I appointed you to go and bear fruit, fruit that will last, so that the Father will give you whatever you ask him in my name. (John 15:12–16, emphasis added)

Jesus was explaining to his disciples what friendship looks like and who he considers to be his friends. He also wanted his disciples to see him as their friend and brother, not their master. Rather than the relationship between that of a servant and a master, Jesus identified his disciples as his friends and, even closer, as family members.

The concepts of siblinghood and friendship are not mutually exclusive for Jesus. Matthew reports this: "And pointing to his disciples, he said, 'Here are my mother and my brothers! For whoever does the will of my Father in heaven is my brother and sister and mother" (Matt 12:49–50). In the days of his flesh, Jesus belonged to a biological family.

He was considered one of the sons of Joseph the Carpenter. In Matthew's account, the people who came looking for Jesus were his biological family (Matt 12:46–47). In his response, Jesus did not deny his biological family, but he expanded his family to include all who followed him (Matt 12:49–50). He pointed to his spiritual family where only those who followed him by serving others belonged. Jesus saw his disciples as friends and siblings with a shared task to go and befriend others. Paul continued Jesus's emphasis on friendship, making more disciples and including all those who followed Jesus during and after the time of the disciples (Rom 14:15, 21; 1 Cor 8:13).

The body of Christ consists of a family of believers, and every member of the family is a brother or a sister to one another. Samuel Ngewa explains, "Each group [in Africa] traces its origin to a particular hero."[2] For African Christians, Jesus is the hero of the community, serving as the community's cornerstone and the reason it exists. Just as any person belongs to a family with which they identify, Christians belong to the body of Christ. Christ welcomes them into this community by the power of the Holy Spirit. All those belonging to Christ's body are members of one family and one community—the community that is expansive, inclusive, and gathers together to worship Christ. Whoever does the will of God— irrespective of tribe, nation, and tongue—belongs to this community.

Friendship and Brotherhood as Cultural Values

Although this expansion of who is considered to be one's family is driven by Scripture for the Christian, it also resonates with traditional African cultural values. Friendship and brotherhood[3] are intertwined in their meaning. Though there are distinct words for friendship and brotherhood in most of the African languages, the two concepts are occasionally used interchangeably. In the Swahili language, for example, there are the words: *Urafiki* and *Undugu*. *Urafiki* means friendship or companionship. The word also refers to the relationship between associates, colleagues, or people who turn to one another for help in times of need. *Undugu*, on the other hand, means brotherhood and refers to a close family association

2. Ngewa, *What is the Church?*, 1431.

3. I use the term "brotherhood" rather than "siblinghood" here because of the translation from Swahili into English. However, I do not mean to exclude women from my use of this term.

by blood. Though the two Swahili words are distinct in their connotation, one can still call one's friend a brother or a sister and vice versa. Practically speaking, there is not a big gap between a friend and a brother or sister in the two Swahili terms.

Africans are conditioned by their culture to view non-biological family members as brothers and sisters, and the same concept is extended to non-community members—unless there is a reason not to do so. In other words, people who are not from one's community are not enemies until they are proven to be enemies; they are friends until proven to be otherwise. It is commonplace for many Africans to consider their friends to be their brothers or sisters. For example, although Iningo was my close childhood friend and not a relative, my mother would often allow me to visit Iningo and spend a few nights with him in his family's home. Iningo and I slept on the same bed because we considered one another as brother and friend. An African proverb says, "To be without a friend is to be poor indeed." Failure to have a friend is a failure to have a brother. He or she who does not have a brother is poor. Although economic poverty is loathed, one should not be blamed for this; however, if one lacks friends, many would conclude that the individual is to blame for this much more serious form of poverty. Friendship is wealth: wealth of wisdom, advice, companionship, and much more. Just as a financially wealthy person is able to eat decent food and pay medical bills, a person with friends often enjoys protection, security, and assistance in times of need. When one is in trouble, friends come to help; when one has lost a relative, friends come to dig the grave and bury the dead; when one seeks to be married, friends contribute their resources to make it possible. Friends even help defend one another when an enemy arises. For these reasons and many more, one is only whole amidst one's friends.

Friendship with Christ and *Wiri Nina*

The term *Wiri Nina*, used by the Azande people of South Sudan, literally means "son or daughter of my mother." The term is also used to refer to a close friend. Although *Bakure* is the common word for friend among the Azande, *Wiri Nina* is semantically stronger. *Wiri Nina* expresses proximity more than *Bakure*. Consider the following uses of *Wiri Nina*:

- The term is used to refer to a blood sibling. When people are born into one family, have stayed in one place for a long time, and have eaten together, the people are considered to have developed a strong relationship which cannot be easily broken. The most important element in this relationship is blood. Blood provides a nearly unbreakable bond between siblings. In a traditional African community, blood is considered the most precious element in the human body. Blood is also believed to carry one's being. In other words, my blood is me and I am my blood. In some communities, if a person wanted to get into a very close relationship with another person, the two would cut themselves to the point of bleeding. They would then bring their wounds into contact and slightly rub them against each other. This act means the two bloods have become very close if not joined together as one. Siblings take pride in a blood relationship and are there to help, care for, and defend their siblings when needed.

- The term is also used to refer to a close associate or colleague. Communities consist of members who are not necessarily blood relatives, but these people are able to contribute positively to the life of the community. These people can still be called *Wiri Nina* because of their significant contributions to a particular person, family, or community.

- The term is used to refer to a close friend. Friends call each other *Wiri Nina* because they know their relationship is even stronger than that of siblings. Hebrew poetry implies this when it says "a true friend sticks closer than one's nearest kin" (Prov 18:24). Friendship is based not on material benefit, but mutual support and care for one another.

- The term is also used among lovers. When you love a person, you can call the person *Wiri Nina*. This type of love is the kind that exists between friends, community members, relatives, siblings, etc. It is the kind of love where one cares about and takes care of another. This love does not normally apply to romantic love. Instead, romantic lovers would use the term *Bakure* (for a male) or *Nakure* (for a female) to refer to each other rather than the term *Wiri Nina*.

The common thread running through the concept of *Wiri Nina* is love. Love is reflected in the proximity between a person and the care they show for the other. A person cannot call another person *Wiri Nina* when there is an absence of love, proximity, and care. *Wiri Nina* is a strong term used when referring to a friend.

Wiri Nina is also used among Christians and carries a similar significance and meaning. However, when used among Christians, it expresses a deeper bond than that which is formed by blood, community, friendship, or love. This bond is found in Christ and unites Christians as equal members and friends no matter where each individual comes from. Friendship with Christ necessitates that Christians are friends with the members of Christ's body and makes it possible for all Christians to be called *Wiri Nina* despite their location, culture, skin color, or language.

As *Wiri Nina*, Christians are expected to care for one another because of the special bond they have as members of Christ's body. According to Paul Wadell, friendship with God does not end with God, but teaches Christians to practice friendship among themselves as one community.[4] God is a good God and whoever comes to him learns from him. Approaching God, one finds a faithful friend who does not change. If Christians are friends with God, they should learn about friendship from God and implement the same in the community of believers.

Friendship in the body of Christ is not meant to be confined among isolated pairs or groups of individuals; rather, it is meant to unify the body of Christ as one community. The goal of *Wiri Nina* not only among some Christians but among a united community is difficult to achieve, yet it resonates with a deep cultural value of community. In his book, *Biblical Christianity in African Perspective*, Wilbur O'Donovan highlights the importance of community in many African contexts. He says that

> the community is where you get your values and beliefs and your early training in life. It is the community where you establish the deepest and most enduring relationships of life. It is the group of people from which you derive your name and your identity as a person. It is the community in which you find a sense of purpose in life because you help to make it what it is.[5]

In light of the importance of community, the significance of the *church* community takes a central role in the life of many African Christians. O'Donovan continues, identifying that

> the church is the community where you are to get your values and beliefs and your early training in the Christian life. It is the

4. Wadell, *Becoming Friends*, 21, 27.

5. O'Donovan, *Biblical Christianity*, 155–56.

community where you will establish the deepest and most en-during relationships in life. It is the group of people from which you derive your name as a Christian and your identity as a child of God.[6]

"The body of Christ" is a metaphor developed by Paul (1 Cor 12:1–31). In the metaphor, Paul identifies his fellow followers of Jesus Christ as the key ingredient that makes up the body. The body is composed of the people of God who are united in Christ through the baptism of the Spirit (1 Cor 12:13). These people are repentant, converted, and united with Christ.[7] The body of Christ does not only give these people a sense of belonging with other individuals in the present; it also connects Christians to a larger body of believers in the past, present, and future. Samuel Kunhiyop explains that the community of the body of Christ

> resonates with Africans because of the scope of this community. It includes all believers worldwide and each local community (church) and is also connected to the past (believers who have died) and to the future (those who have yet to be born spiritually). This way of seeing the church acknowledges the role of our spiritual ancestors. These ancestors are the believing dead (Hebrew and Christian) who are interested in our lives and exert influence over them, serving as examples and encouragements for us.[8]

Just as an individual is integral to the formation of the community, a Christian is integral to the formation of the body of Christ in the present and connected to the body of Christ in the past and future. The community nurtures the individual with values, a sense of belonging, and other necessities that enable them to live a flourishing life.

The Community of Christ's Friends and *Ubuntu*

The spirit of togetherness many African Christians value and find present in community is supported by the cultural concept of *Ubuntu*. The concept originated from a Nguni Bantu term which simply means "humanity." Semantically, the word expresses value for humanity, unity, and togetherness. *Ubuntu* underscores oneness in a community, challenging

6. O'Donovan, *Biblical Christianity*, 155–56.

7. Davis, *The Local Church*, 103.

8. Kunhiyop, *African Christian Theology*, 146.

any human attempt to live alone, isolated from others, and estranged from human community. Pragmatically, the concept promotes unity, generosity, love, and the support of one another.[9]

Oko Elechi observes that, "Ubuntu . . . captures the underlying African world-view that expresses Africa's egalitarian, humanistic, interconnectedness, communitarian and participatory democratic values."[10] The way of life captured by the concept of *Ubuntu* is so captivating that many Africans have come to believe that Africans could be the next catalyst for good relationships in the world. Steve Biko, a well-known South African politician and anti-apartheid activist, believed that Africans would help the world create and sustain stronger relationships. "We believe that in the long run, the special contribution to the world by Africa will be in the field of human relationships. The great powers of the world may have done wonders in giving the world an industrial and military look, but the great gift still has to come from Africa—giving the world a more human face."[11]

Ubuntu helps illuminate why friendship is so integral to the African way of life. This is also why the concept of *Ubuntu* is typically summarized as, "I am because we are, and since we are, therefore I am."[12] Desmond Tutu echoes the same sentiment by saying, "A person is a person through other persons. None of us comes into the world fully formed. We would not know how to think, or walk, or speak, or behave as human beings unless we learned it from other human beings. We need other human beings in order to be human."[13] This means that when I hurt another person or work against them, I actually hurt and work against myself. Instead, I should love the person as a brother and friend, forming bonds with others in my own community deep enough to be called *Wiri Nina*.

Childhood and Ubuntu

Ubuntu is instilled at childhood. A child is taught to live as part of a community not as an individual, but as one who shares whatever one has—especially commodities such as food, drink, and clothing. In South

9. Tutu, *No Future Without Forgiveness*, 31; Eze, *Race*, 32.

10. Elechi et al., "Restoring Justice," 73.

11. Coetzee and Roux, *The African Philosophy Reader*, 30.

12. Mbiti, *African Religions*, 113.

13. Tutu, *God Has a Dream*, 25.

Sudan and many other parts of Africa, it is common that a child lives and is taken care of by an aunt or an uncle, even when the parents of the child are alive and present. This helps the child understand that everyone in the family and community is equal to and as important as his or her parents. As a child, I lived with my mother's eldest sister. Growing up, I understood that my aunt was my mother and my mother was *also* my mother! One day, my aunt bought a local cake for her biological daughter, Annie. After letting Annie know the cake was hers, my aunt divided the cake into pieces and distributed it among the five other children who were present, including me. As she was distributing the cake she said to Annie, "You need to share it with the rest of your own because they are also my children—just like you!" My aunt was teaching us the importance of siblinghood, and was trying to discourage a spirit of individualism. She stressed the fact that we were more than kids playing together in the neighborhood; we were to see one another as close family, as friends, and as equal members of the community. She was helping us see one another as *Wiri Nina*.

Belonging to one communal family while coming from different biological families is a central characteristic of African family life. Extended families include biological and non-biological children, cousins, aunts, uncles, and many others. For this reason, African families tend to be large. Living in extended families ideally trains children not to be selfish and abhorrent to the non-biological fellows in the community. This is a fundamental element in the concept of *Ubuntu*, where people must live for one another, not only for themselves. Child upbringing does not fall on the biological parents alone, but every adult in the family. This means every adult is responsible for the upbringing and training of every child. That is why it is commonly said in Africa, "It takes a whole village to raise a child."

A child is encouraged to befriend the "good" children in the neighborhood. In fact, a child can be scolded or punished for sitting in the room alone, eating alone, and not playing with the rest of the children in the neighborhood. Many children spend more time with their friends and other community members than with their parents. This type of child upbringing helps the child to understand the importance of life together with people in a community. Since the idea of extended family helps the child to embrace non-nuclear family members, friendship with outsiders becomes easy as long as it is between people who pose no danger to one another. These values instilled in children help them place significant value on friendship and community throughout their lives. These cultural values are practiced by both Christian and non-Christian families. For the Christian families, they consider such values to be promoted by Proverbs 22:6: "Train children in the right way, and when old, they will not stray."

Respect of Strangers

Ubuntu shapes many values within the community including how members of the community should treat strangers. By "stranger," I mean a person who does not live in one's immediate community or have a blood relationship with the family he or she interacts with. For example, a missionary may come to a small town in Uganda for a medical outreach program. The missionary is not a family member but has come to the village for a good cause. As long as the missionary is in the territories of the local people, he or she is a stranger and deserves the respect of the indigenous community. The stranger must not only be respected but treated well and taken care of by the community. Everyone in the community including the children should greet the person with signs of love, care, and hospitality. A familiar example of this can be seen when children and adults stand by roadsides leading in and out of villages to greet visitors with welcoming gestures and chants. Whoever does not offer hospitality to strangers in these ways and others works against the values and health of the community.

Approaching Enemies of the Community

Strangers are different from enemies. Strangers hail from different tribes or communities and are to be respected by the local community members. A stranger may or may not be friendly—possibly an enemy. Culturally, an enemy of a community is any person who stands against the progress or cultural values of a community. Likewise, an individual's enemy is anyone who works against the individual's progress or welfare. An enemy may choose to show or hide his or her antagonistic attitudes toward the one he or she hates. Enemies are not *Wiri Nina* because they have broken the fundamental tenet of *Ubuntu*—social togetherness and support for one another. Because of this, from a traditional cultural perspective, an enemy is to be hated and, if possible, be destroyed.

Enmity can be historical between the ancestors of different communities, tribes, or clans. This type of enmity can exist for decades and be passed on to the next generations. In this case, all members of one rival clan or community are enemies of the other clan. The two communities live in antagonism, and fighting can occur periodically, even over petty issues. In West Africa, for example, it is believed that one's misfortunes are always caused by an enemy. That is why a person in trouble seeks help from a diviner—a person who will reveal the identity of the enemy responsible for one's misfortunes.[14]

A close family or community member may even turn out to be an enemy. Even more troubling is when a seemingly devoted *Wiri Nina* turns out to be an enemy. It is also possible that the person who pretends to be your friend is actually your worst enemy, and Africans know this very well.[15] A Ghanaian writer expressed this in a powerful way:

> for it may happen that your most intimate of friends
> Can turn out the most treacherous of friends
> Actually at the helm plotting your downfall;
> At the helm of the mechanics planning your death.
> There is no man without an enemy.[16]

However, central to the Christian faith is a challenge to how one treats not only their friends and neighbors, but also their enemies. Although *Wiri Nina* is limited to only those who support and care for others, Christians are given the additional task of extending love to their enemies—even to the point where they might reconcile and become *Wiri Nina*. While the shared cultural value is to respect strangers, the Christian value calls love to be extended to the stranger and enemy alike (Luke 6:27). This love of neighbor and enemy is at the heart of the ministry of reconciliation that should be the defining characteristics of the church community—ministry that the church learns from their *Wiri Nina*, Jesus Christ (2 Cor 5:18–20).

Wiri Nina and Ubuntu in the Body of Christ

In its essence, the church cannot be an entity comprised of individuals, nor does it belong to or can be dominated by one person. Ina Gräbe

14. Adams, *The Cultural Grounding*, 949.

15. Adams, *The Cultural Grounding*, 949.

16. Kyei, *No Time to Die*, 72.

explains that Paul's metaphorical phrase, "you are the body of Christ" (v. 27), consists of two fundamental parts: (1) The "you" as we read it today, which includes all generations of people in the body of Christ to the present, and (2) The vehicle which is the body of Christ. It is through this vehicle that Jesus's body remains active in the world to the present.[17]

Paul's metaphor of the body of Christ highlights the dependence of the diverse parts of the body on each other. If members of the body of Christ do not depend on one another, different parts of the body will run the risk of atrophy and death. Robert Saucy has drawn three important truths from the analogy of the relationship between the natural body and members of the church as follows:

1. *Unity*: just as a natural body is composed of many members, the church is comprised of different individuals and communities.[18] In 1 Corinthians 12, Paul emphasizes the importance of the gifts of the Spirit in the church. Though the members have different spiritual gifts, they still have the same Spirit that unites them. This resonates with the concept of *Ubuntu*, where different community members are to live in unity, care for one another, and contribute their unique gifts for the overall good of the community.

2. *Diversity*: the fact that one body consists of different parts shows that the body is diverse. The diversity of the body of Christ is good and beautiful; the different backgrounds, nations, tribes, and tongues make the flourishing of the church possible. The inclusive and diverse nature of the church is a strength built upon biblical principles—principles reflected in the orthodoxy and orthopraxy of Christians. In other words, those who believe in Christ must also follow and act like him who is "the head of the body, the church" (Col 1:18). This is not to say that following Christ means to assume the role of the head of the body; that is Christ's position alone. Faith entails both belief in Christ as the head of the church and a commitment to learning through practice in diverse community what one's unique role is in Christ's body.

3. *Mutuality*: just as different body parts depend on all other parts of the body to live and make possible the ongoing vitality of the body Christians must depend on one another to serve God. Love must be central in order for Christians to live together. *Wiri Nina* regards love as the central element for friends, relatives, and siblings to live together.

17. Gräbe, *Aspekte van poetiese taalgebruik*, 12.

18. Saucy, *The Church in God's Program*, 26–27.

This love makes the stronger family members care and help the weaker members. In the same way, the different gifts, weaknesses, and inabilities among some Christian members are strengthened and supported by other members—and by this the whole body remains strong. 1 Peter 4:10 reads, "Each one should use whatever gift you have received to serve others." Each member needs and depends on another member's gifts. By the usage of metaphors, Paul wanted to communicate the importance of unity among Christians wherever they are. Metaphors are not used by Paul for mere illustration; they are there to inform and create reality.

In addition to these lessons from Paul regarding the body of Christ, John 15 contains four important elements that must exist in the community of Christ's friends—concepts which resonate strongly with the type of bond entailed by those who know and call one another *Wiri Nina*. The first is love. Jesus said, "Love one another as I have loved you" (John 15:12). Scripture is full of love among friends. For example, 1 Corinthians 13 speaks to love among the members of the body of Christ; we read that Jonathan loved David like himself (1 Sam 18:1); and Proverbs says, "A friend loves at all times, and kinsfolk are born to share adversity" (Prov 17:17). Love must have humility and be the driving force for Christians to meet the needs of others. Whereas worldly love can be emotional and object-oriented, true Christian love is sacrificial and practiced among friends and enemies within and beyond the body of Christ. Christians are tasked with not only loving their friends and relative, but also, as I have stressed before, their enemies. Christ said, "Love your enemies, do good to those who hate you" (Luke 6:27). Loving one's enemies is what differentiates Christians from others. As Jesus told his disciples, "If you love those who love you, what credit is that to you? Even sinners love those who love them" (Luke 6:32).

The second element is sacrifice. Sacrifice means the readiness and willingness to offer oneself up to harm, adversity, struggle, or unpleasant circumstances for the sake of one's friend. Jesus said, "Greater love has no one than this: to lay down one's life for one's friends" (John 15:13). A true friend does not look for what benefits him at the expense of his friends, but he looks for what benefits his friends even at his own expense.

The third element is obedience. Obedience among friends cements the friendship. Friends ought to obey and support one another: "You are my friends if you do what I command" (John 15:14). Obedience among friends is the evidence that the friends are considerate of each other.

Obedience entails listening and supporting one another in all of life's circumstances.

The fourth element that must exist is sharing. Friends share their own possessions, time, and passions with their friends. Jesus told his disciples that he was now letting them know they were his friends and that he shared with them everything he received from his Father (John 15:15). John is one biblical example among many others which illuminate the life Jesus calls his *Wiri Nina* to live out of obedience to Christ and as an outworking of what life with Christ entails. Because Christ has made us his *Wiri Nina*, friendship is at the center of Christian practice. It is commonly said, "Show me your friends and I will show you who you are." As Christians, it is through the faces and lives of our *Wiri Nina* that others can see Christ.

Conclusion

In this chapter, have discussed the body of Christ and how the members of the body are not siblings and friends. The body of Christ is a union of friends—of *Wiri Nina*—brought together by the head of the body, Jesus. They are friends even if they have never met physically. Friendship is valued so highly among African Christians both because of their Christian faith and because of the cultural value on friendship, community, and *Ubuntu*. Because the body of Christ is meant to serve Christ, it should not boast or be egocentric. The body of Christ should work for the betterment of every member of the community. Members of the body of Christ should also think of others beyond their local borders. Each *Wiri Nina* is to be concerned with and participate in the advancement of the kingdom of God throughout the whole world.

In regard to friendship, three points should be remembered: First, friendship is fundamental to the life of African Christians; it is not an option but a way of life. Life is meaningful in the presence and company of friends. An African proverb says, "Between true friends, even water drunk together is sweet enough." Second, status and color should not be barriers in forming and sustaining friendships. Friendship is built on history, mutual benefits, or a common goal. Status does not matter because people from different economic and social statuses can be friends. In most cases, wealth is generated by the poor and the wealthy depend on the poor for creating more wealth. True wealth is the wealth of friendship.

Third, friendship is often strong between people from different cultures. For example, if I have friends in the United States of America, I am a strong man because I am able to make and keep friends from a distance. Fourth, respect is paramount in friendship. Respect here includes valuing what one's friend values and viewing one's friend as an equal partner. Respect is crucial especially in relation to the elderly in the community. A younger person is expected to respect an older person. The younger should serve the older.

Friendship is indispensable because it is more related to being (who a person is) rather than doing. This friendship goes beyond the borders of the continent of Africa. It is a friendship that embraces people from all over the world. To make friends outside the continent of Africa in the body of Christ has been my joy and pride. Such friendship has contributed to the cementing of the Christian faith in my own life and ministry as mutual teaching and learning have taken place. Friendship makes members of the body of Christ feel like they belong to one tribe. All Christians are tribesmen. Tribesmen fight together and help each other in times of need. As an example, a western Christian friend is able to assist an African Christian friend to attain training for ministry. Likewise, an African Christian friend is able to help a western Christian friend learn more about living as a true community member of the body of Christ. *Wiri Nina* support one another without expecting a reward; we do so as the body of Christ always for the sake of the kingdom of God.

Bibliography

Adams, Glenn. "The Cultural Grounding of Personal Relationship: Enemyship in North American and West African Worlds." *Journal of Personality and Social Psychology* 88 (2005) 948–68.

Coetzee, P. H., and A. P. J. Roux, eds. *The African Philosophy Reader*. London: Routledge, 1998.

Davies, John Keith. *The Local Church: A Living Body*. Durham: Evangelical, 1998.

Elechi, O. Oko, et al., eds. "Restoring Justice (Ubuntu): An African Perspective." *International Criminal Justice Review* 20.1 (2010) 73–85.

Eze, Chielozona. *Race, Decolonization, and Global Citizenship in South Africa*. Rochester: University of Rochester Press, 2018.

Gräbe, Ina. *Aspekte van poetiese taalgebruik: teoretiese verkenning cn toepassing*. Potchefstroom, Suid-Afrika: Potchefstroomse Universiteit, 1984.

Kunhiyop, Samuel Waje. *African Christian Theology*. Nairobi: Hippo, 2012.

Kyei, Kojo Gyinaye. *No Time to Die: A Book of Poems*. Accra: Catholic, 1975.

Mbiti, John. *African Religions and Philosophy*. 2nd ed. Oxford: Heinemann, 1990.

Meilaender, Gilbert. *Friendship: A Study in Theological Ethics*. Notre Dame: University of Notre Dame Press, 1985.

Ngewa, Samuel. "What is Church?" In *Africa Bible Commentary*, edited by Tokunboh Adeyemo, 1420–41. Nairobi: Word Alive, 2006.

O'Donovan, Wilbur. *Biblical Christianity in African Perspective*. Carlisle: Paternoster, 2000.

Ridderbos, Herman N. *Paul: An Outline of His Theology*. Translated by John Richard de Witt. Grand Rapids: Eerdmans, 1975.

Saucy, Robert L. *The Church in God's Program*. Chicago: Moody, 1972.

Simon, Caroline. *The Disciplined Heart: Love, Destiny, and Imagination*. Grand Rapids: Eerdmans, 1997.

Tutu, Desmond. *God Has a Dream: A Vision of Hope for Our Time*. New York: Doubleday, 2004.

———. *No Future Without Forgiveness*. New York: Doubleday, 1999.

Wadell, Paul. *Becoming Friends: Worship, Justice, and the Practice of Christian Friendship*. Grand Rapids: Brazos, 2002.

11

Of All These Friends and Lovers
Remembering the Body and the Blood

Craig Keen

1

Dennis Okholm and I shared an office wall at Azusa Pacific University from late summer, 2003, until my retirement in May, 2017. We were hired at the same time to fill two recently vacated slots in the Theology Department and moved to Los Angeles from two different institutions in the Chicago area. We hadn't known each other previously, but we quickly became friends. We shared similar views, theologically, politically, and socially. That no doubt helped. We were not, however, in complete agreement. For example, I think I was and am more Protestant than Okholm, even if oddly, Wesleyan that I have long been. Still, I am a Wesleyan whose first love was the quite Lutheran Søren Kierkegaard. Okholm's theological inclinations are a mixture of Reformed and monastic spirituality and theology.[1] The importance of the virtues in monasticism inclined Okholm to put considerable weight on the phenomenon of *friendship*.[2] I, too, am a great fan of friendship and, more concretely, of friends. However, I fear that I am less inclined than he is to find smooth continuity between

---

1. We both have trouble distinguishing the terms "spirituality" and "theology."

2. See Okholm, *Monk Habits*; Okholm, *Dangerous Passions, Deadly Sins*. One of Okholm's favorite courses to teach is his senior seminar on friendship and community.

friendship and the strangely ambiguous events, "neighbor love" and "faith."[3]

2

It is good to enter into the life of someone whose ideas and practices resonate with the ones that are most at play in one's own life, to spend time working and talking and thinking together, laughing and crying, remembering and planning, studying and hypothesizing—together. It is good to trust another with your secrets and to find her over time not to have betrayed your trust. It is good to be trusted with *her* secrets and not to have betrayed *her* trust. It is good to have been so implicated in one another's history that you both know that, however long you may live and work apart, no warmup will be necessary when once more you find yourselves in the same close space and time. Not every phenomenon called friendship has come to such intimacy, but even casual acquaintance is drawn in that direction, it seems to me.

Of course, friends must differ, if only that there be room for deference. A friend is never one's clone, never *simply* another *me*. One of life's delights is to be surprised by a friend. And yet, to be delightful, a surprise must resonate with something in me. A disturbance in the Force has to be quickly sublated and unity restored, preferably enriched, or a friendship has been wounded, if not killed. That is, friendship has a certain nonuniform integrity. It moves with the vitality of anticipation, tending reconcilingly. It is the laughter after a punchline, the sigh after the relaxation of tension, the applause after a hot saxophone solo. The difference of friendship must yield in the end, however complexly, to one or another variety of "again." In friendship, difference never *overwhelms* identity.

The beauty of friendship is due in part to its contingency. Most of the persons we meet will never be our friends. Even when we spend extended periods of time with another person—on a committee, on a work crew, in a class, in a prison cell—there is no guarantee that when we part we will have had more than a formally collegial relationship, if that. It is also a sad, but ordinary feature of friendship that it ends. One with whom I once enjoyed a trusting, jovial, resonant relationship, I may now find cold and distant or not to have changed with life as I have, so that we no

---

3. I'm thinking of Søren Kierkegaard's account of the former and Karl Barth's account of the latter.

longer nourish each other. Even if this does not occur, odds are that one of us will die before the other. There are loves that may outlive the beloved, but friendship is not one of them. There may be a longing for a lost friend, but friendship requires at least the prospect of a return of affection and without it, friendship will wither and die. It is the conditionality and ephemerality of friends that marks the relationship's desirability. It is no wonder that Aristotle spoke of friendship so highly as he thought through the patterns that make for a richly happy life.[4]

And yet, the gospel is not to be confused with a report of a happy life, however well explained. Certainly, the gospel concerns peace, and the Hebrew *shalom* is not in every respect different from the Greek *eudaimonia,* both naming something like *well-being.* And yet *eudaimonia* offers itself to be *understood,* it is thought as continuous with the other goods of a life well-lived, of a cosmos well-ordered. The *shalom,* the *eirene,* i.e., the peace, of the gospel "passeth all understanding," the gospel tells us. It does not fit neatly as a puzzle piece in the jigsaw puzzle of phenomenal and supra-phenomenal life. In fact, the peace that makes the news of Jesus good is a peace that clashes with what any reasonable human being would mark as "happy," as is signaled with even the most casual consideration of the mutilated body that comes out of the tomb on Easter morning. What, then, does friendship signify for *theology*? How is the *theologian* to understand good and true and beautiful phenomena, such as this one? What is the place in particular of friendship in a *cruciform* life, one that takes up its *cross* and follows *Jesus,* one that has "the mind of Christ," one that heeds the hard saying of Jesus, "Whoever comes to me and does not hate father and mother, wife and children, brothers and sisters, yes, and even life itself, cannot be my disciple" (Luke 14:26)? Does this not foreclose for one faithful to the gospel the possibility of friendship? And yet, what could be good about the news that life is to be lived without friends?

4. Aristotle, *Nicomachean Ethics,* 7:2–3: "[To] a friend we say we ought to wish what is good for his sake. But . . . goodwill *when it is reciprocal* [is] friendship. . . . To be friends, then, they must be mutually recognized as bearing goodwill and wishing well to each other . . . . Perfect friendship is the friendship of men who are good, and alike in virtue; for these wish well alike to each other qua good, and they are good themselves." Emphasis added.

3

It has been argued that among the most epochal of the outcomes of the economy that first emerged in Greece with the era of the Pre-socratic philosophers was the drive to think and imagine all things together in a gap-less, *calculable* whole.[5] Indeed, each of the "first philosophers,"[6] the first to think in the way we habitually name "philosophy," pressed hard to situate everyone and all within an idea that would provide them with a neatly apportioned home. And it does seem true that in about 600 BC, for the first time in human history, certain officials, first in the vicinity of Lydia, then throughout Greece,[7] assigned a monetary exchange value to everything within their jurisdiction and by the threat of violence imposed that valuation on everyone living there. If a soldier wanted a goatherd to give him a wedge of cheese and some onions, he would know the monetary value assigned to them and would have been issued coins for just such an exchange[8]—an exchange that the goatherd would be authoritatively coerced into accepting. The goatherd might then use those same coins to pay taxes or might purchase one or more items with them from someone else, at the official price. In this way all things of use to the masters of usefulness came to be situated within an abstract quantitative economic system. And since items within systems entail one another, even their relationships would be determined by the logic of money.

Thus we might say that Greece of the seventh or sixth century BC became the world's first *thoroughly* monetized economy/society/culture.[9] Its mode of life thus differed decidedly from the economy, say, of a tiny, isolated village of three households, of fifty people, all struggling together to survive, none of them regularly, if ever, meeting a stranger, never imagining the concrete affairs of daily life to be translatable into monetary exchanges between neighbors or members of a household.[10]

5. This is one of the most important conclusions of Richard Seaford in his important work *Money and the Early Greek Mind*.

6. That there were *first* philosophers might call quite a lot of the assumptions of Western Civilization into question.

7. And later throughout Europe and then the lands colonized by it.

8. Coins worth more than the material into which an authorized image had been pressed.

9. Of course, there was money long before this, but not, it is argued by Seaford, a thoroughly monetized economy.

10. Barter seems to be secondary to monetization. In any case barter already operates within the logic of money, quantifying economics and imagining mathematical

In a *thoroughly* monetized economy there could by definition be nothing that might slip through its interlocked fingers, which by decree would hold everything. Food, drink, shelter, hearth, and home; indeed, all goods would thus translate to money. There would be nothing outside the system, except perhaps a not yet or no longer organized raw material, electrum, say, a kind of chaos, an indefiniteness waiting for a craftsperson-accountant (a *dēmiourgos*) to give it or restore it to value. Is it good? Is it true? Is it beautiful? Thought and imagination would, at its best, respond not crudely, but delicately, and yet still monetarily, i.e., calculatively, however sublimely, according to the tilt of the scales. And so, the noblest of categories, *justice*, might be depicted as a goddess brandishing a sword and a pair of scales—and Anaximander's sole surviving fragment, written in the morning of this era of "new money," might gesture toward such an economy of justice: "But from whatever things is the genesis of the things that are, into these they must pass away according to necessity; for they must pay the penalty and make atonement to one another for their injustice according to Time's decree."[11] Friendship, a kind of justice, would in a monetized logic be unthinkable without reciprocity. In a thoroughly monetized economy, scales must always balance.

4

Of course, 600 BC was a long time ago. Monetization spread slowly. It takes time and adequate administrative technique to lay hold of and command all exploitable hectares of a planet the size of the Earth. And if some acres have not yet in every respect yielded to its accounting, they, too, lie within its bullish acquisitive gaze. At least in terms of our imagination we have, for a little while now, come to live and move and have our being in the comprehensive, planetary advent of this Lydian lord. That is, the logic of money has in our time come to so dominate our ambitions that we can hardly imagine life otherwise. It was a long march from a sparsely populated world of tiny, widely separated, and desperately poor villages to the unimaginable concomitant density and loneliness of the modern megacity and the wealth it has (selectively) generated. It took centuries of expansion of the empires of Macedon and Rome in antiquity, centuries of cultural experimentation amid the rubble of Rome's dissolution, centuries to rise in the Renaissance—face turned to the imagined

---

equivalences between goods.

11. Jaeger, *The Theology of the Early Greek Philosophers*, 36.

faint glow of a golden age—and centuries of the prolonged outworking of a program carried out by gunboats, developers, missionaries, and deep hold cargo vessels.[12] It took a long time, but the journey in our time is all but over.

But what if even now there were not only such a system holding us together, insisting on mutual benefit, balanced books? What if even now one's meeting another really were meeting an *other*—one who would not succumb to the logic of debt and repayment, of investment and return, of an echoing "like calling out to like"? What if even now there were no way from *me* to *you* or from *you* to *me* except across what calculation would always dismiss as unbridgeable, as a void? What if behind or beside or after calculation there were no *analogia entis* binding neighbors together, no system of reciprocity to which they must conform? What if even in the act of exchange every coin were counterfeit, better rasped away and consigned to the dust of the ground, than paid to another human being for the fruit of her labor, however honorably and beautifully? What if, that is, there was a way to a neighbor that could never be purchased, but only gifted, for-given, freely, without strings or contract?

5

Forgiveness, according to the gospel, is not by good will overcoming resentfulness or pretending one has not been wronged. It is not magnanimously carrying the weight of another's misdeed, humbly bigger than one's offender. It is a slippage out from under the weight of deeds and misdeeds, a letting go of any and all debt, of all that gravity would drive to a crushing end. It is a deferral to an outside roomy enough for us all, an outside in every respect nonetheless terrifyingly righteous, i.e., holy.

The God of the gospel is indeed holy, as high and lifted up, as fearfully inaccessible, as "the Lord of hosts" whom Isaiah confronts in the temple.[13] Isaiah, humiliated by the encounter survives only because seraphs with fire burn away his "uncleanness." Jesus, by no means less obeisant to the holy God of Israel, is a more complicated story. According to every standard of purity in which his work is situated, anyone is rendered unclean—and thus barred from the holy God—who moves into intimate

---

12. Kipling, "The White Man's Burden," 323: "To seek another's profit / And work another's gain."

13. Dunn, "Jesus and Holiness," 169.

solidarity with the unclean: every contact with a leper or a menstruating woman or a corpse, every meal with tax collectors and sinners, and certainly every lacerating blow at the hands of the enforcers of Empire and temple, tearing deeply into and mutilating one's body—above all if that body breathes its last nailed to a cross alongside no-accounts.

Of course, the gospels energetically place Jesus at the heart of such scenes. Yet in doing so they work a reversal.[14] They are confident, in spite of the evidence, that this Galilean peasant lived his humble life and died his humiliating death in unbroken intimacy with the holy Yahweh. Thus they are emboldened to go out of their way to declare that, contrary to expectations, Jesus is not disgraced by what well established legitimization structures deem disintegration. Indeed they declare that God has come fully to dwell in his rent body. This is the way Good Friday, Holy Saturday, and Easter Sunday spill into each other in the gospel. Indeed, the holy God so unrestrictedly dwells here that Jesus is made the avenue of purification for all.[15]

Of course, that a rent body might be the avenue of purification requires a new understanding of purity. The unclean are made clean by Jesus's embrace, the gospels say. But they speak not from a past-to-future, expanding temporality, but a time that comes without our help: an apocalyptic time. Two covenants contend both in what Jesus did and what was done to him. It could not have been clear, as his history took shape, whether he would in the end be shown to be the Son of Beelzebul or of God. A time-honored past leans to the former, a barely precedented hope leans to the latter. It is Holy Week that marks new purity. According to the gospel, Jesus—whom the law of Israel would stamp as unclean and thus unholy—is in crucifixion/resurrection the advent of the Holy Yahweh. That is, one might say, the reversal of the order of purity declared by the gospels occurs in the retroactive apocalyptic power of the Spirit of the glorification of Yahweh where the mutilated body of the crucified Jesus rises unmended.[16] "But the death and resurrection of Christ, as an event

14. Dunn, "Jesus and Holiness," 187.

15. Dunn, "Jesus and Holiness," 192: "Holiness was more important for Jesus as a power which cleanses uncleanness and dissolves impurity than as a status (of person or place) constantly threatened by the 'common' and profane."

16. Barton, "Dislocating and Relocating Holiness," 206: "For the author of Hebrews, the holiness of God revealed in the death of the Son of God is a holiness offered, ironically and paradoxically, through the profanity and defilement of a corpse. Now, that which sanctifies is precisely the dead corpse outside the camp. . . . Holiness as separation—of life and death, male and female, priest and lay, Jew and Gentile, purity

which inaugurates the coming near of God in salvation and judgement, comes to be seen as a new act of creation, indeed, the bringing into being of a new creation (*kainē ktisis*) remade "in Christ" (cf. 2 Cor. 5.17). This new creation is an unmaking and remaking of the old. The extent of this unmaking is almost unimaginable. In fact, its perception and recognition required a transformation of the imagination of the kind which only the language and thought-forms of apocalypse could bring about."[17]

6

"Whenever you stand praying, forgive . . . so that your Father in heaven may also forgive you" (Mark 11:25). I am to pray, that is, in order that everyone might *get in the way*—my neighbors and my enemies, everyone against whom I could justly bring charges. I am to pray in such a way that they rise together in judgment against any entreaty that would exclude them. Indeed I am to pray in such a way that *without them* a Godward outpouring would be no prayer at all, whatever else it may be. That is, there is a certain audacity, a foolhardiness, in bowing one's head before the wildly unpredictable, apocalyptic Yahweh and exposing the back of one's neck to a possible fatal blow. And yet we are invited to pray to this God not only with fear and trembling, but also boldly. We are not just to pray alone, not even in some secret closet. Our neighbors and enemies are to press upon us wherever we go, even if they are nowhere to be seen—and there, we are told, they are to be forgiven. And we are told this because praying in this earthy apocalyptic field of combat is acknowledging that the future of all creation lies not in our hands, but in Yahweh's.

This command to forgive is not, however, to be followed thoughtlessly, perhaps out of a disdain for lawlessness and esteem for authorized dicta, such as biblical ones.[18] Forgiveness has a reason, even if it does not draw from a logic of similitude. It does not say,[19] "God has forgiven you. Be like God and forgive others!" It rather says, "The forgiveness showered upon you is also the forgiveness showered upon *every act* and *every actor*."

---

and impurity—is displaced by *holiness as solidarity*: the solidarity of Jesus the great high priest in sharing human nature as flesh and blood and, above all, in accepting the defilement of death (cf. Heb. 2:14–15, 17)."

17. Barton, "Dislocating and Relocating Holiness," 209.

18. ("Do what you are told!")

19. (Jean Valjean's priest notwithstanding.)

To say, "Yes!" to the God who forgives us is to say, "Yes!" to all to whom and to which God's forgiveness flows, to all God redeems, particularly to *whom* and *what* strike us as irredeemable. It is this, perhaps above all, that makes the reason for forgiveness appear so unjust, indeed, moronic.

No one in the two-millennia-old mainstream of theological ortho-doxy would deny *that* our sins are forgiven by the work of Jesus. Contro-versy and the spilling of ink have come from the more specific question of *how* forgiveness is worked through him. Quite often it has been assumed that the theologian must rise above God and creation and with an eternal synoptic gaze discover what logic would explain *why* God would come for us at all, and in particular in such a violent manner. And this approach is just what one would expect if it were assumed that all thinking were to be kept tightly within a calculable system, a thoroughgoing, authoritatively compelled economy of money, say, in which God is thought to operate, to which God, too, is thought to comply. The question, then, becomes, "How in our ledgers do the figures denoting God's transactions balance?" Let us say that this is the wrong question, that there is a non-monetary logic at play here, an apocalyptic logic of for-giveness.

How might such an apparently moronic logic begin? Perhaps with an exclamation: "Thomas answered him, 'My Lord and my God!'" (John 20:28). This is a doxological utterance. Doxology may arise from some great benefit that is articulated/understood as God's work. It is like a prayer of thanksgiving in that. The difference, though, is that the link to the deed for which a people are justly grateful grows thin, to the breaking point, in doxology. Doxology need not forget, e.g., the mighty deed by which God has saved us from our enemies, but it does not dwell there. It rather gives itself to God in such an unqualified way that the ground falls away from under its feet and ours, we who voice it. *God* is the only reason for doxology, i.e., for *words* (*logoi*) that yield to God's *glory* (*doxa*). The words of doxology come untethered and rise as if held by the winds of a storm, as if held by nothing at all. They speak of God as needing no external justification nor rationalization nor computational resolution nor balanced figures on a (perhaps, metaphysical) spreadsheet. To the question, "*Cur Deus Homo?*" doxology replies, "My Lord and my God!" This is an apocalyptic logic and the apocalyptic discourse of the gospel is nothing if not doxological.[20]

---

20. See LaCugna, *God For Us*, 348–68; Bauckham, *The Theology of the Book of Revelation*, 43, 60.

Thomas is not in the upper room fixating on Jesus, however. He is not slapping the label "God" onto him. Thomas has lost his equilibrium and, staggering, slips into God's act of solidarity with this broken body. Thomas's encounter with the ruptured body of Jesus ruptures him as well, and in that rupture God is glorified, God's very holiness is manifest. It is as if there in this upper room there occurred a "beyond *in* the world,"[21] a beyond that will not leave the world and will indeed never leave the world *intact*.

Jesus performs all of this neither simply actively nor passively. What he does, God does. What God does, he does. He so gives himself to the coming of God that he and his work become an empty place, awaiting without demand to be the site of the arrival of a holy justice, a righteousness, a Reign of God, that would give a future even to this battered Galilean body and thus to every battered body. When he appears to Thomas in the upper room, Jesus embodies and works *forgiveness*. However, *n.b.*, he does so first and last in *his being forgiven*. Jesus is the savior because—dead and damned, consigned to hell and forgotten, cut off from the Father he never forsook, defiled, broken, shredded, and dumped in a ditch—he is himself saved by an unspeakable apocalyptic in-breaking of a wildly unpredictable, wildly merciful holy God.

Jesus is not the noble hero who meets the condition that must be met in order for God to forgive us. He is rather the *deed of forgiveness*, the *event* in which forgiveness—in all its earthiness—*occurs*. Certainly, hope has always imagined a future in which even the most final of all defeats will have been undone, the most desperately conclusive of damnations will have been harrowed, the deepest, darkest sea will have given up its dead. Apocalyptic literature is the literature of just such hope. But it is the resurrection of the mutilated body of Jesus that is *forgiveness in the flesh. Here* the alpha and omega over all creation, the creator of all, the almighty one, is shown to have sovereignty not only to work light and darkness, but also to overcome death and damnation, what time has with all its power consigned irrevocably to the past, to have sovereignty to contact and exalt what a holy God could never contact and exalt—but here *does*, here *hallows* the utterly unclean. The shock of the event of the resurrection of the body of Jesus—wet wounds agape—arrives with the disclosure of a God whose deeds will never compute in the monetized logic of balanced scales, who does too much for the gatekeepers of purity

---

21. To use a phrase from Rivera's *The Touch of Transcendence*, 38.

to manage or even entertain. And so, "Thomas answered him, 'My Lord and my God!'" (John 20:28). There is nothing more that can be said of God than what is said here and it is said of the very place where the life story of Jesus was given a hard period: on Golgotha. The resurrection of Jesus is not the erasure of his crucifixion, but its glorification, its exaltation. It is the coming of peace, *shalom, eirene,* to this world's horrorfest marked as it is by casualty figures, despair, and corpses. But this apocalyptic peace requires no closure of wounds or of graves. It is rather the coming of a new world in which there is sanctity, life, freedom, love, and laughter, but without competing with the binary opposites that in our old world could never reconcile with them: mutilation, death, slavery, hatred, and tears.

7

The ruptured body of the resurrected Jesus rises as the New Jerusalem descends, each repeating the other. And so, unsurprisingly, the body of the New Jerusalem is a ruptured body, as well. Certainly, it is ringed by a wall, as cities, nation states, and other defensible creatures want to be. Its wall is interrupted by huge gates, however, that stand perpetually and invitingly open, keeping nothing out, deconstructing the logic of exclusion/inclusion with which walls are erected, deconstructing the walls themselves. The New Jerusalem is an enormous city, larger than the known world of the time, larger thus, *we* might say, than the universe. It is so large that nothing could even *be* outside it. Nonetheless, oddly, "the nations" are outside . . . but only that they, too, might come in, gratefully, unhanding there their "glory and honor," "purified" the way all things are purified, i.e., by entering the body that in faithfulness to the coming of God and in solidarity with us became impure.[22]

To say "pure" is in ancient Israel to say "intact." Purity is integrity, wholeness.[23] Oozing sores make the *person* impure, because they break the skin, the body's protective identifying boundary. The outside gets in, as the inside gets out, and wholeness is lost. The *household* is imagined as similarly vulnerable. A stranger threatens to pierce and corrupt the integrity of the family line, e.g., by impregnating through seduction or rape a patriarch's daughter, sister, or mate. The invasion of an enemy army

---

22. Yet without impurity (cf. 2 Cor 5:21).

23. See Berquist, *Controlling Corporeality.*

threatens the unity of the *nation* not only by the inevitable slaughter it swears to inflict, but even more by its destroying patterns of righteousness kings and priests had long managed.[24] There is nothing significantly unfamiliar to us about this, at its heart. We, too, are quite publicly anxious about dangers to our health, just as we are about threats to our national identity and the stability of the family. We all want not only to survive, but also to thrive, to flourish. We know in our bones that any threat to the wholeness of those we hold dear is a mortal threat.

However, in ancient Israel purity was never an end in itself. It was a great good, but it was by no means the reason for being alive. Israel and through Israel all of creation are here, their prophets and sages declared, in order that they might be holy—and that for no other reason than that Yahweh is holy (Lev 11:45). What is it to be holy? In Yahweh's case there is no extrinsic standard. Yahweh is holy in that Yahweh is not any other god and is not to be circumscribed by any account, especially by an account of the cosmos. Yahweh is *other than* the cosmos, *other than* anything and everything, living or dead, *other than* all things "in heaven and on earth and under the earth" (Phil 2:10), we might say. "I am God, and there is no other; I am God, and there is no one like me, declaring the end from the beginning and from ancient times things not yet done" (Isa 46:9–10). It is not that Israel and, through Israel, all creatures might become holy by imitating God, e.g., by achieving some human version of aseity or some set of moral traits. The sin of Adam and Eve lies in their desperate attempt to make themselves "like" God.[25] Being holy is being *set aside to the one God*, to *follow the one God*, to *lean out into* the coming of *the one God*. It is, i.e., to "love the Lord your God with all your heart, and with all your soul, and with all your might" (Deut 6:5). Purity without such abandonment to the coming of God is vanity.

The moment in which God *raises* the mutilated body of Jesus from the grave, the moment in which "all the *fullness* of God [is] pleased to dwell" in that mutilated body (Col 1:19), the moment in which God is *glorified* in the mutilated body of Jesus, the moment in which the *holiness* of God shines through the wounds agape all over that body, in *that*

---

24. Therefore, God puts up a hedge around Israel to protect it and, on the other hand, gives it up to be conquered, when it has already abandoned the way of righteousness.

25. Our being created "in the image of God" in Genesis 1 is not our being made similar to God, no matter how inadequately. It is rather our being created to live out into the coming of God, i.e., faithfully.

moment God has made a new arrangement with us, the creatures who swarm upon the earth (cf. Lev 11). That moment is the event in which it is no longer necessary to be whole in order to have lived well. It is the event in which the gates of hell have been kicked off their pivots from inside and any who would may walk out into the light: "Ride on King Jesus / No man can a-hinder me!"[26] Thus the New Jerusalem is agape, wide open, a "Yes!" to all God's forgotten children, those still staggering through the streets and alleys of this present evil age, those who long ago crumbled into dust, and those who have not yet been granted their first breaths. This is the *event of forgiveness*, the wide open expanse in which every action and passion is held in hands more capacious than space and time. It is, e.g., the event in which a theology of friendship is to do its work.

8

The liturgy of the eucharist is the work *in, with, and under*—but not cir-cumscribed *by*—this space and time, work where the outcry of Thomas and other members of a grateful church is liberatively upheld. Liturgy is a corporate—i.e., corporeal and social—work. It remembers the body and blood of Jesus as it eats and drinks bread and wine, but it is neither a memorial nor an object lesson. It feels the weight, temperature, and texture of the actual body of Christ, as it holds, eats, and drinks bread and wine, but it is subject neither to an ontology nor to a presence. It is an economic movement that unsettles all such things.[27] Into the liturgy of the eucharist bodies carry all the moments of a long week—all that they have done and all that has been done to them—and there they let it all go to the coming of the New Jerusalem into which they (liturgically) step. It is an entry into and a concurrence with the body of Christ, an entry, that is, into the world—past, present, and future—the world he has taken in and glorified, his body rendered borderless, above all on the way to and upon Golgotha.[28] He is thus the capaciousness of the New Jerusalem. It is in him that there is room for all.

26. Lomax, *Ride On, King Jesus.*

27. Cf. Schmemann, *The Eucharist.*

28. Barth, *CD* 3/3:90: "Therefore nothing will escape him: no aspect of the great game of creation; no moment of human life; no thinking thought; no word spoken; no secret or insignificant enterprise or deed or omission with all its interaction and effects; no suffering or joy; no sincerity or lie, no secret event in heaven or too well-known

In him, in this city of glory, enemies are set free to embrace . . . and so are friends. Just as enmity undergoes a radical change when there is no longer winning or losing, when the first become last and the last first, so also does friendship when there is no longer exclusion or inclusion, no longer closure of any kind. That is not to say that there is no trace of enmity or friendship on those streets of gold. The faces that we meet are the faces that we met. The New Jerusalem is populated by the resurrected bodies of the dead, by lost time renewed. Old friends and enemies are for-given and loved alongside old lovers and strangers. In this body, in this city, in this expanse, "There is no longer Jew or Greek, there is no longer slave or free, there is no longer male and female; for all of you are one in Christ Jesus" (Gal 3:28).

But there is also the liturgical prayer, "Let us depart in peace!" That is, the journey out into the coming New Jerusalem—the city in which every lost coin, sheep, and child, every lost moment, is gathered into God's glory and redeemed—that journey is also a journey out into the world yet to be redeemed. These are not two worlds. Redemption does not have to wait. There is no future event that exceeds the complex, *Good Friday/Holy Saturday/Easter Sunday*. In its glorification the mutilated body of Jesus has opened more widely than space and time. And yet, everywhere a child of God looks, there lies the crumpled heap of the remnants of the damage—targeted or collateral—inflicted by an order of profit and loss, of good and evil, an order of insiders and outsiders: of Jew or Greek, slave or free, male and female, friend and foe.

The conflict between "the present age" and "the age to come" is not an opposition between orders of ethical demand. It is not that relationships in an unredeemed world are to be cast aside in order to achieve an abstract integrity. Integrity as a condition for holiness died on the cross. And yet living in an unredeemed world is living in ambiguous acquiescence to its schema (1 Cor 7:31), schema that will not have prevailed on the Day of the Lord. Thus it is not necessary to live in constant refusal of the pleasures of fragmented time. I don't have to turn up my nose at a plate of fried catfish. I don't have to withhold my affection from my friends and lovers. And yet, living in the mission of the eucharist is living freely in relation to all that we are trained daily to grasp and hold,

---

event on earth; no ray of sunlight; no note which has ever sounded; no color with has ever been revealed, possibly in the darkness of oceanic depths where the eye of man has never perceived it; no wing-beat of the day-fly in far-flung epochs of geological time." Cf. Schmemann, *For the Life of the World*, 42.

as Adam and Eve grasped and held the fruit of the Garden. "I mean, brothers and sisters, the appointed time has grown short; from now on, let even those who have wives be as though they had none, and those who mourn as though they were not mourning, and those who rejoice as though they were not rejoicing, and those who buy as though they had no possessions, and those who deal with the world as though they had no dealings with it" (1 Cor 7:29–31).

It is a mistake to imagine friendship as a reciprocal interchange that an accountant might track via entries in a ledger. It is a mistake to imagine it as an artful transaction between honorably satisfied sages. It is a mistake to imagine it as among the calculable goods that make life worth living. This is not to deny the joy of friendship, of labor and affection shared, of secrets entrusted, of concurrent understanding. It is not to say that a life without friends is not a dreadfully painful life. It is to say, however, that the categories by which we wisely classify the good and the bad in daily life do not determine the future. The future is roomy enough even for the friendless. Even now, the hope that there is room in *what is to come* for the lonely and forgotten relativizes not only enmity, but also friendship. And on the sad day when one has been forsaken by a friend, the gospel makes room for her still to be loved, i.e., with a love that says "Yes!" to *her*, even if a former affection will never return.

Bibliography

Aristotle. *Nicomachean Ethics*. Translated by W. D. Ross. New York: Oxford University Press, 1925.

Barth, Karl. *Church Dogmatics 3/3: The Doctrine of Creation*. Translated by G. W. Bromley and R. J. Ehrlich. Edinburgh: T. & T. Clark, 1960.

Barton, Stephen C. "Dislocating and Relocating Holiness: A New Testament Study." In *Holiness: Past & Present*, edited by Stephen C. Barton, 193–213. New York: T. & T. Clark, 2003.

Bauckham, Richard. *The Theology of the Book of Revelation*. New York: Cambridge University Press, 1993.

Berquist, Jon. *Controlling Corporeality: The Body and the Household in Ancient Israel*. New Brunswick: Rutgers University Press, 2002.

Dunn, James D. G. "Jesus and Holiness: The Challenge of Purity." In *Holiness: Past & Present*, edited by Stephen C. Barton, 168–92. New York: T. & T. Clark, 2003.

Jaeger, Werner. *The Theology of the Early Greek Philosophers: The Gifford Lectures, 1936*. Translated by Edward S. Robinson. New York: Oxford University Press, 1947.

Kipling, Rudyard. "The White Man's Burden: The United States and the Philippine Islands, 1899." In *Rudyard Kipling's Verse: Definitive Edition*, 323–34. London: Hodder and Stoughton, 1940.

LaCugna, Catherine Mowry. *God For Us: The Trinity and Christian Life*. San Francisco: HarperSanFrancisco, 1991.

Lomax, John A., et al. *Ride On, King Jesus*. Recorded in 1939. Huntsville, Texas, 1939.

Rivera, Mayra. *The Touch of Transcendence: A Postcolonial Theology of God*. Louisville: Westminster John Knox, 2007.

Schmemann, Alexander. *The Eucharist: Sacrament of the Kingdom*. Translated by Paul Kachur. Crestwood: St. Vladimir's Seminary Press, 1988.

———. *For the Life of the World: Sacraments and Orthodoxy*. Crestwood: St. Vladimir's Seminary Press, 1998.

Seaford, Richard. *Money and the Early Greek Mind: Homer, Philosophy, Tragedy*. New York: Cambridge University Press, 2004.

12

Is It OK to Be Proud of Your Humility?

ROBERT C. ROBERTS

THE IDEA OF FEELING proud of your humility seems at first glance paradoxical. But the paradox dwindles if we distinguish vicious pride, which
would invalidate a self-assessment as virtuously humble, from pride that
is virtuous, or at least not vicious. In a recent book on humility, Kent
Dunnington calls this distinction into question on the basis of a reading of the desert hermits and early Christian monasticism. I defend the
notion of virtuous pride and argue that it is possible for a Christian to
feel proud of her humility, or the progress she has made toward virtuous
humility. The argument turns on an analysis of the concept of love and
examination of some passages in the New Testament that make room for
a virtuous kind of pride.

In a fine book on the seven deadly sins as explored by the early desert fathers and mothers, Dennis Okholm writes,

> Pride lays low the proud one by his own "spear." The virtues of
> the one whom pride attacks are simply supplying the soul with
> "new fuel" for vanity. It is a vice "interwoven" with our virtues,
> as Evagrius puts it: "Vainglory is an irrational passion and it
> readily gets tangled up with any work of virtue." The one who
> has forsaken the world and abandoned temporal honors and
> sought humility is wounded by the "shaft" of vainglory and falls
> the more fatally from on high.[1]

1. Okholm, *Dangerous Passions*, 165, citing Evagrius, "On the Eight Thoughts," 7.1,
in Sinkewicz, *Evagrius of Pontus*; Cassian, *Institutes* 11.7–9; and Gregory, *Morals on*

In Okholm's account of the desert hermits' struggle against and comments on vainglory, they don't distinguish virtuous from vicious pride. They seem to think that all pride is vicious, inasmuch as it implies a lack of the all-important virtue of humility.

Consider two scenarios in which the doer of a virtuous action might feel proud of his humility:

Scenario one:
I have been struggling against vanity for a while. I realize that I have a strong urge to *display* what few excellences I have for people to *see*. And when I get compliments, I take intense pleasure in them (though I try not to show it too much), a pleasure that fairly swamps whatever pleasure I got simply from performing the good action. I have been meditating, with compunction, on this tendency of mine and asking the Lord to take it from me: "Help me, dear Lord, to be perfectly willing to do good anonymously, to be glad simply in the acting and in observing the good that flows from it." But now I find a time-consuming opportunity to help a colleague avoid an error in her work, and I do so without anyone knowing of my sacrificial action. And I feel completely OK about it—serene, no need to have it known. And I think to myself, "Moral progress! I see improvement in my character!" And, without exaggerating it or overestimating the depth of this improvement of myself, I delight in it.

Scenario two:
It is the same as the first scenario, except for one more delight: I think of my friend Alfredo who, though dear to me, is a bit of a braggart. Whatever he does that's impressive or good he shares with anyone who'll listen, though the biggest kick is the one he gets from hearing the compliments of *high-ranking* people. And with delight I think of my serene anonymity *in its contrast with Alfredo's frenetic self-display*. I delight in the comparison that sets me above Alfredo.

If pride, as an emotion, is delight in the association of oneself with something admirable, then both of these scenarios exhibit pride, because in both, what I am delighted about is *my* humility—an excellent trait. Notice that it makes no essential difference to the claim that scenario one is a description of pride, whether I acknowledge God's hand in working my moral improvement. I may even take no credit at all for having

---

Job, 40:16.

achieved this bit of humility; let's say I think it's entirely and exhaustively a work of God. A person can be proud of things he had no hand at all in bringing about: I can be proud of my sister's artistic prowess without thinking I had a hand in producing it; all that pride in her requires is that she appear to me admirable and that I see myself as associated with her. Pride in being the *author* of my moral improvement is one kind of pride, but neither scenario stipulates *that* condition. So either scenario may presuppose that God is either involved in my moral improvement or is the sole cause of it. The difference between the scenarios, obviously, is the more particular description of what I take delight *in*: In scenario one, I delight in my improved humility (simply), and in scenario two I delight in my humility *as a way of being morally superior to Alfredo*. As Okholm comments, "Ultimately, [vicious] pride is our craving for superiority and the beliefs we harbor about ourselves that fuel such a craving."[2]

Scenario two illustrates Evagrius's point about how sinful pride can get tangled up with a work of virtue: in priding myself on my progress against my vanity, I fall into the perhaps even worse sin of self-righteousness. Scenario one, by contrast, seems to me to describe an episode of pride that is spiritually compatible with the humility that it's about. It is pride because the excellence that I see as *admirable* I also see *as my own*. But it involves no invidious comparison with anyone else; it does not arrogate credit where credit is not due (say, by denying that credit to God); it does not seek to be seen and admired by others; nor do I see it as an occasion for dominating others.

Spiritual disciplines such as the hermits undertook when they went into the desert to vanquish the evil spirits and the spirit of evil in themselves seem to presuppose a self-directed concern—a concern to become holy. Joy, as I have argued elsewhere,[3] is seeing something as satisfying our concern for it. If you want your sick child to get well, then when he gets well, you rejoice; when you want to find your lost coin or your lost sheep, and you find it, you rejoice. So it seems that, if you want to become holy, and you see in yourself progress in the endeavor, you will naturally

2. Okholm, *Dangerous Passions*, 162. The "craving" for superiority is *dispositional* pride, pride as a trait; delight in my superiority is episodic, *emotional* pride. Emotional pride is related to dispositional pride as the satisfaction of the craving. I'm not sure that the sense of superiority is the only mark of a joy that makes it a case of sinful pride. For example, another possible mark is radical or ungrateful autonomy—what I will call "radical autonomy." In the case of that kind of pride, the difference *will* be that I grudge God the credit.

3. Roberts, "Joys."

experience joy in your progress. Since this joy is about something admirable attributed to yourself, this joy will be pride. But the desert hermits thought pride a bad thing, inconsistent with humility. On the view of emotions that I have applied in this paragraph (that they are satisfactions or frustrations of our concerns[4]), the desert hermits had two options for avoiding this forbidden joy: They could maintain their concern to become holy, but refuse to recognize any progress in themselves, or they could seek to quell the underlying concern to become holy. Interestingly, Kent Dunnington seems to opt for the second solution.

Dunnington on Humility in the Desert Hermits and Early Christian Monastics

In a recently published book on Christian humility, Dunnington offers a picture of humility that would logically and morally rule out being proud of it (or, indeed, of anything else). He distinguishes the Christian virtue, which he calls "radical humility," from a secularized analog of it that he calls "mundane humility." Radical humility involves a complete ("radical") absence of concern for one's own value, one's own excellence, one's own importance; so it is a "no-concern" kind of humility. Mundane humility, by contrast, allows for such concern, and so is compatible with such "prides" as self-confidence, secure agency, aspiration, pride in one's work, a sense of one's dignity, self-respect, and a sense of personal authority.

Dunnington cites sayings from early Christian monks that apparently reject such versions of positive self-esteem. *Contra* self-confidence, Benedict of Nursia says, "The sixth step of humility is that a monk is content with the lowest and most menial treatment and regards himself as a poor and worthless workman in whatever task he is given."[5] *Contra* secure agency, "we hear of Abba Cronides that 'such was the humility that he had guarded right into old age that he considered himself a nonentity.'"[6] *Contra* pride in one's work, "we are told of a nobleman's daughter, who was possessed by a devil. Her father asked a monk for help. The monk said to him, 'No one can cure your daughter except some hermits I know:

---

4. Roberts, *Emotions*, chapters 3–5.

5. Dunnington, *Humility*, 66, citing Benedict, *Rule*, 7.49.

6. Dunnington, *Humility*, 67, citing Ward, *Lives*, 106.

and if you go to them, they will refuse to do it from motives of humility."[7] *Contra* self-respect, Bernard of Clairvaux comments, "If you examine yourself inwardly by the light of truth and without dissimulation and judge yourself without flattery; no doubt you will be humbled by your own eyes, becoming contemptible in your own sight as a result of this true knowledge."[8] And so on, for each of the prides.

This humility that is incompatible with any kind of pride whatsoever, says Dunnington, is the ideal of Christian humility. It is a virtue very difficult, if not impossible, to attain in this life; nevertheless, this radical loss of all positive self-regard is every Christian's calling. "The path of humility, which leads to our beatitude, calls for the relinquishment of precisely what contemporary psychology and virtue theory tells us is necessary for the moral life—namely, pursuit of a secure sense of self."[9]

A "Mundane" Conception of Humility

I will briefly sketch the evolving concept of humility that I have promoted over the last couple of decades, and say why it is compatible with virtuous pride. Like Dunnington, I say that humility is a kind of absence. But absences are defined by what they are absences *of* and *in*. For example, purity, as a quality of water, is the absence of pollutants, but it is not the absence of hydrogen or oxygen; indeed, it is the absence of pollutants *in* H_2O. Similarly, humility is the absence of ego-pollutants in a human personality or character. Dunnington's conception of humility differs from mine in what we take humility to be the absence of. Dunnington takes humility to be the absence of self-directed concern, whereas I take it to be the absence of a *specific kind* of self-directed concern—concern for what I term *self-importance*. Self-concern is not itself a pollutant, but

7. Dunnington, *Humility*, 67, citing Ward, *Fathers*, 153. These hermits seem to be motivated by a desire to protect their humility against the temptation to think highly of themselves in case they did this good service to the father and his afflicted daughter. But isn't this motivation a concern for their own excellence (the excellence of humility), and a perverse one at that, since it moves them to refuse to do good? Aren't they laying themselves low by their own spear? They seem to exemplify exactly the ethically defective self-concern that some critics take to be endemic to the enterprise of virtue ethics.

8. Dunnington, *Humility*, 67, citing Foulcher, *Reclaiming*, 1.

9. Dunnington, *Humility*, 69.

an ingredient in a healthy personality; self-importance is the pollutant of which humility is the absence. What is self-importance?

Self-importance is the kind of personal "importance" that people care about and seek when they exhibit what I call the vices of pride: arrogance, pretentiousness, conceit, presumption, envy, invidious pride, vanity, selfish ambition, domination, radical autonomy, snobbery, and racial/ethnic supremacy.[10] These vices all have in common that they entail a concern to have the pseudo-value that I call self-importance. In English, "self-importance" is a rough synonym for the vice of conceit; but I use the expression more broadly to designate the "value" that the conceited person thinks he has a lot of, the envious person feels she is deficient in, the arrogant person thinks he gets from his special entitlements, the vain person seeks in displaying her excellences, etc. Self-importance is strongly related to the clinical category of narcissistic personality disorder,[11] though people who are driven by self-importance may never become so socially dysfunctional as to be officially diagnosed or forced into therapy. Indeed, a person beset with an extreme case of the vices of pride—a person consumed and obsessed with his self-importance—might even manage to become President of the United States.

Humility is the absence of the concern for self-importance. The purpose of using the word for conceit as the name of this "value," as well as the quotes around "value" and "importance," is to mark that self-importance is not a real value and is not a real kind of human importance. The less concern a person has for his or her self-importance, the better the person's character and the healthier the person is. Having a lot of satisfaction of the concern for self-importance (say, in the form of being conceited or arrogant) is not a desirable kind of self-esteem. Unfortunately for the human race, none of us is perfected in the virtue of humility; none of us is perfectly without the concern for self-importance. Thus, when we speak colloquially of someone as being virtuously humble, we are talking about his or her *relative* lack of concern for self-importance. We aren't claiming that she is perfectly humble.

10. For an overview of both the virtuous and the vicious prides (as well as the corresponding humilities), see Roberts, "Virtues of Pride," and Roberts and West, "Jesus and the Virtues."

11. In my "Humility and Human Flourishing," I compare the vices of pride with the criteria for narcissistic personality disorder in the fifth edition of the American Psychiatric Association's *Diagnostic and Statistical Manual of Mental Disorders*.

The humility that I have just sketched is "mundane," to use Dun-nington's word, because it is not the absence of self-concern; it is not the absence of the concern to be important; and thus it is not the absence of all pride. It is the absence only of vicious pride. What is the essence of virtuous pride, and what has it to do with Christianity? Virtuous pride is essentially connected with love—in particular, *being* loved; and the "greatest" of the Christian virtues is love in which human love reflects God's love.

When you say to someone, "*I* love *you*," you say, among other things, "You *matter* to me," "You are *important* to me." This is to say something not merely about the lover, but also about the beloved, at least as the lover sees him or her. Thus, when the beloved "receives" this love, in the sense of acknowledging, accepting, feeling, and appreciating it, the beloved says to herself, as it were, "I matter to him," "I am important to him." Of course, she may not *say* this, or even explicitly think it, but the point is that this affirmation of herself, which speaks to a concern of hers, a con-cern to be important, becomes part of her emotional self-understanding, implicit though it may be. To be important in this sense is one of the deepest concerns of the human heart. But a *sense* of one's own impor-tance, a *satisfaction* of this deep concern, is a kind of pride.

A sense of one's own importance has a *character*. Its character—the *kind* of sense of one's own importance that is in question—is a matter of the reasons behind it, the way one thinks about, or would think about, this importance. To specify the kind is to specify the reasons I would give if challenged to articulate them (and if I am self-aware enough, and cognitively adept enough, to articulate them accurately). If the reasons that give its character to my pride are those that are characteristic of the vices of pride—superiority to others, empty self-display, domination of others, radical autonomy—then my sense of my own importance is vi-cious and sinful and contrary to Christian character and the Christian way of living. But if my pride is born of love—of someone else's love for me—then it is virtuous and consistent with Christian character. If it is born of God's love for me, and the love of my Christian brothers and sis-ters for me, then my pride is not just consistent with Christian character, but is *characteristic* of it.

The vices of pride distort features of human life that are quite basic, and therefore not necessarily distortions, though they are subject to dis-tortion. Some of these features are: (1) We are agents, doers of actions; (2) We are people-watchers, and in watching we evaluate; (3) We are diverse in many ways; (4) Social organization among us requires that special entitlements or privileges be assigned to some. As Okholm points out, the sense of superiority to others pervades the vices of pride: conceit, arrogance, snobbery, and self-righteousness are examples. But a person who keeps firmly in mind that he is the object of God's gracious, undeserved love, can recognize and appreciate the fact that he is superior to others in some way—more intelligent, perhaps, more beautiful, more capable, a better chess player, or whatever—and be grateful for his attribute, without basing his sense of personal importance on *being better than these others*. In the vices of vanity and pretentiousness, the feature of being people-watchers (in particular, the sense of *being observed and evaluated by others*) is salient. But one who has a firm sense of being loved by God and fellow human beings will not base the sense of her importance on other people's admiration of her, except to the extent that admiration is a quality of love.

Arrogance is the disposition to value and arrogate special entitlements and privileges for the sake of the self-importance they symbolize. Some special entitlements are justified, such as a doctor's entitlement to prescribe medicines or a teacher's entitlement to choose the materials for a course. But some entitlements are "empty," for example the special entitlements in our society that go with having light-colored skin, or the privilege of the wealthy to immunity from some kinds of inconvenience. The virtuously humble will value justified entitlements for the reasons that justify them, and not for the prestige they entail, and will feel uncomfortable with having empty entitlements. It is a symptom of vicious pride to cherish entitlements for their prestige value. Virtuous pride is an implicit sense of secure agency, of self-respect, of self-confidence, of pride in one's work, of aspiration to excellence, and so forth, that is begotten of an awareness of being cherished for one's own sake. And that awareness does its work in forming these attitudes in a person by virtue of the person's having a natural need and desire to be loved—a self-oriented need and desire that find satisfaction in being loved.

Hints of Virtuous Pride in the New Testament

My first argument against the radical no-concern conception of humility is that love, the "greatest" of Christian virtues, attributes importance to the beloved, and that when love is properly received, the beloved attributes that importance to himself; and that this attribution is ethically, psychologically, and spiritually significant because the human soul is fundamentally and properly concerned to be loved. If these premises are true, then "radical humility" is inconsistent with the very heart of Christian doctrine and life—the life of loving God and fellow human beings and being loved by them. A Christian conception of humility must be compatible with love, and thus with proper self-concern and a related self-understanding in which each person attributes importance to herself.

A more particular kind of self-attribution of approval is contexts in which a Christian sees himself or herself as worthy because of some action or type of action. In the fifth chapter of the book of Acts, Luke reports that the apostles were causing quite a stir with their ministry in Jerusalem, preaching Jesus and healing sufferers. Many people were being converted and were availing themselves of the apostles' ministry—so much that the religious authorities became alarmed and "arrested the apostles and put them in the public prison" (Acts 5:18). During the night, an angel released them from prison and sent them back to continue their public ministry. When the authorities found out what had happened, they arrested the apostles again, and told them to stop their activities. But Peter told the authorities that he and the others must obey God rather than human authorities, and preached the gospel to them. This made the authorities angry, and they were on the verge of doing the apostles violence, but Gamaliel persuaded them to be careful. So they just flogged the apostles, exhorted them once again to desist their ministry, and released them. "As [the apostles] left the council, *they rejoiced that they were considered worthy to suffer dishonor for the sake of the name* [of Jesus]" (5:41, emphasis added).

By their rejoicing, the apostles show that they wholeheartedly endorse the attribution of worthiness to themselves on account of their obedient defiance of the authorities and the consequent dishonor that they suffered at the authorities' hands—a dishonor that resembles what Jesus suffered for their sake. But rejoicing in one's own excellence is episodic (emotional) pride. Despite their bruises and wounds, the apostles feel good about themselves and about how they have conducted themselves. In a holy way, they are feeling proud of themselves. Luke reports their rejoicing without the least hint of disapproval or hesitation. He seems to think it perfectly appropriate. If the desert hermits or Simone Weil[12] think the apostles are here compromising their Christian humility, they seem to be at odds with Luke.

12. See Dunnington, *Humility*, 149–52.

The verb καυχᾶσθαι and its noun cognates καύχημα and καὶ ̄ ̄ ̄
are translated in a variety of ways including "boast" (noun and verb),
"pride," "glory" (verb), "glorying" (noun), "rejoice" (verb), and "rejoicing" (noun). The NRSV translates καυχᾶσθαι mostly as "boast," while the
KJV uses a greater variety of English terms, including "glory" and sometimes "rejoicing" (remember that emotional pride is a kind of joy). The
occurrences of καυχᾶσθαι and its cognates are almost all in Paul, with a
few in James and Hebrews. Here are some examples:

> Romans 5:2
> "and we boast [καυχώμεθα] in our hope of sharing the glory of
>   God." (NRSV)
> "and [we] rejoice [καυχώμεθα] in hope of the glory of God."
>   (KJV)

> 1 Corinthians 4:7
> "And if you received it, why do you boast [καυχᾶσαι] as if it were
>   not a gift?" (NRSV)
> "now if thou didst receive *it*, why dost thou glory [καυχᾶσαι], as
>   if thou hadst not received *it*?" (KJV)

> 2 Corinthians 1:12
> "this is our boast [καύχησις], the testimony of our conscience."
>   (NRSV)
> "For our rejoicing [καύχησις] is this, the testimony of our
>   conscience." (KJV)

> 2 Corinthians 1:14
> "on the day of the Lord Jesus we are your boast [καύχημα] even
>   as you are our boast." (NRSV)
> "we are your rejoicing [καύχημα], even as ye also are our's in
>   the day of the Lord Jesus." (KJV)

> 2 Corinthians 7:4
> "I have great pride (καύχησις) in you." (NRSV)
> "great *is* my glorying (καύχησις) of you." (KJV)

> 2 Corinthians 10:17
> "Let the one who boasts (Ὁ δὲ καυχώμενος), boast (καυχάσθω)
>   in the Lord." (NRSV)
> "But he that glorieth (Ὁ δὲ καυχώμενος), let him glory
>   (καυχάσθω) in the Lord." (KJV)

The NRSV shies away from "glory" (verb) as a translation of καυχᾶσθαι, perhaps because it rings antique. Instead, the NRSV makes heavy use of "boast." I think something is lost thereby. For one thing, to glory is clearly to be in an emotional state, namely, joy about something excellent that is significantly associated with oneself. The association can be various in type. The one who glories may glory in an action she responsibly performs—say, an action of ministry. Or it may be in a state of oneself for which someone else is responsible, say, to glory in one's hope of the kingdom of God. Or it may be in a relationship, say, to glory in the Lord (the Lord being one's *own* Lord). "Glory," then, is a good translation of καυχᾶσθαι inasmuch as it suggests emotion (joy) in excellence with a self-reference. The association with *oneself* in this attitude toward the Lord is what justifies the more recent translation of "boast," and thus the suggestion of a kind of pride. To associate the Lord's excellence with oneself is to cast a reflection of excellence on oneself which, in the emotion of glorying, one feels with pleasure. This connection to self-evaluation, which is essential to καυχᾶσθαι and its cognates, is normatively ruled out by the radical no-concern conception of humility.

"Boasting," by contrast, is not an emotion, but an action. Although boasting essentially expresses glorying, not all glorying is so expressed. This fact makes "boast" an unfortunate substitute for "glory" (verb) in some contexts. Boasting is *pointing out*, usually verbally, one's excellence, or that the excellent thing is associated with oneself. Boasting requires an audience, someone *to whom* one points out the exalting excellence. The relation between boasting and glorying is that boasting requires glorying, but glorying doesn't require boasting. That glorying is essential to boasting is evident in the fact that praising one's own attributes without glorying in them—say, listing one's excellences on a job application purely with a view to securing work—doesn't (or shouldn't) count as boasting.

Another reason that "glory" (verb) is better than "boast" is that in English boasting has a bad reputation. It's usually taken to express one or more of the vices of pride: arrogance, envy, vanity, self-righteousness, and the like. But many of the contexts of καυχᾶσθαι in Paul's writings are not censorious. English is perhaps unfortunate in lacking a better word than "boasting" to express explicit self-celebration. The excellent reader of the NRSV will thus supply implicit quotes around "boast" in some contexts of Paul's writings.

To be sure, Paul is sometimes palpably uneasy with his καύχησις, suggesting that the word can also denote a species of unhealthy and damnable pride. In chapters 10–12 of 2 Corinthians, Paul appears to be combatting the influence in the Corinthian congregation of people claiming to be "super apostles" who are belittling Paul's apostolic authority, as well as one another's. In response to their activity, Paul passionately defends his apostleship. He is properly proud of his accomplishments and qualifications as an apostle of Jesus Christ, but seems to judge that he is sometimes "carried away" with his boasting—carried away from proper humility and apostolic decorum. He admits that he may glory "a little too much [in] our authority" (2 Cor 10:8), and he several times calls himself a "fool" for the way he boasts (glories) of his apostolic service (2 Cor 11:1, 16–23; 12:11).

Paul's moral identity as an apostle is a matter of deep and intense concern to him. This would put him low on the scale of holiness according to the radical no-concern conception of humility. But Paul doesn't think of his concern for his moral identity as *in itself* a spiritual defect, and instead offers criteria, along the way, to distinguish proper from improper concern for one's moral identity. One criterion is that the self-commendation not be "beyond measure," that is, based on something for which someone else should get credit. "We do not boast beyond limits, that is, in the labors of others" (2 Cor 10:15). This criterion might be seen as an instance of the general one that a person should take credit only where he or she merits it; truth should be respected in credit-taking (2 Cor 12:6a; 13:8). A second criterion is that, speaking of the "super-apostles," Paul says, "when they measure themselves by one another, and compare themselves with one another, they do not show good sense" (2 Cor 10:12). Here the more general criterion might be that feeling proud should not be based on superiority to someone else, as though being superior to the other is what makes one worthy of admiration. (This would be "invidious" pride.) This is the criterion that generates most of Paul's self-attributions of foolishness. In commending his own apostleship, he verges on wrangling childishly with the super-apostles. He thus verges not only on invidious pride, but also on devaluing his own apostleship. A few verses after pointing out that the super-apostles "do not show good sense" when they compete with one another in claiming authority, he says, "I think that I am not in the least inferior to these super-apostles" (2 Cor 11:5).

It is important for the Corinthians to know the difference between Paul's genuine apostleship and the false apostleship of the super-apostles. The Corinthians' very Christianity may be at stake. That justifies Paul's impressive implicitly comparative recital of deeds and sufferings; it tends to establish the genuineness of his apostleship in contrast with their spurious apostleship. So there can be no doubt about the practical pastoral usefulness of Paul's "boasting" (2 Cor 11:2–4; 12:19c; 13:9b) on the understanding of pride and humility that I am promoting. The question whether this "boasting" expresses sinful pride or not is a question about motivation: Is Paul motivated by a *vain* or *invidious* concern to assert, defend, or establish his importance (that is, his *self*-importance), or is he motivated by a *genuine* and *loving* pastoral concern to defend his role as apostle in relation to the congregation at Corinth (and, no doubt, elsewhere)? Given that Paul is a serious pastor but also a flawed human being like the rest of us, it is likely that his motivation is a mixture of these two kinds. His uneasiness about his motivation (is he being a "fool" or an apostle?) suggests that he is aware of being pulled in both directions. His virtuous humility will be perfect only if his self-concern involves *nothing* vain, invidious, or selfish.[13] Human beings do perhaps exhibit such purity of self-concern episodically, but it is doubtful that anyone exhibits it with full consistency—that is, as a fully reliable trait.

Let me briefly mention one other New Testament concept that bears on proper pride, δόξα (glory).[14] In the New Testament, glory is manifest excellence. It carries a suggestion of visual obviousness: radiance, splendor, shining, light. It is thus impressive excellence, though not everyone may be impressed; it may require "eyes to see," a spiritual preparation. But if something is glorious, it will impress those whose faculties are properly formed; and if it doesn't impress, the fault is not in what is glorious. Glory is primarily an attribute of God and of Christ. But it is (or will be) also an attribute of human beings. The author of Hebrews quotes Psalm 8, "You have made [human beings] for a little while lower than the angels; you have crowned them with glory and honor" (Heb 2:7). Paul says that "God chose to make known how great among the Gentiles are the riches of the glory of this mystery, which is Christ in you, the hope of glory" (Col 1:27), and "When Christ who is your life is revealed, then you also will be revealed with him in glory" (Col 3:4), and "we speak God's wisdom, secret and hidden, which God decreed before the ages for our glory" (1

13. On the distinction between self-concern and selfish concern, see Adams, "Pure Love." Adams couches the distinction in terms of the contrast between self-concern and self-interest.

14. Another, for which I won't have room in this paper, is παρρησία (bold confidence).

Cor 2:7). God "called you through our proclamation of the good news, so that you may obtain (περιποίησιν) the glory of our Lord Jesus Christ" (2 Thess 2:14). He also notes that "When we cry, 'Abba! Father!' it is that very Spirit bearing witness with our spirit that we are children of God, and if children, then heirs, heirs of God and joint heirs with Christ—if, in fact, we suffer with him so that we may also be glorified with him" (Rom 8:15b–17).

If glory is manifest excellence and the children of God are destined to be glorious, it would be odd if they were constitutionally unable to notice it. But seeing excellence *as excellence* presupposes caring about it. I suppose someone might be able to identify excellent woodworking by some markers, without at all finding joy in considering it. But would she thereby see the woodworking's excellence *as excellence*? She might be able to distinguish excellent pieces from those that are not excellent by checking for the markers, but if she didn't take delight in them, their excellence would not be *manifest* to her. She wouldn't see it *as excellence*. To delight in the excellence of the woodworking, she would need to love it, to care about it. Similarly, the children of God can be expected to perceive their own glory only if they care about it. On the radical no-concern understanding of humility, the humble child of God will not care about her glory and so will be blind to it. This is not a happy theological result, so the radical no-concern account must not be the right account of Christian humility.

Taking Pride in Your Humility

In scenario one that I sketched at the beginning of this paper, we see a person who has been struggling with his vanity, taking delight in seeing the fruits of his efforts (or of God's grace, or both). We noted that he may attribute these fruits entirely to the work of God, or, alternatively, he may think he himself had some hand in producing them. But in either case, he *delights* in *his own* emerging *excellence*. He apprehends a prefiguration of his promised glory. Joy in excellence because it is one's own is episodic pride (an emotion). I have argued that there is nothing morally or spiritually untoward about such delight.[15]

15. This paper has focused on episodic pride, the *feeling* of pride in or about something. An interesting question it has not addressed is about the relation of such episodes to such virtues of pride as secure agency, high aspiration, self-confidence, and entitlement serenity.

Bibliography

Adams, Robert M. "Pure Love." *Journal of Religious Ethics* 8 (1980) 83–99.

American Psychiatric Association. *Diagnostic and Statistical Manual of Mental Disorders*. 5th ed. Washington, DC: American Psychiatric Association, 2013.

Benedict. *The Rule of St. Benedict*. Edited by Timothy Fry. Collegeville: Liturgical, 1981.

Dunnington, Kent. *Humility, Pride, and Christian Virtue Theory*. Oxford: Oxford University Press, 2019.

Foulcher, Jane. *Reclaiming Humility: Four Studies in the Monastic Tradition*. Collegeville: Cistercian, 2015.

Okholm, Dennis. *Dangerous Passions, Deadly Sins: Learning from the Psychology of Ancient Monks*. Grand Rapids: Brazos, 2014.

Roberts, Robert C. *Emotions in the Moral Life*. Cambridge: Cambridge University Press, 2013.

———. "Humility and Human Flourishing." In *The Routledge Handbook on the Philosophy of Humility*, edited by Mark Alfano et al., 49–58. New York: Routledge, 2021.

———. "Joys: A Brief Moral and Christian Geography." *Faith and Philosophy* 36 (2019) 195–222.

———. "The Virtues of Pride and Humility: A Survey." In *Virtue & Voice: Habits of Mind for a Return to Civil Discourse*, edited by Evan Rosa and Gregg ten Elshof, 113–34. Abilene: Abilene Christian University Press, 2019.

Roberts, Robert C., and W. Scott Cleveland. "Humility from a Philosophical Point of View." In *Handbook of Humility: Theory, Research, and Applications*, edited by Everett Worthington et al., 33–46. New York: Routledge, 2017.

Roberts, Robert C., and Ryan West. "Jesus and the Virtues of Pride." In *The Moral Psychology of Pride*, edited by Adam Carter et al., 99–111. Lanham: Rowman and Littlefield, 2017.

Roberts, Robert C., and W. Jay Wood. "Understanding, Humility, and the Vices of Pride." In *The Routledge Handbook of Virtue Epistemology*, edited by Heather Battaly, 363–78. New York: Routledge, 2018.

Ward, Benedicta, ed. *The Desert Fathers: Sayings of the Early Christian Monks*. London: Penguin, 2003.

———. *The Lives of the Desert Fathers: Historia Monachorum in Aegypto*. Translated by Norman Russell. Collegeville: Cistercian, 1981.

13

Dennis Okholm

MICHAEL McNICHOLS

ONE OF MY MOST significant theological influences was Dr. Ray S. Anderson, who taught theology at Fuller Theological Seminary for over thirty years. Ray taught as a practical theologian, and his classes were usually filled to overflowing. While he taught primarily at Fuller's main campus in Pasadena, he was the only full-time faculty member who also taught on a regular basis at Fuller's regional campus in Orange County, California.

When I came to work at Fuller as Director of the Orange County campus in 2006, I learned that Ray was retiring from teaching. I couldn't imagine who could take Ray's place, and I wondered how in the world I would find a way to fill that void. To ease my troubled mind, my predecessor informed me that she had already made arrangements for someone to take Ray's cherished role in Orange County: a theology professor who had come to Azusa Pacific University by way of Wheaton College named Dennis Okholm.

Wait a minute, I thought to myself. *I know this guy.*

I didn't really know him, but I was familiar with his work. In my prior role as a pastor I was reading anything I could get my hands on that addressed the apparent shift in western culture that was ominously categorized as *postmodernity*. There was a book on my shelf with the title *Christian Apologetics in the Postmodern World*, edited by Timothy Phillips and Dennis Okholm. I recognized that this Okholm person was engaged with issues that I believed were vitally important to the church today, and I was thrilled and expectant that he would address those issues with our students with depth and theological integrity.

I was right about that, but what I didn't expect was to meet a notable scholar with the uniqueness of Dennis Okholm. He popped into my office just before the new term began to make sure he had everything he needed to get started. He was full of laughter and fun, and before he departed he let me know that we really needed to go out to lunch together. Very soon, we did just that.

Professional academicians are, in my view, amazing people who contribute great value to the world. However, they tend to be more comfortable in the cloisters of research and study than in social engagements with chatty strangers. Dennis, however, challenged that stereotype. He was an energetic social animal, a lover of gatherings, eager to drop into a conversation quotes from old Seinfield episodes, bold in his invitations to his home for dinner or to search for theological themes in a Coen Brothers movie, and excited to invite his friends into new adventures, like climbing Mount Kilimanjaro (which he did, but, alas, without his timid friends) or spending an evening at a local arena to watch women's roller derby.

Over the years I've had to wonder: What is it that motivates my friend Dennis Okholm to not only produce profound academic work but also to wrap his arms, so to speak, around so many people? The students we shared in common soon discovered that a question posed after class could result in a shared lunchtime the following week (his students often affectionately refer to him as "Doc Ok," a nod to the nefarious Doctor Octopus from the Spiderman comics). The servers we encountered at our regular dining spots (Dennis seemed to know these people all by name) were always pleased to see him and were obviously touched when he asked them about their families or their ambitions. He also left generous tips, which probably enhanced his popularity. Why did he do these things?

One could speculate that there might be some relational voids in his life that he sought to fill with a lot of social activity. But I don't think that's the case. As I've come to know Dennis, I think he operates out of a deep sense of hospitality. In the New Testament, the Greek word *philoxenia*, meaning *friendship with* or *love for the stranger*, is usually translated as *hospitality*. Over the years I have learned that Dennis does not abide strangers for long because he quickly turns them into friends. Hospitality is not simply a thing that he does as the occasion arises; hospitality is, for Dennis, a practice of his life.

That may be why he is deeply committed to that complex, scattered, divisive, loving, sometimes confused, global network of communities that we call *the Church*.

✦

Huntley and Barbara Okholm were church people, and their faith community of preference was Assemblies of God. But by the time Dennis reached his early teens, they had moved to Arcade Baptist Church in Sacramento, California. It was under the attentive care of Pastor Lee Toms that Dennis was mentored and nurtured in his Christian faith.

Lee Toms was known as a visionary leader, speaking to congregations around the world and to his local community through regularly broadcasted messages over the local radio station. He founded the Arcade church and led it from a small group of twenty-seven to several thousand by the time of his retirement in 1992. Toms's stature, however, did not distract him from the work of personally investing in those who would follow him as he followed Jesus. It was in his invitation-only, early morning Bible study that young Dennis Okholm would find in Pastor Toms a mentor who cared deeply for him, encouraged his journey of faith and learning, and helped to create a safe and nurturing space for a young man just beginning to wrestle with the inklings of a calling that would lead to a lifetime vocation of ministry.

This time of deep influence, however, was not limited to the cloister of the pastor's study. It was the life of the church itself that offered Dennis a place of belonging; Arcade Baptist Church became a place of connection for Dennis that would transcend the challenges of his home life and create a new and expansive definition of the word *family*. He took seriously Jesus' challenging words in Mark 3:33–35: "'Who are my mother and my brothers?' And looking at those who sat around him, he said, 'Here are my mother and my brothers! Whoever does the will of God is my brother and sister and mother.'"

Dennis's understanding of the church as his first family would lead him toward a ministry with young people, a vocation of deep commitment and focus that would, he believed, require him to remain single in order to be faithful to God's calling in his life. With the Spirit of God as his guide and the church as his family, he would never truly be alone. So, upon completing high school, he set off for Chicago where he would enroll at Wheaton College to pursue his bachelor's degree. During his studies at Wheaton, he would encounter two people who would change the direction of his ministry and his life.

The first was Robert Webber, professor of theology at Wheaton. Webber was a controversial teacher, fearless in his engagement with American culture as it was shifting and contorting in the late 1960s. Even before his first semester, Dennis had been encouraged by his friends to take courses from Webber, which he did. He was captured by Webber's willingness to exegete American culture and to challenge the church's immersion in the assumptions of modernity that were already beginning to crumble. Dennis discovered that Webber was, like him, a follower of Jesus on a journey that had not yet been clearly charted. He describes the effect of those early encounters with Webber:

> [Webber] was a fellow pilgrim—an honest Christian inquirer, reared in fundamentalism like most of his students, trying to figure out how to be an honest evangelical in the culture that had grown out of the 1960s, a world our parents never knew.[1]

Webber's influence would, at least in part, lead Dennis toward an awareness of the church's tension with the larger culture and with its own identity as God's people. The rapid change that was characterizing the western world was not, for Webber, a call for the church's accommodation to the culture, but rather a call for the church to remember and demonstrate the profound nature of its shared life.[2]

This awareness would flourish years later when Dennis and Robert Webber became colleagues at Wheaton. Over time, Dennis would see theology as expressed through liturgy as a possible remedy to the church's lack of identity and to the effects of the formative powers of the world. As he would later write,

> It is in the church that we learn the language and engage in the practices or rituals that will train us to see reality as disciples of the crucified, risen, and ascended Christ. This happens especially as we rehearse the biblical narrative, particularly that

---

1. Johnson, *The Conviction of Things Not Seen*, 199–200.

2. Gerhard Lohfink makes this point succinctly: "The most important and most irreplaceable service Christians can render society is quite simply that they truly be church." Lohfink, *Jesus and Community*, 168.

part of the narrative centered on Christ. Our moral conceptions depend on the way that this ecclesiastical language-using community shapes the way we as moral people see the world by recounting and reliving the story into which we have been baptized.[3]

For Webber, engagement with the liturgy was not limited to the colors, readings, and prayers that would be expressed in a service of worship. Liturgy also needed to include deep reflection on the way that the ongoing rehearsal and celebration of the story of God's redemptive work in and through Jesus Christ would shape the church's demonstration of the gospel through redemptive, healing acts such as hospitality. Reflecting on the season of Epiphany, Webber described how the enactment of God's story through worship forms the church as a hospitable people:

> Christ is manifested in us when we live by the fruits of the Holy Spirit—love, joy, peace, patience, kindness, goodness, faithfulness, gentleness, and self-control. In the early church the fathers saw these fruits of the Spirit expressed in the gift of hospitality. Hospitality is a very special gift because it is a unique means through which Christ can be manifested.[4]

The seeds of hospitality had long ago been planted in Dennis's life. Through the relationship with Webber, those seeds would sprout, take root, and grow into a theological construct that would shape Dennis's thinking in the classroom, the church, and the world.

The Christian life is a trajectory that arcs its way toward the ultimate purposes and intentions of God. Along the way, the pathway of our lives may be modified, nudged, and reconfigured as we experience new things, gain fresh insights, and encounter influential people. Webber was one of those people whose influence had the effect of altering Dennis's life trajectory. But Webber was not the only one. There was another.

Dennis met her at a salad bar.

Trevecca Newsom had just transferred to Wheaton from a college in San Diego and was enjoying dinner in Wheaton's dining hall with her new friends. After introducing himself to Trevecca at the salad bar, Dennis finished dinner and promptly returned home to call her, requesting that she walk with him to a local diner favored by Wheaton students. She

---

3. Okholm, *Learning Theology*, 6.

4. Webber, *Ancient-Future Time*, 92.

accepted his invitation. They continue to celebrate the memory of this first date every October 29th.

Falling in love with Trevecca created a challenge for Dennis. He had convinced himself that the single life would suit his sense of God's calling. Remaining single would also give him the freedom of mobility—in both his academic pursuits and his vocation of ministry in the church. The prospect of a possible life partner complicated his plan.

Dennis wisely reached out to Lee Toms for counsel. After exchanging a series of letters, Dennis accepted the possibility that having Trevecca in his life would not be a violation of his calling, but instead a fulfilling of it.[5] Instead of living out God's calling in singleness, Dennis would see the trajectory of his life altered as he experienced that calling from the vantage point of the community of marriage. Dennis and Trevecca were married on August 24, 1973.

Marriage may have been the way that Dennis's thinking about the life of faith as a shared life, a common life, was formed and shaped. Yes, he had experienced and valued the church as his family, but now he would experience that ecclesial family through his lifelong companionship with Trevecca. As they welcomed each other into marriage, they would, together, extend that welcome to their children and to the sojourners they would encounter along the way. It would be this shared, common life that would convince Dennis that such a life was the environment where the voice of God could be heard and obeyed.[6] It was also the environment where the practice of stability, "the commitment to stay with the same community for the rest of one's life,"[7] would be experienced and demonstrated. As he would later write,

> This is something I tell each of my classes at the beginning of the semester: I am just enough of a Calvinist to believe that God has called together this *particular* constellation of people to speak to and hear from each other what is needed for their mutual growth in Christlikeness. . . . Stability means being *faithful*

5. Dennis also asked Pastor Toms if he thought it was acceptable for him to tell Trevecca that he loved her. Toms thought that such an action would be just fine.

6. "It is involvement in the *coenobium*—the common life—that makes it possible for me to grow into a deeper awareness of God's will for me. This is why the oft-heard sentiment of Protestants that it's just 'Jesus and me' is dangerously misguided. Left to myself (even with Jesus), I am easily deceived and very unreliable." Okholm, *Monk Habits*, 60.

7. Okholm, *Monk Habits*, 89.

where we are—really paying attention to those with whom we
live and to what is happening in our common life.[8]

After Dennis's graduation from Wheaton with a bachelor's degree
in philosophy, he and Trevecca headed off to Trinity Seminary where he
completed a Master of Arts in Church History and a Master of Divinity
degree. The next stop was Princeton Theological Seminary, where Dennis
would complete a Master of Theology degree and a PhD in Systematic
Theology.[9] Along with his academic accomplishments, he also made an
important step in his ecclesial life: he became a Presbyterian.

It was at Hopewell Presbyterian Church, just a few miles away from
Princeton, that Dennis and Trevecca met Pastor Bob Berringer. Pastor
Berringer introduced them to this new congregation and family of faith
that seemed to be a natural home for Dennis, whose intellectual gifts
and academic desires would find kinship and appreciation. Now official
members of the Presbyterian Church (USA), Dennis and Trevecca would
both find greater clarity than before in their shared sense of calling. They
would flourish in this new family of faith for many years.[10]

As much as Dennis relished the rich flavors of the academic life, this
next season of life would bring something new to savor. It came from a
family of devoted Christians whose rhythms of life had roots in an ancient world undiscovered by many Protestants. Dennis's understanding
of the life of the church, an understanding shaped by Pentecostal, Baptist,
and Presbyterian tribes, would now be re-fashioned by a group of Benedictine monks.

Upon completion of his PhD at Princeton, Dennis taught for three
years at Western Kentucky University, and then took a position at Jamestown College (now University of Jamestown) in North Dakota, where he
would serve as both professor of philosophy and college chaplain. While
the college was Presbyterian, it also served a number of Roman Catholic

8. Okholm, *Monk Habits*, 90–91.

9. His dissertation was titled, "Petitionary Prayer and Providence in Two Contemporary Theological Perspectives: Karl Barth and Norman Pittenger." The credentials
he earned at Princeton Seminary turned out to be shocking disqualifiers when he was
released after four years in his tenure-track position at Western Kentucky University.
His new department chair decided that a seminary degree was incompatible with the
values of a public university. Dennis's fifth year there would be his last. Okholm, *Monk
Habits*, 16.

10. Dennis was ordained in the Presbyterian Church (USA) from 1984–2011, and
Trevecca was a Certified Christian Educator (1997) with an emphasis on children and
family ministry, working in full-time ministry in the PC(USA) from 1986–2012.

students, many of whom worshipped at a local parish where a Benedictine nun named Sister Michaeleen Jantzer had been assigned to minister to the students. Sister Michaeleen had been a nun for many years, and she and Dennis became fast friends. When Dennis inquired about a good place for a private retreat, she referred him to a Benedictine monastery with an ethereal name that challenged the young intellectual with its *new age* implications: Blue Cloud Abbey.

His two days with the monks of Blue Cloud were life-changing. The initial experience of sharing meals, joining with the monks throughout the day in prayer, and luxuriating in deep conversations about faith and life would deepen his love for the Christian community—not only for what it was, but also for what it could be. He revisited his friends at the monastery, and soon took a major step in his life by becoming an oblate[11] of Blue Cloud Abbey.

Church life in the USA is complicated. While regular church attendance is declining overall, there are still plenty of people who attend multiple times each month with a desire to be close to God. But there are others who find attendance difficult because, for the most part, they prefer a form of individualized spirituality or just can't seem to find a church in which they feel comfortable. When it comes to church, a deep sense of belonging can be hard to come by. When you add in the realities of busyness and the tendency for church to be viewed consumeristically in American culture, the words "church" and "community" are not always synonymous.[12]

Christian college and seminary students are notorious for putting church attendance on hiatus during their years of study. So, when Dennis made the two-hour drive from Blue Cloud Abbey back to Jamestown, he had plenty of time to sort out how the trends in Protestant church life might be impacted by what he had learned from his new friends at the monastery. In other words, how might the people he served, in both

11. An oblate is a person devoted to God's service and, while not a monk or a nun, affiliates with a particular monastic community. To learn more about Dennis's journey as an oblate, see Brother Benet Tvedten's epilogue in this volume: "At the Advice of a Sister," 213–19.

12. In a brief conversation with Dallas Willard, I asked him if church membership was a passing reality. He responded by saying, "If we don't give people a way to belong, then we leave them to the ravages of consumerism."

the academy and the church, learn how to truly do life together, not as a religious requirement, but rather as a gracious gift?[13]

These experiences in the life of the church would form Dennis's sense of his vocation in a way that would ultimately lead him to value worship, liturgy, mission, and the possibility of a shared life in the church more than he had ever anticipated. He had already learned the significance of making vows; he had made them to God, to his wife, and now to a community of Benedictines. How would those vows play out in his vocation?

It is often difficult for people with advanced degrees in theological studies to sit through a church service without employing their skills in analytical and critical thinking. Dennis would certainly have his times of challenge as he listened to sermons over the years, but he experienced those challenges within the life of the church rather than on the outside of it. He worked hard to become a respected scholar in the academy, but he was also a scholar of the church, from the church, and for the church. Throughout his career he would dive deeply into his family of faith, regardless of its location, and seek to orient his life around Jesus within the community of God's people.[14] He would come to recognize that the church throughout its checkered history had been the primary context in which the Christian faith was preserved, witnessed, and learned. He realized that the church was necessary[15] to the faith journey of all followers of Jesus, and would claim that

13. As Dietrich Bonhoeffer observed as he served a young group of seminarians just under the radar of the Gestapo in Germany: "So between the death of Christ and the Last Day it is only by a gracious anticipation of the last things that Christians are privileged to live in visible fellowship with other Christians." Bonhoeffer, *Life Together*, 18.

14. The centrality of Christ within the life of the church was at the heart of Dennis's service. Legend has it that he was confronted one Sunday by a parishioner who was concerned that his morning sermon did not focus on the theme of the national holiday that had fallen on that weekend. The well-meaning person suggested that the reason we were all here was because of the sacrifice of the courageous patriots who had gone before us. As the story goes, Dennis responded, "No. We are not *here* because of them. We are *here* because of Jesus."

15. While Catholics and Protestants might debate the nature of such necessity, they would probably agree that the church factors significantly in the Christian tradition. As James Davison Hunter affirms: "It is true that there are religious virtuosi who maintain strong beliefs on their own with little or no social support but these individuals are rare. Most of us, however, need the reinforcement that social institutions provide to believe coherently and live with integrity. There is a sociological truth, then, to the statement *extra ecclesiam nulla salus*; that 'there is no salvation outside of the church.'"

the church is the community *within* which the Christian pro-
fesses her faith. It is the community in which faith is born, nourished, lived out, and proclaimed. . . . It is impossible to *become*
and to *be* a Christian apart from the church. To be a Christian is
to be part of Christ's body. There is no individual Christianity.[16]

Almost thirty years after being introduced to the liturgical life of the
Benedictines, where Dennis experienced faith being nourished and lived,
he would explore a faith community that, while new to him, would bring
him to a fresh understanding of the relationship between the rhythms of
worship and the flourishing of Christian faith. As a scholar and a pastor,
he would find a new home among the Anglicans.

After meeting with Bishop Todd Hunter, Dennis entered the ordination process with the Anglican Church in North America (ACNA),
in a non-geographical diocese called Church for the Sake of Others
(C4SO). This was more than a simple denominational relocation based
on personal preference; it demonstrated Dennis's deep conviction that
our devotion to Jesus Christ must be more than a shared creedal affirmation. It had to be a shared life where, in worship, we submit ourselves
to the ongoing formation that comes from the very hand of God. In the
rhythms of the liturgy—rhythms with roots in the ancient church—wor-
shippers not only learn theology, but their bodies enact theological realities in community.

This is where the church community comes in. It is in the church
that we learn the language and engage in the practices or rituals
that will train us to see reality as disciples of the crucified, risen,
and ascended Christ. This happens especially as we rehearse the
biblical narrative, particularly that part of the narrative centered
on Christ. Our moral conceptions depend on the way that this
ecclesiastical language-using community shapes the way we as
moral people see the world by recounting and reliving the story
into which we have been baptized. Our worship—our liturgy—
plays a central role at this point, centered in the Eucharist (the
Lord's Supper or communion).[17]

This movement toward an ecclesiastical context where both liturgy
and mission were vital realities should have been no surprise to Dennis
or to those who had journeyed with him. Robert Webber had influenced

---

Hunter, *To Change the World*, 202.

16. Okholm, *Learning Theology*, 180.

17. Okholm, *Learning Theology*, 6.

Dennis in settings both academic and collegial, and Webber's journey toward a worshipping community where liturgy and sacraments were apparent could be seen throughout his writings. Webber describes his own early movement (after preaching a controversial sermon during a Wheaton College chapel service) from his roots in evangelicalism to the sacramental environment of Anglicanism:

> If God cannot be contained in a system, where can he be encountered? I didn't know it at the time, but this experience, because it forced me to seek God seeking me, pushed me in the direction of worship and the sacraments. Since neither worship nor the sacraments were given high priority in the local evangelical churches, I had to look elsewhere. My journey into the Episcopal Church and into the mystery of God's saving presence in Christ communicated through worship and the sacraments had begun.[18]

The influences of Webber and the Benedictines would help to nudge Dennis toward seeing the worship life of the church as richer and more meaningful than he had ever imagined. It could very well be that his early exposure to the spiritual expressions of the Pentecostals created an unexpected link with the sacramentalism of the Anglicans where both families of faith, in their own ways, expected corporate worship to be an engagement with the mystery that is God.[19]

It is no small thing to be a follower of Christ who is called to reconcile a love for scholarship with the fractured and unsteady life of the Christian community. So, it seemed natural that Dennis would find himself in the role of Canon Theologian[20] in the Anglican Church. In this new vocational phase of his calling, Dennis would bring a depth of theological inquiry into congregational life with a group of people made up of university and seminary students, faculty, seekers of faith, and those hoping to give church just one more try. In the liturgical practices of worship, Dennis's commitment to his academic vocation would find a new kind

18. Webber, *Evangelicals on the Canterbury Trail*, 14.

19. Ray S. Anderson makes the link between mystery and sacraments: "The Greek word *mysterion* was translated as *sacramentum* by Jerome in the Vulgate (Latin) Bible (e.g., Eph. 5:32). The word *mysterion* as used by Paul does not mean a mystery in the form of a hidden secret, but a revealed reality: God is present in the form of a human person, Jesus of Nazareth." Anderson, *The Soul of Ministry*, 167.

20. A priest and scholar who assists the bishop in theological matters, trains ordinands, and communicates on behalf of the bishop through writing and speaking.

of expression, articulating his own definition of theology: "Theology is a human response to the revelation of God, done within and for the Christian church, which engages in critical reflection for responsible talk about God."[21] This "human response" is one done in the hospitable environment of the Christian community, where the continuous re-enactment and rehearsal of faith finds expression in the gathering of worship—in the liturgy of the church.[22]

It is an interesting possibility that there would be a link between hospitality and liturgy. For some Protestants, to use the word *liturgy* is to describe a ritual drained of life, a mind-numbing nod to Christian faith that not only fails to warm the heart but instead freezes it solid.[23] Of course, all churches have regular practices that could be categorized as liturgy, whether in high church services or hipster gatherings in the off-hours of a local pub. It is what we Christians do when we come together as a worshipping community, but it isn't simply about *us*. In a footnote, Dennis gives clarity to the definition of liturgy:

> The word that Christians use to speak of worship is *liturgy*. It is often misunderstood (etymologically) as "work of the people" (*laos*)." It comes from the Greek word *leitourgia*, which comes from the Greek *leitos* (public) and *ergon* (work). In other words, it is a secular Greek word for public work done on behalf of the people by another person or group appointed to the task. In the New Testament the primary use of the term refers to Christ himself: Hebrews 8:2 designates him as our *leitourgos*. In other words, we join a liturgy already in progress—the Son, our high priest, renders worship to the Father, and we participate in that worship as we offer ourselves to Christ.[24]

21. Okholm, *Learning Theology*, 25.

22. Aiden Kavanaugh offers this description of liturgy: "The liturgy is not some thing separate from the church, but simply the church caught in the act of being most overtly itself as it stands faithfully in the presence of the One who is both object and source of that faith. The liturgical assembly's stance in faith is vertiginous, on the edge of chaos. Only grace and favor enable it to stand there; only grace and promise brought it there; only grace and a rigorous divine charity permit the assembly, like Moses, to come away whole from such an encounter, and even then it is with wounds which are as deep as they are salutary." Kavanaugh, *On Liturgical Theology*, 75.

23. The word *ennui* (borrowed from the French) is probably the best descriptor here, since it comes from the Latin *inodiare*, "to make loathsome."

24. Okholm, *Learning Theology*, 4n4.

The hospitality of the Christian community doesn't begin with greeters at the door of the church or free coffee and doughnuts before and after the service. It begins with Jesus Christ, who summons his church to join him in the ongoing worship of the Father. We are the strangers beloved by God and welcomed by the Son to worship in Spirit and in truth. For Dennis, the work of theology, as expressed in and through the liturgy, is not done *to* the church, but rather gives framework to the Spirit-created, shared life that *is* the church.

Dennis once told me how grateful he was for the academic life that had characterized his career. Over the years I've heard him teach and preach, I've watched as he's helped others grow in their life of faith, I've read his books, and I've enjoyed many a meal with him and his valued friends. I've come to realize that his vocational life can't be captured in the single identifier, *academic*. Dennis is more of a Renaissance scholar, one who can't help but put his hand to a variety of things and then pursue them with gusto. He is, to put it simply, one who relishes life.

This life, however, is not one that survives on its own. It is a life in Christ, a shared life expressed in Christian community, to the glory of God and for the sake of the world. As Karl Barth declared,

> [s]olidarity with the world means that those who are genuinely pious approach the children of the world as such, that those who are genuinely righteous are not ashamed to sit down with the unrighteous as friends, that those who are genuinely wise do not hesitate to seem to be fools among fools, and that those who are genuinely holy are not too good or irreproachable to go down into "hell" in a very secular fashion. . . . Since Jesus Christ is the Savior of the world, [the church] can exist in worldly fashion, not unwillingly nor with a bad conscience, but willingly and with a good conscience. It consists in the recognition that its members also bear in themselves and in some way actualize all human possibilities.[25]

Dennis's hospitable reach is like that described by Barth. Existing in "worldly fashion" is not, for Dennis, to simply co-opt whatever trends are blown his way by the winds of the culture. This hospitality, this "solidarity with the world" leads him to stand alongside those often considered to be *others*—strangers held in suspicion—because of gender, or race, or ethnicity, or religious convictions. He does not fear descending into the

---

25. Barth, *Church Dogmatics* 4/3.2:774.

hell that is systemic injustice because he believes that those who suffer
still have a seat reserved for them at the table of Jesus.

Dennis seeks to remain in Christ, and to live faithfully in the world.
Both words—*remain* and *live*—are both used in scripture to describe the
life to which we are called as followers of Christ. Certain versions of the
Bible continue to use the term *abide*, a word that seems to capture a variety of meanings, as in the words of Jesus in John 15:4–5:

> Abide in me as I abide in you. Just as the branch cannot bear
> fruit by itself unless it abides in the vine, neither can you unless
> you abide in me. I am the vine, you are the branches. Those who
> abide in me and I in them bear much fruit, because apart from
> me you can do nothing.

To abide, to live, to remain. We are summoned, drawn into the very
life of Christ. To abide is to rest in the love of God that is shared in the life
of the Father, Son, and Holy Spirit.

A vital way in which we are regularly drawn into our abiding in
Christ is in the Eucharist. The celebration of the Eucharist is at the heart
of the Anglican liturgy. While there may be many diverse views about the
nature of the elements shared in the Lord's Supper, it is still and undeni-
ably the table of Jesus. At its origin, this table was populated by young
Jewish men,[26] most of whom were confused and at least one was treach-
erous. Jesus knew this and yet included them all. It was a small group of
participants, but we can find something of ourselves in each one.

I've watched Dennis a number of times as he has led the church in
the celebration of the Eucharist. I've extended my hands to receive the
bread as he has looked me in the eye and called me by name, reminding
me that this is the body of Christ. In those moments I couldn't help but
think of the people we've encountered together over the years—servers
at pubs and restaurants, confused and aspirational students, conversation
partners from other religious faith traditions—and wondered how they
might receive this invitation to come and dine. I think I'm on safe ground
in suggesting that Dennis would like for this table to not be representa-
tional but instead actual, an expansive table that invites even the least
of these to find a place and abide in the life-giving mystery that is Jesus
Christ.

---

26. To put a fine point on it, there were no Christians at the last supper.

It's a good word, abide. It captures the ideas of living of constancy, of journeying, of bearing, and doing all of those things together, abiding as the church, the body of Christ. It's good to abide.

My friend Doc Ok abides. I don't know about you, but I take comfort in that.[27]

Bibliography

Anderson, Ray S. *The Soul of Ministry: Forming Leaders for God's People.* Louisville: Westminster John Knox, 1997.

Barth, Karl. *Church Dogmatics.* 4/3.2: *The Doctrine of Reconciliation.* Translated by Geoffrey Bromiley et al. Edinburgh: T. & T. Clark, 1962.

Bonhoeffer, Dietrich. *Life Together: The Classic Exploration of Christian Community.* San Francisco: HarperOne, 2009.

Coen, Joel, and Ethan Coen, dir. and writ. *The Big Lebowski.* 1998. United States: Gramercy Pictures (I).

Hunter, James Davison. *To Change the World: The Irony, Tragedy, and Possibility of Christianity in the Late Modern World.* New York: Oxford University Press, 2010.

Johnson, Todd E., ed. *The Conviction of Things Not Seen: Worship and Ministry in the 21st Century.* Grand Rapids: Brazos, 2002.

Kavanaugh, Aidan. *On Liturgical Theology.* Collegeville: Liturgical, 1984.

Lohfink, Gerhard. *Jesus and Community.* Minneapolis: Fortress, 1984.

Okholm, Dennis. *Learning Theology through the Church's Worship.* Grand Rapids: Baker Academic, 2018.

———. *Monk Habits for Everyday People: Benedictine Spirituality for Protestants.* Grand Rapids: Brazos, 2007.

Webber, Robert E. *Ancient-Future Time: Forming Spirituality through the Christian Year.* Grand Rapids: Baker, 2004.

———. *Evangelicals on the Canterbury Trail: Why Evangelicals are Attracted to the Liturgical Church.* New York: Morehouse, 2012.

27. Thanks to the Coen Brothers and their movie, *The Big Lebowski*, for the use of this line.

Epilogue

At the Advice of a Sister:
The Benedictine Way for the Unexpected

Benet Tvedten, OSB

When Reverend Dennis Okholm arrived in Jamestown, North Dakota in 1987, he was introduced to Benedictine Sister Michaeleen Jantzer from Mother of God Monastery in Watertown, South Dakota. She was stationed at the Catholic parish in Jamestown and tended to Catholic students at Jamestown College where Dennis had been hired to teach and to minister to Protestant students. Although the college was founded by Presbyterians, it was welcoming of other denominations. Dennis, a Presbyterian at the time, asked the nun about a good place to take a retreat. Sister Michaeleen suggested that he try Blue Cloud Abbey in Marvin, South Dakota, a community of Benedictine men. He would be welcomed as a retreatant at the abbey, she assured him.

He was made to feel so welcome that on April 30, 1989 he affiliated himself with the abbey by becoming an Oblate of St. Benedict. I was the oblate director. Most oblates are lay people affiliated with a particular monastery of men or women. Like the monastics, they pray the daily psalms in the Divine Office, but usually an abbreviated version, and they adapt in their own lives the teachings contained in Benedict's *Rule* for monastics. The monks had been welcoming clergy from other denominations, individually and in groups, ever since the Second Vatican Council (1962–1965).

Dennis became an oblate at a time when people outside the Roman Catholic Church were discovering the Order of St. Benedict and Benedict's *Rule* via the popular writings of two lay women: Esther de Waal,[1] an Anglican married to the former Dean of Canterbury Cathedral, and Norvene Vest,[2] an Episcopalian married to a priest. Shortly after the significant contributions of de Waal and Vest, a plethora of books dealing with Benedictine spirituality began to appear, written by both Protestants and Catholics.

In 2007, Dennis's superb book appeared: *Monk Habits for Everyday People*. In it he writes: "When I first began to explore the roots of contemporary Benedictine monasticism, it dawned on me that in one sense Benedict belongs to Roman Catholics no more than he does to Protestants. His life preceded the Reformation by a millennium, and the same Protestants who revere and learn from Augustine (b. 354) may just as legitimately, and without feelings of betrayal and guilt, appeal to Benedict (b. 480)."[3] It was a custom for oblates to choose a patronal saint on the occasion of oblation; Dennis chose Anselm, the Benedictine abbot who became the Archbishop of Canterbury in 1093 and was known for his mystical writings.

Around the same time Dennis was discovering Benedictine monasticism, another Dakota Presbyterian was being introduced to it. Kathleen Norris, who lived in Lemmon, South Dakota, was a frequent visitor to Blue Cloud Abbey. Once when we were leaving the monastery chapel, she dipped her finger in the holy water font and made the sign of the cross. Her lapsed Catholic husband commented, "Of all the Catholic things you do, Kathleen, that is the one John Calvin would find most despicable." Kathleen became an oblate at Assumption Abbey in North Dakota, the monastery to which I now belong.[4] In the foreword she wrote for Dennis's book, Kathleen identifies Dennis and herself as being in a grassroots movement of American spirituality in which many Protestants were

1. See de Waal's *Seeking God*, which was selected to be the Church of England's book for Lent the following year. De Waal later wrote a commentary on the *Rule* titled *A Life-Giving Way* and also established the "Benedictine Experience," an ecumenical retreat in which participants work and pray in the Benedictine manner.

2. See Vest's *Preferring Christ* and her *Friend of the Soul*. Vest is now an oblate of St. Andrew's Abbey in Valyermo, California.

3. Okholm, *Monk Habits for Everyday People*, 24.

4. I came to Assumption Abbey in 2012 following the closure of Blue Cloud Abbey which had decreased in membership. Only twelve monks were left, two of them under the age of seventy.

finding spiritual renewal at Catholic monasteries. "My attraction to monastic liturgy did not mean that I was becoming a Catholic," says Kathleen. "Instead, it threatened to turn me into a better Protestant, one who was more attentive to the power of the Word."[5] Her book, *The Cloister Walk*, is an account of a year she spent at St. John's Abbey in Minnesota. I was and continue to be quite pleased with the interest in Benedictine piety shown by so many people from various Christian denominations.

While at the Jamestown College, Dennis brought students to Blue Cloud Abbey twice for a monastic experience. They prayed and worked with the monks for a week and spent one day visiting the Benedictine Sisters in Watertown—Sister Michaeleen's community. Dawn Linder, a student in the first group who was at the time seeking ordination in the Presbyterian church, was changed by this experience. Now the Reverend Dawn Linder, Dawn retained a relationship with the abbey even when she lived some distance from the place. She became an Oblate of St. Benedict and faithfully attended the annual retreat at the abbey. Dawn was present among the great number of people who came to Blue Cloud Abbey on August 5, 2012, the day the monastery closed.

When Dawn became the pastor of a rural Minnesota parish a couple years after her ordination, she asked me to deliver the homily at her installation. I informed the congregation about the very young nephew of one of our monks who was riding with his mother through a largely residential area in Indianapolis, Indiana. He read a sign advising motorists: "Beware of *Presbyterians*." His mother informed him of the correct wording: "Be Aware of *Pedestrians*." I assured Dawn's congregation that I felt safely and enthusiastically welcomed by all of them. It was moments like these that reminded me that the hospitality people like Dennis and Dawn had found at the abbey was a two-way street. Now in the context of Dawn's religious community I had received that gift as well.

Even after Dennis left Jamestown in 1989 to teach at Wheaton College he remained involved as an oblate. In 1997, for example, the North American Association of Benedictine Oblate Directors (NAABOD) welcomed the participation of oblates at their biannual gathering. Until then only a few oblates of the community hosting the event would attend. I had been elected coordinator of the organization and I invited Dennis to give the keynote address at the gathering at St. Meinrad's Archabbey in Indiana. He was a success, as I knew he would be.

5. Norris, "Foreword," in Okholm, *Monk Habits*, 8.

The next NAABOD gathering was in 1999 at Conception Abbey in Missouri—and Norvene Vest was a speaker. It was becoming a reality in most Benedictine communities that one need not be a Roman Catholic when wishing to affiliate with them as an Oblate of St. Benedict. It was also a reality that while oblate membership was on the increase, the profession of religious vows in Benedictine communities was on the decline. An elderly priest who was the oblate director for his community had written to me expressing his concern that I had been accepting people who were not Roman Catholic. However, I did not see any compelling reason to exclude my Christian brothers and sisters from learning from and participating in the life of the community in their own ways. The doors to the abbey were opened and the people coming in—Roman Catholic and non-Roman Catholic alike—received the hospitality that is so central to Benedictine spirituality.

A lawyer from Sioux Falls, Robin, was the first of our non-Roman Catholic oblates. She was an Episcopalian who came to the abbey for private retreats. Within a few years, monthly oblate meetings were being held in Sioux Falls at Robin's parish church, Calvary Episcopal Cathedral. The bishop, a priest, and a deacon from that cathedral had all become Oblates of St. Benedict affiliated with Blue Cloud. Meetings were held on a Saturday and began with praying Vespers, followed by a potluck supper, and then a conference. In later years, we met at the Episcopal Church of the Good Shepherd in Sioux Falls where the rector and his wife were Oblates of St. Benedict as were several parishioners. The Sioux Falls gatherings were ecumenical: Episcopalian, Roman Catholic, Lutheran, and Methodist. When the abbey closed in 2012, among the oblates there were six Roman Catholics, seven Episcopalians, three United Methodists, six affiliated with the Evangelical Lutheran Church in America, two from the Association of Free Lutherans, three Presbyterians, and one from the United Church of Christ. This ecumenical diversity illuminated the reality I had come to know through people like Dennis: Benedictine hospitality welcomes everyone.

This diverse array of Christians was a window into the diversity of the Christian faith; each oblate found refuge and nourishment in Benedictine spirituality regardless of what they did in their own communities of faith. An Episcopalian oblate was on the board of an AIDS hospice in Sioux Falls and another Episcopalian oblate helped prepare a meal there once a week; a United Methodist oblate, although he used a walker, ministered to hospital patients every week; and a Lutheran oblate, who was a county agent opposed to hog confinement parlors, sought refuge at the abbey when the situation got too heated for him to handle.

The presence of these Christians from different traditions and backgrounds who spent time at the abbey and affiliated with it also contributed to the life of the community with their fellowship, insights, and commitment to the community. One Roman Catholic oblate of Blue Cloud Abbey, the novelist Jon Hassler, would come to the monastery yearly to spend a week working on his current manuscript. On an evening near the end of the week, he would read for the monks and guests what he had accomplished during his time with us. One year while Jon was with us, students from Gustavus Adolphus, a Lutheran college in St. Peter, Minnesota, were also at the monastery for their annual visit. Jon kept a journal of his time at the abbey, and here is what he overheard while working on his manuscript:

> Brother Gene is lecturing the students on the monastic life. They are gathered in the lobby down the hall from my room, and I hear his husky voice as he describes the *Rule* and the ordered day of the monk. It occurs to me that the Benedictines have survived for 1500 years by paying attention to form. Lots of form in their lives. Lots of ordered routine. More than necessary, it might seem to an outsider. But maybe that's why they've endured. Maybe if they'd grown careless about form, the substance would have disintegrated and there would be no abbeys for people like me and the Gustavians to visit.

What Jon overheard and took the time to write down helped me better understand my own life with my brothers.

What is it that Oblates of St. Benedict find in the *Rule*? One oblate, Cathleen Curry, summed it up this way:

> The warm welcome of visitors to the monastery made me realize genuine hospitality was an important virtue in Benedict's eyes. His emphasis on stability, fidelity, moderation, and continual conversion to Christ settled in the low spots of my psyche, filling the holes and smoothing out my path. As my grandchildren might say: "Benedict's your bag, Grandma!"[6]

I seldom saw Dennis after he and the family moved to Wheaton, Illinois. Besides his one trip to Blue Cloud Abbey with students, I met him again at a meeting of the American Benedictine Academy when it held its

---

6. Quoted in *How to Be a Monastic*, 82.

biannual meeting at Sacred Heart Monastery in Yankton, South Dakota and he had been one of the speakers. Dennis had the distinction of becoming the first board member of The American Benedictine Academy who was not a Roman Catholic nor a professed member of a Benedictine community. He was a board member of the American Benedictine Academy from 2000 until 2004.[7]

Between 2014 and 2016 Father Martin Shannon, an Episcopal priest, was elected as President of the American Benedictine Academy. He is a member of the monastic Community of Jesus in Orleans, Massachusetts. His community of men and women identify themselves as Benedictine. They are ecumenical in membership and operate The Paraclete Press, which publishes a number of monastic titles. Father Martin said, "We all have stories to tell." He said that his and Dennis's stories have something to do with, "[t]he new expressions of the Benedictine charism, like Protestant oblates and ecumenical monasteries. And the American Benedictine Academy has spread out its tent pegs to make room for such daughters and sons of Benedict."

Several years ago I was at my local post office when a man and woman came in and asked if there were any interesting sites to view in the neighborhood. The postal clerk asked if they had seen "our abbey." I was pleased to hear her use the possessive pronoun. Now the new owners advertise the Abbey of the Hills Inn and Retreat Center as reflecting "the reverence and peace sustained here by Benedictine monks for more than sixty years."

Dennis was one of the Protestant pioneers to unexpectedly find his way into the doors of Blue Cloud Abbey and immerse himself in Benedictine spirituality. Dennis and his wife, Trevecca, through their friendship, commitment, and prayers, have helped sustain *our* Benedictine community for the decades since then. Dennis dedicated his book *Monk Habits* to Sister Michaeleen who got him started and to me who kept him going. It has been a very joyful journey.

---

7. The American Benedictine Academy was founded in 1947 with the purpose of cultivating, supporting, and transmitting Benedictine values. A gathering of members occurs every other year at a Benedictine monastery of either men or women. Papers are presented by members on various monastic topics. See https://americanbenedictine.org.

Bibliography

de Waal, Esther. *A Life-Giving Way: A Commentary on the Rule of St. Benedict.* Collegeville: Liturgical, 1995.

———. *Seeking God: The Way of St. Benedict.* Collegeville: Liturgical, 1984.

Norris, Kathleen. *The Cloister Walk.* New York: Penguin, 1997.

Okholm, Dennis. *Monk Habits for Everyday People: Benedictine Spirituality for Protestants.* Grand Rapids: Brazos, 2007.

Tvedten, Benet. *How to Be a Monastic and Not Leave Your Day Job: An Invitation to Oblate Life.* Brewster: Paraclete, 2006.

Vest, Norvene. *Preferring Christ: A Devotional Commentary and Workbook on the Rule of St. Benedict.* Naperville: Source, 1991.